Designing AI Companions

How to Create Empathetic AI Experiences

Designing AI Companions

How to Create Empathetic AI Experiences

CANSU HIZLI

DESIGNING AI COMPANIONS
How To Create Empathetic Ai Experiences

iUniverse books may be ordered through booksellers or by contacting:

iUniverse
1663 Liberty Drive
Bloomington, IN 47403
www.iuniverse.com
844-349-9409

ISBN: 978-1-6632-4348-5 (sc)
ISBN: 978-1-6632-4349-2 (hc)
ISBN: 978-1-6632-4350-8 (e)

Library of Congress Control Number: 2022914131

Print information available on the last page.

iUniverse rev. date: 03/30/2023

Contents

Acknowledgements
Preface
Introduction

Acknowledgments

I would like to thank the following persons who helped me a lot during my work on my master's degree and events that help me to grow.

Hey, Maslo, Ross Ingram, and Russell Foltz-Smith, amazing people I had the chance to meet during my research. They gave me the possibility to discover more about this topic and supported me from thousands of miles away. I am really thankful to discuss with you empathetic companions and expand my knowledge about empathic computing. My book arrived at this point thanks to your amazing ideas and hard work. I believe that Maslo will change our perspectives to release our inner heroes!

My colleagues at Maslo! You are the most amazing people that I have ever met and worked with. Thank you for pushing the limits to be an expert in the field. I am so grateful for all your support to bring this dream to a life.

Professor Margherita Pillan, course coordinator of MSc. Digital and Interaction Design of Politecnico di Milano, thank you for giving me a chance to join the master's program and improve my knowledge for my future career.

To my supervisor, Davide Spallazzo, I want to thank you not only for the research process but also for my overall MSc. journey at the Politecnico di Milano. You were always kind and supportive, and I learned a lot from you. Together we made discoveries in the process, and thanks to this exploratory journey, I have completed my research. There was always room for me to discuss my ideas with all my excitement. I am so grateful for this and for many other reasons. I could not have made it without you.

Riccardo, whatever I am writing for you will be never enough. My greatest support, my motivator, my magician, and an emotional hero in my life. You gave me the courage to realize my endless excitement, and I learned again how to build dreams and believe in them. You are an amazing companion and love in my everyday life.

My amazing and crazy family, thank you so much for your emotional support. You always believed in me under any conditions. It was a hard journey to be away from home, from you. I challenged myself with many difficulties, but you were always there with all of your love. Thank you for always being crazy, lovely, and supportive.

Melisa, an idol and a friend with whom I shared a home in Italy with all the challenges. You, with your unbelievable ideas and endless curiosity, are one of the pillars on this journey who made me excited to select this path in my career. Thank you for everything.

Friends support each other. I learned that this is so true. A big thank-you to all my friends who made my days in Italy and Turkey amazing.

Thank you with all of my heart!

Preface

The use of artificial intelligence (AI) is increasing, becoming more prominent in our lives. People mostly prefer to use virtual assistants to reduce the complexity of their daily basis and make the process faster to directly reach the desired result. Smart artificial assistants already have the potential to make someone's life easier, but at the same time, they are not active devices as might be expected. In addition to that, with the increase in the use of these intelligent devices, many problems have occurred related to trust. According to a new report from Microsoft based on consumer adoption of voices and virtual agents, 41 percent of voice-assisting users were concerned with trust, confidentiality, and passive listening (Olson & Kemery, 2019). Researchers are focusing on emotional intelligence and empathy in AI agents to make these assistants more like personal companions and better able to establish more trustful interactions. Along with empathy, relationships between human and the machine will be redesigned in more transparent and trustworthy ways by reducing the complexity of technology. It will be possible to create more personal, emotional, and empathetic experiences that have an impact on individuals, improving their self-growth, awareness, and courage.

The aim of this research is to understand the expressions of emotions and empathy as they relate to psychological, cognitive, and social theories; emotional intelligence in terms of personal and social competence; interactions between humans and machines; the role of design in AI and

empathetic companions to build trustful companionships and interactions with digital products.

Introduction

AI is a powerful science to help people with their basic needs and to create new experiences. Today, AI is used in many fields as a tool to shape someone's actions and reach the expected goals in the easiest possible way (Holbrook, 2017). One needs to take care of a machine's intentions, aims, and competences to know its limitations, understand the machine's abilities, and communicate with the machine in a better way (Bodegraven, 2019). On the other hand, with emotional intelligence, machines will have the possibilities to comprehend users' goals, motivations, and pain points. Making AI more human-centered will create room for intelligent agents to manage the unpredictable situations in a better way, which means that in time, the machine will learn from the user, and the user will learn from the machine.

Virtual personal assistants are probably most likely to see AI in the shape of the interactions to reflect human behaviors, like smart speakers, as conversational AI and domestic robots. According to *TechCrunch,* in 2018, the smart-voice AI industry was a crucial landmark with nearly 41 percent of US consumers owning an activated voice speaker, a growth of 21.5 percent over 2017 (Perez, 2018). These intelligent agents already have the potential to make our lives much easier, at least regarding our basic daily needs. While these agents aim to complete the goal, during the learning process, they are not only part of the experiences but also learning from them and interpreting the information autonomously by making predictions, suggestions, or recommendations on the path to reaching the goal.

Every human has different communication skills, social abilities, and thoughts while they are following social norms. With the rising usage of technology, people, especially from the younger generations, have fewer social and emotional actions. Not only in human-to-human contact but also in personal communications and interactions. Having better knowledge and understanding of the characteristics that regulate one's emotions, AI will change, with virtual agents becoming more like companions with different personalities, and individual self-awareness will increase. AI must leave its passive role and become a design material to shape user experiences rather than to be defined as a tool. Thus, emotionally intelligent agents will provide improvements in social interactions and increase their efficiency in acceptance, success, and trust (Fan et al., 2017).

In time, AI agents will build emotional connections with users and improve interactions between humans and machines, leading them to have more trustful relationships. With this consideration, they will be able to better understand the user's personal needs and develop openness and closeness to create more trustful relationships and personalize the user's experiences so they function more effectively and efficiently.

This project investigated how we could establish trustful relationships with digital empathetic companions through developing personalities. The first part of the book contains a detailed description of the emotions and power of empathy and explanations of personality models and traits that are designed and implemented to construct onboarding experiences for the first meeting with companions. It also provides a method for testing and evaluating the personality of the model. The second part of the book consists of an experiment to investigate whether personality has a positive effect on the user experience to create trust with an empathetic companion through onboarding experiences. The experiment found that to create trustful experiences, the companion's personality, which is built using personality frameworks, had a significantly improved effect on user experiences.

Emotions
and Power
of Empathy

Chapter 1
Emotions and Power of Empathy

Expressions of Emotion

Antonio Damasio, a Portuguese-American neuroscientist, talks in his essay about the relationship between emotions and their brain substrates. He mentions that feelings are capable of sensing whether nature and situation are compatible or not. And we have acquired our own development by way of interactions with our social surroundings, both consciously and unconsciously, through genetic adaptations and nature. Feelings, as well as the emotions, act as internal guides. They assist us in communicating with other signals that can lead them as well. On the other hand, feelings are neither intangible nor difficult to catch (Damasio, 2004).

Emotions are described as abrupt distresses and passing agitations induced by acute anxiety, shock, or happiness. Mental feelings and affinity were also described as separate from cognitions or volitions like pain, willingness, hope, and so on. These definitions are the basic dictionary descriptions and reflections of several experiences. In basic, they are the way of showing someone's feelings. According to Darwin, the English naturalist, geologist, and biologist, the speech or the expressions of emotions in themselves are relevant to the well-being of the human race (Darwin, 1872). The fundamental message by Darwin was the evolution of emotional expressions and adaptation. Hess and Thibault explain Darwin's emotional phrases regarding these expressions as a significant communicative function and part of an emotional mechanism that protects or prepares the body for action. The expressive behavior described by Darwin as part of the emotional state is the expression of emotions that reproduce their communicative value from being external manifestations of an inward state. These are some important highlights from his book *The Expression of the Emotions in Man and Animals* in terms of being validated intercultural observations and the first evaluation research, which later initiated the scientific observation and the research related to emotional expressions (Hess and Thibault, 2009).

Moreover, according to Cannon, emotions were seen as just somatic reactions (Cannon, 1927). And emotion has been defined as a state of mind by the *Dictionary of Cognitive Psychology* (Oatley, 1994). Moreover, Dantzer classified emotions as solely cognitive and described the visceral and cognitive elements as a part of the mental representation of emotional experience (Dantzer, 1989).

Theories of Emotion

Emotions are linked to a variety of psychological events, including motivation, personality, and temperament. The main motivational theories are classified into physiological, cognitive, neurological, or social categories.

Theories of Emotion   **P1.1**

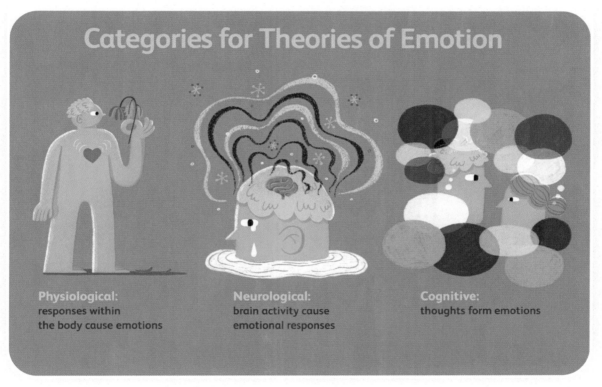

Source: Zhou, 2019

Theories of Emotion (Zhou, 2019)

Evolutionary Theory: Basic Emotion Model

In emotional literature, one of the most ubiquitous ideas is that some feelings have unique positions. They are generally referred to as basic, primary, and fundamental emotions (Ortony and Turner, 1990). The structure of basic emotions clearly shows difference and peculiarity in regards to the overall notion of feelings. This perspective claims to be a tiny amount of so-called main emotions, generally consisting of fear, rage, happiness, sorrow, surprise, and displeasure (Celeghin et al., 2017).

Indeed, there are several theories, approaches, and variable taxonomies about primary emotions. Some considerations that developed are based on the Darwinian approach. This approach indicates feelings by means of automatic processes that have evolved and been chosen due to their adaptive qualities (Tooby and Cosmides, 1990). Moreover, they can regulate the communication with the proximal setting, while at the same time, provide efficient reactions to the appropriate survival scenario, both instrumental and communication (Shariff and Tracy, 2011).

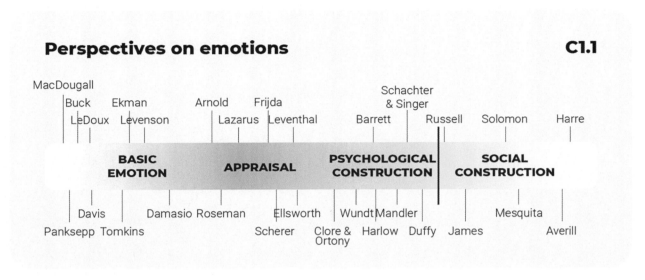

Source: Gross and Barrett, 2011

Perspectives on Emotions (Gross and Feldman Barrett, 2011)

Psychological Construction Theory

Some theories of psychological construction argue against emotional innateness. These theories advocate the consideration that various feelings arise from different building processes. According to this approach, fundamental psychological activities like perception, attention, and memory are combined to produce an emotional significance that is affected by social and linguistic factors (Barrett and Russell, 2015). In this theory, emotions are not described in terms of formal, functional, and causative states of mind like cognition and perception because dedicated mechanisms do not cause the emotions. The continuous and consistently modified constructive method, with more fundamental, nonemotional components, considers all mental states to emerge. Many research studies focus on one or more elements of the mind and leave the emotional notion behind them (Gross and Feldman Barrett, 2011).

One well-known example related to the physiological construction theory belongs to the physiologists William James and Carl Lange; it is called the James-Lange theory of emotion. They announced that emotions arise because of physiological responses to events. Physiological reactions occur when someone sees that the external stimulus leads to physiological responses. So these reactions depend on how someone interprets physical responses. For example, imagine a scary scenario, and a person is trembling because of the fear. The James-Lange theory explains that a person feels afraid because she or he is trembling, not that a person trembles because she or he is afraid (James, 1884).

Another psychological theory is the Cannon-Bard theory, which does not focus on the same aspects as the James-Lange theory. According to Walter Cannon, emotional and physiological responses can be encountered without feeling these emotions. Like, for example, the fact that someone's heart can beat, not because they are afraid, but because of physical activities like training (Cannon, 1987). In accordance with this theory, feelings are proposed resulting from physiological reactions, when the thalamus signals the brain in response to stimulation. The brain receives these signals that stimulate emotional experiences. So both the emotional experience of the physical and psychological development come into existence at the same time instead of one forming the other (Friedman, 2010).

Cognitive Construction Theory

This theory explains emotional phrases as still labeled to privileged mental states that are distinctive in their shape and are formed and triggered by other mental conditions. However, this theory does not label different cognitive processes, like anger, sadness, or fear. Evaluations are like a series of buttons that cause the fundamental biological mental reactions in certain habits, either by stereotypes or by a powerful, almost inevitable tendency to interact in a certain way with the world. In a contextually delicate manner, emotions are considered to be tightly organized responses. Emotions are linked to responding trends, which do not always take place but instead, they are described as arrangements to connect in a specific manner to the world (Gross and Feldman Barrett, 2011).

The cognitive constructive model says that emotions are ways of experiencing the environment. In this respect, emotions are more and more seen as emerging actions, while evaluation models continue to assume that emotions are functional conditions (Barrett et al., 2007).

One of the examples related to the cognitive construction theory is Schachter-Singer theory, also known as the two-factor theory. According to this theory, a person must determine the cause of the excitement and identify it as an emotion that occurred after physiological arousal. A stimulus contributes to a physiological reaction, which is interpreted and marked cognitively and contributes to an emotion (Schachter and Singer, 1962). As a small brief, we can say that for the two-factor theory of emotion, a person needs to define the excitement to feel emotion instead of just feeling excited by reason of interaction between physical excitement and how someone labels this excitement cognitively (Cherry, 2019).

This situation can be explained more clearly with an example. According to Schachter and Singer, if we imagine a person will likely recognize a feeling as fear if she or he encounters a rapid heartbeat or wet hands during a significant moment, like a math test, this moment might be called anxiety. When the individual experiences the same physical signs in a different special moment, like dating someone for the first time, these reactions might be interpreted as love or excitement (Schachter and Singer, 1962).

In addition, this environment plays a role in shaping physical responses besides situational changes. Imagine a person walks to her or his car during the evening, and suddenly, another person appears and quickly comes close. In accordance with the two-factor theory, this person might feel frightened because of the perception of the strange person. First, he or she will realize the appearance of the stranger. Then, the person will feel his or her heartbeat shaping the emotion as fear because of its rapidity. Now, if this situation happens during the day instead of at night, a person can see an elderly woman who suddenly appears. In this scenario, the perception of physical reactions might be related more to curiosity or concern about whether the woman needs help or not, rather than being afraid (Cherry, 2019).

Social Construction Theory

For this theory, emotions are considered to be cultural artifacts or socially prescribed activities, comprising cultural and cultural variables, and restricted by the role of the individual and the cultural background. Especially in psychology, some models of social models treat social configurations like models designed to trigger basic emotional responses and early evaluation models designed to trigger cognitive-emotional principles (Gross and Feldman Barrett, 2011). This theory perceives emotions as sociocultural products and focuses on the effect of human social interactions instead of natural effects. In addition, this theory describes emotions as cultural achievements rather than identify them as inner mental states like other methods. So far, social requirements and limitations are transferred through cognitive processes. These transactions are viewed as learned instead of given by nature in contrast to certain assessments so that these understandings differ from culture to culture. Also, the cognitive and behavioral elements of emotion are believed to coevolve according to local cultural meanings and are mainly regarded for their social roles (Gross and Feldman Barrett, 2011).

According to Averill, professor emeritus in the psychology department at the University of Massachusetts and past president of the American Psychological Association's Division of Theoretical and Philosophical Psychology, as a philosophical doctrine, social constructionism often stands in contrast to reality. Reality occurs in numerous variants, but the truth occurs independently of human ideas and wants. That is what the variations have in common, so it needs to be discovered. In comparison, social constructionism affirms that a particular moment and location always relates to human situations. Averill also claims that cultural convictions and guidelines are one of the main values by which mental syndromes are structured and understood behind a social constructionist strategy (Averill, 2017).

Averill claims that the knowledge of being out of command is an understanding of what we do, but more accurately, this is an understanding of the position of our cultures on our behaviors (Averill, 1982). Many examples of behavior are found that interpret someone's actions in this way. He says in his book *The Social Construction of Emotion* that arranging behavior is part of the responsibility of the social function of emotions. As stated in his book, anger helps someone to regulate interpersonal relations by setting and imposing limits of what is considered correct and improper. In exchange for a stable relationship, romantic or enthusiastic affection permits someone to willingly give up his or her financial and social liberties (Averill, 1985).

Aside from social functions, culture has a crucial role in social constructions. More important, culture offers the content of emotion-generating assessments. Our evaluation contents are cultural, although the evaluation process is described as a biological adaptation. So different cultures and personalities create varieties of emotions. While some actions make a person angry, the same actions can create different feelings for someone who belongs to a different culture. Being aware of the position of culture in our lives helps to understand our emotional actions and reactions, and it brings a broader understanding of emotional social functions (Cornelius, 2000).

To summarize, emotion under the social construction theory is identified slightly differently than other theories. According to social constructivism, emotions are recognized in the fields of neural phenomena and nervous system subsystems, particular cognitions and behavior in terms of interpersonal, cultural, and social events. Thus, emotions are better described with respect to organization or analysis in a more inclusive level.

Emotional Responses

Emotions are determined as episodic dispositions, cognitive arrangements, or social transitional functions. These three overlapping elements, or values, that assist us to comprehend how mental reactions are arranged into consistent syndromes. Averill explains these distinctions with an illustrated example (C.1.2), which shows emotional syndromes, mental structures, emotional states, and emotional responses (Averill, 1991).

Episodic Dispositions (Emotional States)

Emotional states are designed as methods of willingness for intervention triggered by assessments of artifacts or circumstances that are conceptualized. Episodic dispositions identify someone's emotional state at the moment that emotions appear at the same time. These stated emotions are not permanent feelings; they appear and then disappear according to the situations that explain the circumstances of the person. Also, they show variety in many aspects that can depend on a person's personality, culture and cultural effects, and different situations and conditions that they have an effect on, creating emotions and so on.

An emotional state, more formally, is a quick-term, reversible (episodal) inclination (disposition), characteristic of an emotional syndrome, to respond is an emotional state. This explanation looks simple, but it can create misunderstandings in the manner of formulating emotional episodes that are often recognized by allowing part of a syndrome to represent the entire syndrome (Averill, 1991). We can explain this condition using a common example. If we imagine a person's sweaty hands, the general definition is frequently used as a stand-in for anxiety, as a grin for rage, and so on for other emotional syndromes. On the other hand, emotional reactions like fear, anger, and other emotional conditions can be expressed in many ways. For instance, sweating hands can be a sign of anger as well as happiness and excitement or stress. As mentioned before, these reactions might change according to person, culture, conditions, environment, and so on.

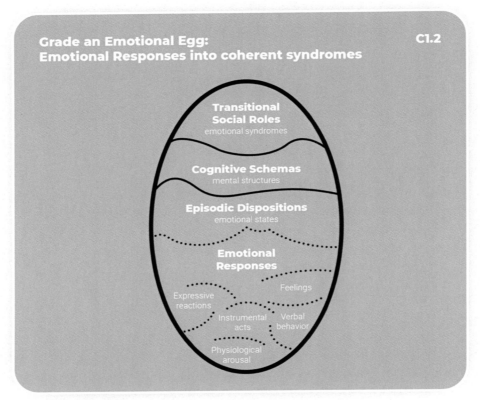

Source: Averill, 2017

Emotional Responses in Coherent Syndromes (Averill, 2017)

Moreover, a person can react in a number of ways in accordance with the emotional syndrome when he or she is in episodic disposition. This condition is called episodic disposition because "episodic" defines a temporary situation with a specified initiation, and "disposition" identifies the state of emotions and willingness to react in accordance with the individual and circumstances (Averill, 1991).

During his interview, Averill also emphasizes the schematic analysis to express aspects of the individual. Schemas are one way to characterize structural factors that allow mental arrangements. With a few exceptions, emotions are considered social phenomena. One of the roles of emotional notion is to provide social transitions to create a connection between individuals and societies that can only be approached socially (Averill, 2017).

The most researched subject in emotional sociology is likely the impact of emotional standards on knowledge and speech (Gordon, 1990). Building on Sartre's traditional differentiation (Sartre, 2001), the writers design emotional experience as comprising two feasible kinds of awareness, namely the first and the second. Reflective (second-order) experience of emotion means awareness of the direct experience (first order) of emotion. For any emotional state, the specific content that defines the possible secondary emotional experience depends on how a person handles the required experience in the first order. As pointed out with this statement, some of the emotional experience can include the reflective experience (second order). However, every emotional state involves emotions in the first order (Aranguren, 2016). While all emotional conditions imply some emotional experience, it is not possible to deduce from the emotional state itself the particular content of the emotional experience (Frijda, 1986).

Empathy

What Is Empathy?

Empathy is usually defined by emotion researchers as the capability to understand another person's emotions, feelings, and thoughts. The witnessing of another's emotional state, learning from another's situation, or even reading can contribute to empathy and spontaneous sharing (Keen, 2006). It is a way to look from the same window to perceive how someone might feel and think about different situations and actions. Empathy helps people to regain their human traits and strengthens their emotional connections to other people and the interactions between them. It creates an idea to better understand other people's situations.

It should be not forgotten that empathy and sympathy are different, even if empathy is believed to be a pioneer for sympathy in terms of mirroring someone else's inevitable emotions and feelings. Mainly, sympathy is a way to share someone's emotional situations or to understand these situations and try to help the other person with this understanding or be happy with them. For example, when someone loses a family member, a friend will feel sorry for the loss and share his or her feelings. The person will understand the friend's emotional situation and share his or her feelings.

In contrast, according to Keen's manifestations of moral emotion, also known as empathic anxiety, they are therefore associated with prosocial and altruistic behaviors. It should be noted that empathy leading to compassion is, by default, a different approach, while an overawakened empathic reaction that causes personal distress, which is a disincentive and self-oriented, leads to a discrepancy between one another's challenging status (Keen, 2006).

More scientifically, with deep historical research on empathy, fundamental aspects of empathy are found in dogs and even rodents among our primate family. Empathy is connected to two pathways in the brain. Scientists have hypothesized that some elements of empathy can be traced to represent neurons, cells in the brain that flame in the same way that others fire when we experience someone else performing an action. Moreover, research has also shown inherited empathy, although studies show that individuals may improve or restrain their empathic abilities (What Is Empathy, 2019).

According to Dutch primatologist Frans de Waal, empathy is usually considered an entirely human characteristic that appears to be seen by humans but also reveals something in apes, and it is shown by other species as well (de Waal, 2005). As de Waal claims, we can say that empathy is not only peculiar to humankind, it also involves other life forms. In addition, people have empathy to the imitated characters we are used to seeing in series, movies, games, and in many other similar fictional scenarios. For example, a person might try to understand this imitated character's feelings and emotions to be happy, sad, or angry for or with the character and from her or his point of view. They can then interpret the character's behaviors and think and empathize against what is happening to the character.

A Perception-Action Model in Empathy

Empathy is described as a specific emotional experience when an individual—the subject—feels a similar emotion to another person—the object—as a result of the perception of another's condition in accordance with a perception-action model (PAM). When the subject pays attention to the object's state of emotion, this process is triggered naturally due to the fact that the subject's emotional status is represented.

First of all, the reason this model is called the perception-action model is because it is based on the same-named tenants of motor actions. The words "perceptual activity" explains the fact that there are specific expectations for the perception and generation of action in motor behavior. Jeannerod and Frank claimed that imagined movements allow common perception and action representations (Jeannerod and Frank, 1999) because the identification and analysis of specific instruments stimulate the imagined movements and image of the motor activity associated with the left premotor cortex. Therefore, the experience of perception-action throughout motor activity applies to direct impressions as well as symbolism, imagination, and action to transparent activities, fantasized actions, and even mental affordances that are cognitively abstract (Preston, 2007).

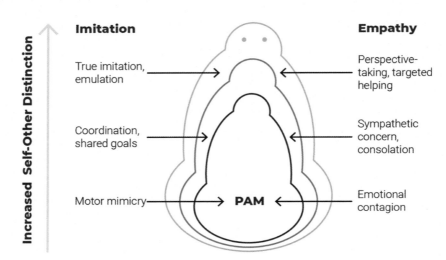

Source: Waal, 2009

Perception-Action Model: The Russian Doll Model of Empathy and Imitation (de Waal, 2009)

PAM can be viewed in circumstances where the issue is clear. This model considers the object and the circumstances in which the subject imagines the object's status. The triggers for empathy may be caused by other people, animals, or even an object in the manner that motor behavior triggers empathy. Based on an original evolutionary model of Preston and de Waal (Preston and de de Waal, 2002a, 2002b), the process developed into live interactions with other people so that living objects better drive the system than imaginary objects, which results in more extreme types of empathy (Preston, 2007).

According to de Waal, empathy causes in the subject a similar emotional state like the object, which is located in the center of the process of perception-action, that produces matching statements. More scientifically, the neural model suggests that the brain areas have their cell structures and connectivities depending on the processing domains. As such, no empathy region is used, and the brain areas are recruited when the appropriate domain is needed for the specific task (de Waal, 2009).

The representation of this theory has been shown in many contexts in psychology. One of the representations shows similarity with the neural network (McClelland and Rumelhart, 1985) in terms of triggering by the same pattern. For this, a representation is a pattern of activation in the brain and body that correlates to a common position and consistently activates the same pattern in repeated instances.

Empathy rises with past experiences and similarities and promotes the significance of similar representations in PAM. For example, if a person has specific experience in her or his past that is related with extremely distressing experiences from childhood, this person has more empathy and compassion (Barnett and McCoy, 1989) when perceiving similar situations in someone else.

All this considered, I found an interesting example that might match the perception-action model in the storytelling field. This is *Russian Doll*, an American comedy-drama television series (Lyonne, Headland, and Poehler, 2019). The protagonist of the story is stuck at a specific time. She keeps dying and coming back to life at the same point, and the story always follows the same memory. All the characters and objects around the protagonist are the same each time she is reborn. In the story, through the protagonist's life and death and life disorder, she finds her alter ego, her co-sick person, and discovers the moment that is related to her mother's death and her necklace, which is a gift from her mother. This situation represents a similar approach on empathy that is represented in the PAM. It claims that when the protagonist realized her experience from her childhood, which has an extremely tragic effect on her psychology, and empathized with the secondary character, a represented model of her alter ego, she finally sets herself free from her repetitive psychological cycle.

Russian Doll   **P1.2**

Source: Netflix,2019

Russian Doll (Netflix, 2019)

Understanding Empathy

In neuroscience, empathy is categorized into three skills of the potential for perceiving, knowing, and experiencing other people's emotional states. According to Derntl and Regenbogen, these skills can be explained as the ability to understand feelings in oneself and others through various communication signals, such as facial expression, tone of voice, or behavior. This mental aspect is also called perspective or mind theory, which defines the capacity while preserving the basic distinctions between oneself and others to adopt another person's viewpoints, and a compassionate dimension that is the ability to experience emotions similar to others thanks to emotional interactions (Derntl and Regenbogen, 2014).

Moreover, Saarikivi talks about these three skills and mentions that they are assisted by different brain functions. She explains these skills as thoughts, feelings, and actions, which are also mentioned above in a detailed way. Thoughts shape a person who tries to understand thoughts that belong to another person or by putting himself or herself in another person's shoes. Our brains have a mentalizing network, and this part of the brain is active when a person thinks about other people's thoughts and his or her own memories and future. Feelings are the vehicle that allows perceiving others' emotions as if they were their own. Human brain structures are highly contagious for emotions (Saarikivi, 2016). For instance, capturing facial emotions is an automatic response by which someone can understand emotional statements, like happiness from a smile. Also, pain can be contagious through seeing individuals as they are cutting their fingers while someone is cutting his or her fingers. This action creates the same effect in the brain, and our brains do not distinguish between the person herself or himself and the others (Lamm, Decety, and Singer, 2011).

Lastly, actions are described as ways to act with the information that is collected while people have the ability to put themselves in another person's place and try to understand what they can do in this situation or to help others (Saarikivi, 2016). An example from scientific research to explain the power of helping others and sharing is related to the part of our brains that is responsible for pleasure and reward. It is more engaged if our friend is rewarding too (Fareri et al., 2012).

Saarikivi also mentions transcranial magnetic stimulation, which stimulates the brain and contributes to brain activity necessary for increasing empathy and clearing away the obstacles causing lack of empathy. She questions about finding new ways to create synergy with other people to increase our emotional connections and interactions; for example, reading to learn about different realities in order to decrease the fear of diversity and differences between us, or music to turn the empathy mechanism in our brains with a rhythm (Saarikivi, 2016).

Listening with Empathy

Communications experts estimate that the words people use constitute just 10 percent of their interactions. Sounds constitute another 30 percent, and body language accounts for the remaining 60 percent. People listen empathetically with their ears, but more important, they listen with their eyes and hearts. They listen for feeling and meaning to track behavior. They use both the left and the right sides—like you think, you intuit, you know, you hear. Empathic listening is important because it helps you to interact with accurate data. With empathy, people truly reflect the reality of dealing with someone's emotions, going deep inside their heads and hearts instead of showing their own feelings and imagining emotions, motivations, and perceptions. Empathic listening is deeply therapeutic and curative, as well as allowing one to invest in his or her own because it supplies the person with psychological air. Covey explains this definition more clearly with an example. If we imagine a person who suddenly learns the air inside the room will be finished soon, he or she will only think about surviving by getting out of the room. This thought will be the only incentive for that person for the moment. However, since we know there is air inside the room, this situation will not motivate us. This is one of the most important insights in the area of human motivation. The answer to what motivates us is the only thing that we can use to reach unfulfilled needs. Thus, we might say that apart from physical survival, since we do not have any great worries about it in our lives, to be recognized, supported, affirmed, and valued by others becomes the main need of human beings (Covey, 2004). When we listen to others with empathy, it gives them psychological air. Completing this vital need, supplying the psychological air, will create an impact on our communications and other interactions between individuals and will encourage us to move forward in our emotional relations more aware of ourselves and others with effective and empathic listening.

Is There a Dark Side of Empathy?

Empathy contributes to positive human experiences and interactions by helping to improve connections between people and groups. It also creates socially deeper cultural understandings. Empathy is a broad and complex emotional subject (Segal et al., 2017). Empathy is a lifelong process that might change when a person meets new people, or it might depend on situations and sociocultural effects. Also, it should not be forgotten to avoid being confused when experiencing someone else's emotions. A person should consider other people's emotions without interpreting them or merging them with his or her own emotions and feelings.

Empathy can be complex, but that does not mean it has a dark side. It is a skill that allows people to feel others' emotions without considering themselves in their situations and imagining a way to handle the situation. Calling wrong definitions empathy can create misunderstandings and make one try to define a dark side of empathy. For example, if someone understands other people's thoughts and then use their weaknesses against them, that is not empathy. This situation just leads to someone reading another person's emotional statement and using that information to bully that individual. It means that a bully can read and understand other people's feelings without participating in their emotions (van Noorden et al., 2015).

Cognitive and Emotional Empathy

Hoffman divided empathy into two sides, cognitive empathy and emotional (affective) empathy (Hoffman, 1977). Cognitive empathy focuses on understanding other people's thoughts, feelings, emotions, and so on while imagining our thoughts about other peoples' positions or experiences. Psychology describes empathy as a high-level cognitive ability that needs language (and is often emphasized on this aspect) and is found only in human beings. On the other hand, this consideration in psychology does not explain the evolution of empathy in human beings.

Animals also have empathy between each other that shows itself in the different ways they express their feelings, moods, and emotional states to other animals. This way of expressing and transferring the emotions is located on the second side, emotional (affective) empathy. According to de Waal, the emotional side is the heart of all empathy, and empathy is first and foremost a psychological interaction between body and emotion. If a person lacks emotions or prefers to stay away emotionally from another person, it is just a way to understand others' perspective instead of having empathy (de Waal, 2009). Understanding other people's emotions can form the motivational foundation for moral development and acceptable behavior (Hoffman, 1990).

In addition, these two sides of empathy have been identified in psychological literature and have influenced many recent research studies in neuroscience. Cognitive and emotional empathy match with type 1, which is defined as being prereflective, stimuli-focused, and uncompromising; and type 2, which is defined as demanding, slow, attentive yet versatile processes in a classic dichotomy of psychology. At first glance, emotional and mental empathy appear to be the same in the field of differentiation in neuroscience as in psychology. However, analysis of this literature shows that cognitive and emotional empathy tend to be related to widely isolated neural systems. Briefly, these two types are likely more clearly reflected in the concept of continuous experiences in an upside, while emotional empathy is more or less consistent and a downward processing flow, which is almost in line with cognitive empathy (Iacoboni, 2015).

Experience of Narrative Empathy

Edward Bradford Titchener, an English experimental psychologist, explores empathy by explaining learning experiences and mentions that people have natural inclinations to immerse themselves in what they see or imagine. They may, in a way, become explorers as they read about the forest, experiencing the gloom, quiet, humidity, persecution, and feeling of looming danger for themselves. Everything is unfamiliar, but it is an odd experience that has come (Titchener, 1915).

With the consideration of emphasizing the emotions with other people or the fictional characters and share experiences, Lee argues that empathy includes imagination and compassion as well as the assumption that has influenced all our conceptions of an outer world and given them to sporadic and heterogeneous experiences from outside the scope of our constant and highly coherent internal experiences, namely our own activities and aims (Lee, 1913).

Different experiences in narratives might create empathy between a person and the fictional characters. Empathy with the fictional character tends not to be particularly complex or rational; it requires only minor components of personality, place, and emotion (Keen, 2006). A person might feel the emotional states of the character or empathize with the character while watching a series, reading a book, or playing a game. Natural compassion toward the feelings of a fictional character can sometimes pave the way for the identification of a character. Not all character emotional states elicit empathy. In addition, empathetic responses with fictional characters and situations can more easily be addressed in the event of negative emotions, whether or not an in-depth match occurs in the experience (Keen, 2006).

It must be remembered that empathy and understanding, under different situations and actions, vary from person to person. Every person has his or her own imagination, expression, and identification that matches the fictional characters. Also, personality, culture, environment, or perception of the emotions might create differentiation in emotional behaviors or affect the intensity of empathy. Thus, we can say that while one person can create an emotional bond and empathetic relationship with the character, another person might not feel empathy and connect emotionally to the character.

Narrator-theorists and specialists in the interpretation of discourses conduct empirical research into literary reading, correlating a range of storytelling methods with empathy. Some theoreticians and researchers regard the formal structures themselves as empathic in nature. Character identification is one of the most widely recognized features in narrative empathy. The possibilities for characterization and, thus, for empathy could be expected to lead to particular characteristic aspects such as classification, definition, indirect inference of characteristics, reliance on styles, relative flatness or openness, representation of behavior, the positions of plot trajectories, the performance of attributed expressions, and the method of consciousness presentations. In addition, fictional characters tend to have independent agencies as commented by fiction authors according to the characters' personalities, a conversation between the characters and the audience, argument about their actions, and consensus on feelings.

In view of the research of Bortolussi and Dixon, character behavior helps to determine features by the people who they are reading, watching, or playing with the character, whereas they stated that there were no self-assessments made by the narrator (Bortolussi and Dixon, 2003). Keith Oatley claims that the personal experiences of emotional response patterns by readers or audiences build empathy with the characters (Oatley, 1995). On the other hand, even if this is not genuine empathy, people who related to the characters in the story through their personal experiences are more likely to report improvements in self-perceptions (Louwerse and Kuiken, 2004).

Perceiving Empathy in Artificial Agents

Social interactions and physical embodiment of emotions can supply information and enable communication with the environment. Computational model creation for emotional development, as well as verification with virtual/real agents and providing new tools or data to better understand the human developmental process, such as a robot as a dependable reproduction tool in psychological research are two of the most used methodologies (Asada, 2015). These approaches and information represent the virtual agents as reliable companions with highly empathetic skills in psychological experiments.

Asada defines the relationship between the development of self-other cognition and empathy in three stages: emotional contagion, emotional and cognitive empathy, and sympathy and compassion.

Emotional Contagion: Having someone's emotions and reflecting them consciously or unconsciously by initiating emotional and behavioral sentiments. Emotional contagion is important because it is a simultaneity of individual relationships. It is closely related to motor mimicry, and it creates automatic attitudes that come from another person's movements.

Emotional and Cognitive Empathy: A broad construct that refers to the personal cognitive (psychological) feature to discover experiences of another and emotional reactions that consist of contagion (motor mimicry) and development of self-awareness and perspective-taking, a range of status square measure evoked by the estimated perspective of someone's mental state.

Sympathy and Compassion: Instead of emotional and cognitive empathy, virtual agents can understand someone's emotional statement and reflect her or his emotions according to the interpretation of these feelings. These feelings are different from those of the other person's, and they simulate the emotional states of sympathy and compassion. For instance, when the artificial agent synchronizes the other's state and then feels totally desynchronized like pity or sorrow.

The relational map in chart 1.4 shows the summary of self-development and differentiation. It describes the evaluation and intersection of imitation and empathy through self-discrimination (Asada, 2015).

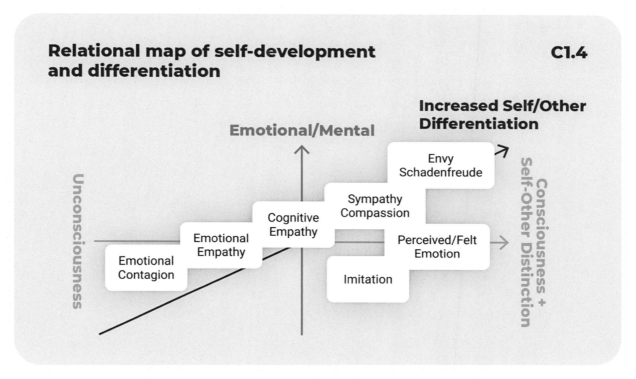

Source: Asada, 2015

Relational Map of Self-Development and Differentiation.
Development of Artificial Empathy (Asada, 2015)

Scientific research in the field of neuroscience has enhanced two theories to explain empathy more completely. The first one is called simulation theory. It is a way of reflecting the emotions and feelings that belong to another person when that person experiences them. This allows the person to understand the other person's emotional situation straight from the person showing her or his emotions.

Some other research supports the theory of mind, which is the opposite idea from the simulation theory. Theory of mind is the ability to understand the other person's thoughts, feelings, and actions while considering these feelings and deciding how to act and show emotions to another person. This theory advises people to use cognitive thought to describe another person's emotional situations and to predict or justify the actions of others by regarding human behavior (Lesley.edu, 2019).

Takeaways

This chapter explained how empathy affected emotional responses and the representation of emotional states. It started with knowing and explaining other people's emotional states, and then it moved to understanding the created effects on individuals from human-to-human interactions. After all, the perspective is changed by focusing on internal experiences of individuals to explain how people create empathetic relationships with their personal experiences.

I used these selected theories to describe the formation of emotions from the birth of humanity to the formation of social order and the definition of cultures, as well as to underline the effect of direct experience of emotions to create awareness on individuals.

In the next chapter, these emotional theories and definitions will be connected to the computing of emotions to explain emotional intelligence.

Affective Computing

Emotional Intelligence

Theories of EI

Verbal and Nonverbal Intelligence

Emotional Disorders

Chapter 2

Affective Computing

Introduction

The general definition of empathy is solely the power to make an associate in nursing an embodied illustration of another's emotion, while at the same time, being responsive to the causative mechanism that elicited that emotion (Gonzalez-Liencresa et al., 2013).

The interaction range between human and computer looks different in terms of finding contexts in which to interact (Riek and Robinson, 2009). But the important thing is to design and create more genuine shapes of artificial empathy (Asada, 2015).

Emotional Intelligence

Emotional intelligence (EI) is an ability to structure feelings and emotions, which includes someone's own emotions and emotions between individuals, and then use that information to create actions and thinking ways that belong to a person. Yale psychology professor John Meyer says that "emotional intelligence is the ability to accurately perceive your own and others' emotions; to understand the signals that emotions send about relationships; and to manage your own and others' emotions" (*Harvard Business Review*, 2004). Research shows that in the near future, the emotional intelligence quotient (EQ) will be more effective than the intelligence quotient (IQ) for building strong relationships with people, other life forms, and machines.

Several theories have been founded about emotional intelligence. For the research of empathetic companions, I mainly focused on three theories for the evaluation of convenient companionship that explain EI with performance (Goleman's model of EI), competencies (Bar-On's model of EI), and abilities (Mayer, Saloyev, and Caruso's model of EI).

Theories of EI

1. Goleman's Model of EI Performance

Goleman describes the EI quotient in five core emotional traits. These traits are related to human success and level of abilities (Riopel, 2019; Executive Partnerships, 2017):

- Know and understand someone's own emotions and reactions.
- Manage, control, and adapt someone's own emotions, reactions, and responses.
- Motivate someone's own emotions and themselves to achieve their goals and take appropriate actions and feedbacks.
- Understand and recognize someone else's emotions, make understandings more valuable, and build more empathy.
- Manage relationships with others, and build social skills in social situations to negotiate conflict and become self-motivated.

Domains of Emotional Intelligence   **C2.1**

	Recognition	**Regulation**
Personal Competence	**Self-Awareness** √ Self-confidence √ Awareness of your emotional state √ Recognizing how your behavior impacts others √ Paying attention to how others influence your emotional state	**Self-Management** √ Getting along well with others √ Handling conflict effectively √ Clearly expressing ideas and information √ Using sensitivity to another person's feelings (empathy) to manage interactions successfully
Social Competence	**Social-Awareness** √ Picking up on the mood in the room √ Caring what others are going through √ Hearing what the other person is "really" saying	**Relationship Management** √ Getting along well with others √ Handling conflict effectively √ Clearly expressing ideas and information √ Using sensitivity to another person's feelings (empathy) to manage interactions successfully

Source: Riopel, 2019

Domains of Emotional Intelligence. Daniel Goleman's Model in Four Quadrants (Riopel, 2019)

Although Goleman explained the EQ as having five sections, there is still disagreement on his model. But ongoing research shows that there is a possibility to improve and develop EI in terms of personal and social competence.

Personal competence involves self-awareness and self-management. Self-awareness helps a person to regulate his or her emotional reactions and understand the impact of his or her behaviors on other people. Besides, self-management helps a person to control these emotions and improve expressing skills to deliver their ideas and thoughts to another person. To make it more effective, a person needs to consider the other person's level of sensitivity when they perceive these actions. It also helps to overcome stressful situations and learn how to solve problems. Thus, people will become aware of being adaptable and learn how to control their emotional responses (Riopel, 2019; Executive Partnerships, 2017). When a person is able to keep in balance understanding their own feelings and aware of how to manage them, social interactions and communications will improve. The most important point is to keep the connection between being aware of and managing the feelings in order to better understand individual emotional states and the effects of these emotions on other people.

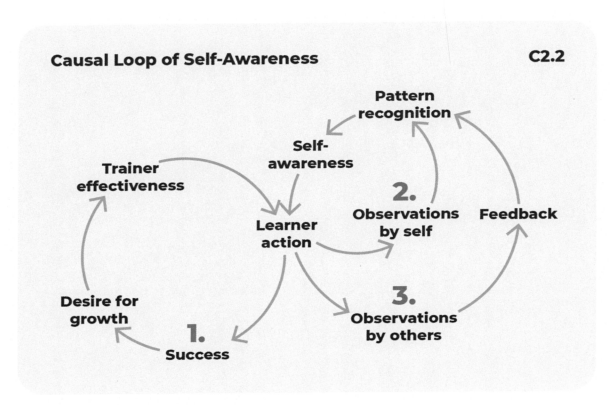

Source: Ramsey and Leberman, 2015

Causal Loop of Self-Awareness: Self-Awareness Growth Model (Ramsey and Leberman, 2015)

Social competence includes social awareness, relationship management, and regulation. Being socially aware means getting into other people's moods, attaching importance to what others do, and carefully listening to what others say. Moreover, the purpose of relationship management is to keep a relationship going by explaining the ideas clearly while communicating with another person and sensitively managing his or her feelings. So people will be able to find new ways of communication and interaction to unlock different abilities.

Gill, Ramsey, and Leberman used self-awareness competency based on Goleman's model of EI to explore the relationship between steps of learning and the way of thinking. Diagram C.2.2 shows the self-awareness growth model to convey a wide perspective of instruction on emotional intelligence (Ramsey and Leberman, 2015).

Another model to explain EI for leadership was developed by Freedman and Fariselli. This model provides a set of unique measures that can help someone to develop his or her own EI. Freedman divided the model into three main research prospects:

- Awareness of emotions and reactions: To know yourself better.
- Responsiveness with intentions: To choose yourself.
- Purposefulness in progressing: To give back to yourself.

Taking these EI models as core values, we can try to understand the position of companions in personal and social competence. When they create a trust and have a position in someone's life, they can encourage that person to grow by transforming technology into the EI models to build more empathic relationships.

2. Bar-On's Model of EI Competencies

Bar-On suggests that EI is connected with a behavior system that comes from emotional and social skills. This model explains emotional-social intelligence as an interrelationship between dealing with someone's daily requirements and their emotional abilities as well as social skills, competences, and facilitators to determine the efficiency of someone's understandings, expressions, and relationship with other people. Most important, this model merges with personal abilities, like self-understanding and awareness of one's personal weaknesses and strengths. Moreover, in line with this model, a person needs to understand herself or himself effectively, communicate efficiently, and deal with difficulties and pressures to ensure the requirements of social and emotional intelligence.

Besides self-awareness and understanding, to be emotionally and socially intelligent, empathy shows itself in order to comprehend other people's feelings, emotions, and requirements. Thus, the person will be able to manage personal, social, and environmental changes efficiently, as well as solve problems and make decisions in a realistic and flexible way. To achieve this, people must handle their feelings and be hopeful, stay motivated, and remain optimistic. All in all, these variables are the components of EI, and they influence human behaviors and interactions (Bar-On, 2006).

3. Mayer, Salovey, and Caruso's Theory of EI Ability

This EI model is used to encourage people's thoughts, lead the decision-making processes, and reflect their decisions thanks to indicated data that comes from perceived emotional understandings and management of emotions.

The four-branch ability theory advanced by Mayer, Salovey, and Caruso focuses on identifying, expressing, and perceiving emotions to manage and engage emotions effectively. They updated this method in 2016 and divided these abilities and skills into four main branches for problem-solving fields that are needed for emotional reasoning (Mayer, Caruso, and Salovey, 2016). These divisions, arranged from emotional awareness to management, are in line with how the capacity fits in an individual's general character (Mayer et al., 2004).

First is an emotional perception that states an understanding and identification of other people's emotions and feelings with their facial expressions or postures. These expressions are connected with nonverbal communication and allow people to empathize and perceive the emotions from others' faces or tone of their voices (Mayer et al., 2004).

The second ability defines simplification of thoughts in that they are cognitively integrated and incorporated with the complicated areas thanks to one's ability to use emotions.

The third branch is the ability to comprehend emotions and to evaluate feelings and consciousness of emotional development, along with the results of feelings that are appreciated (Mayer, Caruso, and Salovey, 2016).

The last one focuses on managing one's feelings, which can be called self-management. This ability includes a personality with objectives, self-confidence, and social consciousness that shapes the management of emotions.

Hot Intelligence

Mayer, Roberts, and Barsade later extended their knowledge about this method and brought new value to the abilities that are called "hot intelligence." This intelligence contains emotional, personal, and social intelligence. It is a useful way to think about the relationship between personal and social intelligence in order to better understand EI by sharing the common concerns for internal knowledge and exterior interactions in the human universe.

Personal intelligence is a new member of this intelligence grouping because to talk about self-satisfaction, courage, and awareness requires showing personal reflections. This is the primary internal pleasure and pain source that describes someone's positive and negative sides. Moreover, hot intelligence encourages people to compare EI with the individual and social intelligence and claim that EI can be placed between these other forms of hot intelligence.

A Comparison of Emotional, Personal, and Social Intelligences.   C2.3

Characterization of intelligence	Type of hot intelligence		
	Emotional	**Personal**	**Social**
Brief definition	The ability to reason validly with emotions and with emotion-related information, and to use emotions to enhance thought.	The ability to reason about personality—both our own and the personalities of others—including about motives and emotions, thoughts and knowledge, plans and styles of action, and awareness and self-control.	The ability to understand social rules, customs, and expectations, social situations and the social environment, and to recognize the exercise of influence and power in social hierarchies. It also includes an understanding of intra- and intergroup relations.
Areas of problem-solving	Understand the meaning of emotions and their implications for behavior.	Guide personal choices with inner awareness, including discovering personal interests and making personality-relevant decisions.	Identify social dominance and other power dynamics among groups.

Source: Mayer, Caruso, and Salovey, 2016

A Comparison of Emotional, Personal, and Social intelligence. The
Ability Model of EI (Mayer, Caruso and Salovey, 2016)

By involving the problem-solving area in this model, we can describe these three intelligences in a different way. The aim to involve the problem-solving areas in this model is not simply to focus on solving problems and creating solutions. Indeed, proof shows that simpler models could describe emotional and personal intelligence as mental skills (Legree et al., 2014). Like EI that is described in four branches, personal intelligence can be analyzed in four steps in terms of the identification of personal information, personality model creation, guidance for personal preferences, and systematization of life aims and plans (Mayer, 2009).

Verbal and Nonverbal Intelligence

We are all different from each other in terms of feelings, emotions, and ways of thinking or acting, so emotional intelligence appears differently in every individual (Mayer and Salovey, 1993). Scarr pointed out that keeping relationships good with other people comprise outwardness, social perception, and low anxiety. They are not being intelligent; they are just associating with intelligence. For example, intelligence creates behavior, but personality traits affect behavior (Scarr, 1989). Also, personal traits might be related to social skills that can be shaped by environmental effects, like the place someone lives, relationships between individuals and family, and other actors. Gardner's argument clearly states personal intelligence—which is the ability to swiftly effect discriminations among one's emotional life, range of effects or emotions, and eventually to label them, enmesh them in symbolic codes, and draw on them as a way of understanding and guiding one's actions—is the basic talent at work here. In its most basic form, intrapersonal intelligence is nothing more than the ability to discern between pleasant and unpleasant feelings. Intrapersonal knowledge, at its most sophisticated level, enables one to recognize and symbolize complex and highly distinct sets of emotions (Gardner, 1983).

EI includes verbal and nonverbal intelligence and expression and regulation of emotions in individuals and others. Nonverbal intelligence is the way to analyze and understand information and then regulate outcomes by using visuals instead of communicating or describing the things with words. Nonverbal tasks may include skills like understanding the meaning of visual information and remembering the sequences of visuals and relationships between each of them. A person with high nonverbal intelligence skills can be more powerful to deal with when using nonverbal messages, which they are able to reduce their needs for previous personal interactions (Penney, Miedema, and Mazmanian, 2015).

Emotional Disorders

The English naturalist, geologist, and biologist Charles Darwin asserts that adaptive emotional regulation has crucial importance in survival and reproduction (Darwin, 1872). With his consideration, many scientists worked on the light of this idea and extended it with another claim. One of the theories that they claimed is related to emotional disorders created by maladaptive behaviors (Gilbert, 1998). As stated in this claim, to experience the right feeling and emotion—like happiness, worry, sadness, and distrust—will improve the organism's congruity if the actions happen in the correct moment and under the right condition. Penney, Miedema, and Mazmanian clearly explain the emotional disorders with an example in their article. According to their example, they claim that emotions might have evolved with intelligence (Penney, Miedema, and Mazmanian, 2015). In view of the fact, emotions can be adapted based on the person's ability to foresee dangerous situations or plan the actions in these situations.

The person can decide wrongly regarding their actions as a consequence of these situations. These factors can create pressure and affect a person's choices abilities to make decisions. For example, a person can easily make the wrong decision under stress or if the level of anxiety is high. Due to feelings of stress and worry, one cannot predict actions happening at that moment or will happen in the next step. Moreover, anxiety will show itself again in the next similar situation. And according to the evolutionary standpoint, people will anticipate these situations because of the threatening worry, and they will not be as able to control their feelings and emotions against the actions. With this consideration, personal companions should be designed and developed carefully to avoid these threats. They should be transparent and trustful enough to encourage users to discover their abilities in decision-making, planning, and controlling their emotions.

Takeaways

This chapter explained how emotions are used to shape interactions between humans and machines to design and create more natural shapes to define artificial empathy. It started with an ability to structure feelings and emotions. Then it moved on to explain the different shapes of these feelings, emotions, and the ways of thinking and acting in individuals. After all, EI is examined in terms of verbal and nonverbal intelligence to describe the way of communicating through human understanding and skills to shape relationships.

I used these theories to describe self-awareness in regulating an individual's emotional reactions and the impact of his or her behavior on others and to encourage people's thoughts on how to improve their emotional understandings and management of emotions.

In the next chapter, these EI theories and definitions will be connected to human-to-human and human-to-machine and other life forms relationships with defining the shared consequences between each of them.

Shared
Consequences

Chapter 3
Shared Consequences

Relationships between Humans

Humans are proven emotional and complicated creatures in their social and personal relationships. To understand each other, empathy showed itself to create a bridge between emotional situations and interactions and help to better understand complex socioemotional behaviors.

According to the theory developed by Salovey and Mayer, new variations of emotional and social abilities can be discovered. These abilities and newly enhanced skills can be improved in terms of using, comprehending, and regulating emotions (Lopes et al., 2003). In order to understand a person's relationships with another person, a testing method, the Mayer, Salovey, and Caruso Emotional Intelligence Test (MSCEIT), is used. According to this testing, they concluded that Emotional Intelligence and personality affect social and personal relationships. Results showed mostly positive in personal and parental relationships, and few negative interactions with close friends.

The result of the MSCEIT showed EI had a relationship with verbal intelligence, personality, and perceived interpersonal relationship quality (Lopes et al., 2003). Briefly, verbal intelligence is the capacity to use language-based reasoning to evaluate data and solve issues. Reasoning based on language can require reading or listening to words, talking, writing, or even thinking.

The Big Five model, also known as the Ocean model, is a taxonomy for characteristics that describe personal traits with openness to experience, conscientiousness, extroversion, agreeableness, and neuroticism (Erder and Pureur, 2016).

The Big Five Model

Openness to experience: In this characteristic, people with a powerful inclination to experience are regarded as imaginative and creative. They are prepared for new experiences and open to discovering new ideas thanks to their curiosity.

Conscientiousness: People with this characteristic are regarded as goal-focused, well-organized, have self-discipline, and take responsibilities. They are also willing to follow laws and plan their activities.

Extroversion: Persons with powerful tendencies toward extroversion are regarded as outgoing, vigorous, and person-oriented. They get their energy from other people and they are described as confident and passionate people, like leaders with high visibility.

Agreeableness: People with a powerful inclination to be caring, kind, and trustworthy are regarded as high in agreeableness. They value and are tolerant in getting along with others.

Neuroticism: People with a strong tendency to be anxious, self-aware, impulsive, and pessimistic are considered high in neuroticism. They are relatively effected by negative emotions.

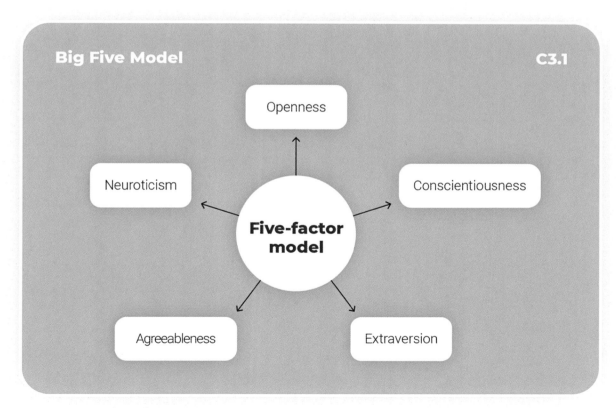

Source: Erder and Pureur, 2016

Big Five Model. Continuous Architecture (Erder and Pureur, 2016)

All these states considered an adult's personality did not shape from the birth. On the other hand, emotional and verbal intelligence have a chance to create an impact on someone's life. Personality can be reshaped with the improvement of interactions with the environment and by supporting personal learning and new experiences (Caspi, 2000).

Myers-Briggs Personality Theory

The theory of Myers-Briggs is an update to Carl Gustav Jung's theory of psychological styles, which is based on sixteen personality styles Jung found using stereotypes (Jung, 1976). Today, this theory is mentioned as one of the most popular psychology instruments in the world (Cherry, 2019).

The aim of this personality-type indicator is to understand and define the personalities that better suit an individual. The Myers-Briggs personality theory is a self-reporting inventory used to classify the type, weaknesses, and interests of an individual. The theory is built on four scales: extroversion and introversion, sensing and understanding, thinking and feeling, and judgment and perception:

Extroversion around people and events, defined with an E, and introversion between ideas and knowledge, defined with an I.

Sensing in terms of facts and truth, defined with an S, and intuition for understanding motivations and possibilities defined with an N.

Thinking with facts and logic, defined with a T, and feeling for defining values and interactions, defined with an F.

Judgment as a well-organized and planned lifestyle, defined with a J, and perception as a flow-related lifestyle defined with P.

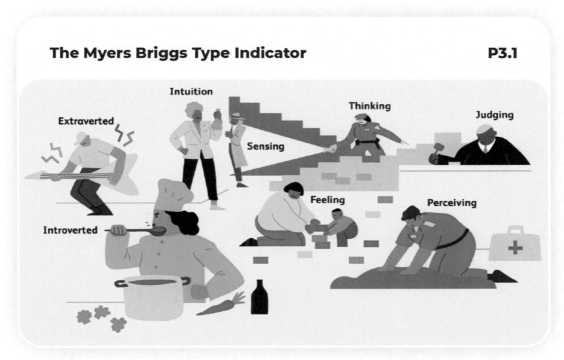

Source: Cherry, 2019

Myers-Briggs Type Indicator. Identify a Person's Personality
Type, Strengths, and Preferences (Cherry, 2019)

All the letters defined above as "E,I,S,N,T,F,J,P" are used to identify a person's personality type by selecting one appropriate characteristic from each scale. After matching, the result shows four matched identities to shape sixteen people's characteristics based on the Myers-Briggs theory. For instance, the variation of INTP is defined as "the thinker" with introversion from the first section, understanding from the second section, thinking from the third section, and perception from the last section. In addition to this, each variation has its own personality. It is important to remember, according to the Myers-Briggs Foundation, each type has importance, and all types are equal. Also, while each form approaches problems differently, and the approach of another person might not be what you choose, each method can be effective (Myersbriggs.org, nd).

The Myers-Briggs theory is not defined as a test. There are no right or wrong answers and all types are equal to each other since one type is not better than any other. These types of personalities do not offer improvement of a person's skills or personality traits. Also, the aim of the theory is not compared to expectations as opposed to many other kinds of psychological evaluations. The instrument seeks simply to offer more data about your individuality instead of looking at your performance relative to the results of others (Myers and Myers, 1980).

Recently, the Myers-Briggs theory was inspired by Adobe to identify people's creative types in terms of simple and related yet robust, science-informed evaluations of creative personalities. With this test, Adobe aimed to identify eight creative types: artist, thinker, adventurer, maker, producer, dreamer, innovator, and visionary to match with personalities based on people's choices (Creative Types by Adobe Create, 2019). The test not only interpreted its findings from this theory but also designed it in a more engageable way, with exciting visual designs, animations, and fictional characters designed for different personality types to unlock someone's full creative potential and be aware of his or her personality characteristics.

Creative types   **P3.2**

Source: Adobe, 2019

Creative Types (Creative Types by Adobe Create, 2019)

Jungian Archetypes

According to Carl Jung's archetypal theory, archetypes are recognized generic patterns, pictorial patterns, and collective unconscious templates and emotional equivalents (Feist and Feist, 2008). Based on this theory, they have inherited potentials that are actualized by entering into consciousness as images or by conduct on the outside world interactions (Wang and Salmon, 2006). Jung identified through these twelve primary archetypes and the associated motivations the four cardinal orientations, which represent a model for our understanding that has a set of values, significances, and individual characteristics. These four cardinals are:

- The ego, which affects the world and leaves a mark.
- The order, which provides a global framework.
- The social, which creates a link to others.
- The freedom that sets someone's mind on being independent and reaching the best.

The model is structured according to a fundamental driving force in three overall categories:

- The Ego Types
  - o The Innocent
  - o The Orphan/Regular Guy or Gal
  - o The Hero
  - o The Caregiver

- The Soul Types
  - o The Explorer
  - o The Rebel
  - o The Lover
  - o The Creator

- The Self Types
  - o The Jester
  - o The Sage
  - o The Magician
  - o The Ruler

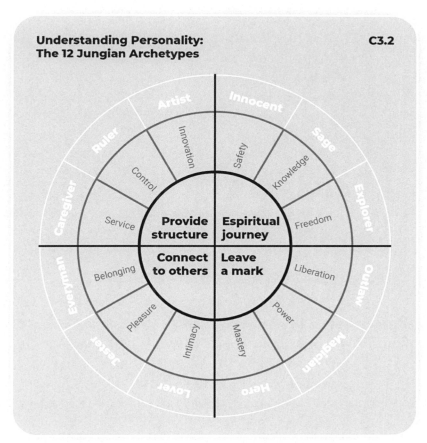

Source: Neill, 2018

Understanding Personality: The 12 Jungian Archetypes (Neill, 2018)

Building Trust

Author and research professor at the University of Houston Brené Brown, in her interview with Devine, mentions that the courage to be vulnerable is about showing up when you can't anticipate or control the results, not about winning or losing (Devine, 2019). According to Brown, people turned their backs to each other and in time, they found themselves lonelier and more scared. One reason for this situation was fear of vulnerability and getting hurt that, in the end, brought a lack of communication between. Strong connections and relationships between humans were lost. Moreover, fear brought other negative emotional states, like criticism, failure, conflict, invisibility, disconnection, and shame. Most people select to protect themselves against fear and move away from humanity, cut their connections with other individuals, or decrease interactions between each of them when they deny their vulnerability and the existence of fear (Brown, 2019).

All these considered, when people take back the feeling of self-actualization, they will be able to create connections between each other without fear. They will learn to listen and share their feelings, not only decent feelings, but also the uneasy and sad ones. At that point, when a person finds a way to connect with herself or himself, the individual will be able to take back the courage they lost and accept criticism. This connection will help to break the disconnection with other people. They will be able to build relationships thanks to their self-courage and self-actualization.

As humans, we need to take time to remember because it is easy to forget about what we have done till today and what we learned from our past actions. To avoid emotional disorders (as mentioned before in the EI section), people need to perceive the actions they learned in their pasts and use their knowledge as everything is not inherent (Brown, 2019). People also need to think about how to shape their thoughts. When someone achieves this point or has success, he or she should celebrate and make these moments memorable for the next possible actions.

With this consideration, these states arrive at one of the main questions that this research focuses on: How we can design personal companions to improve self-engagement and actualization, vulnerability with empathy, and find a way of creating better individual communications?

Relationship between Human and Machine

Presentation of emotional empathy between human and machine is difficult enough if we consider that human-to-human communications are not definitely accurate. To understand the emotional states of a person is complex because everyone shows and interprets emotions differently way. Under some conditions, understanding someone's real emotional situation can be difficult according to the different personalities. For example, some people smile when they are frustrated, cry when they are happy instead of being sad, or look indifferent instead of being angry about the situation. As reported by Bill Mark, president of Information and Computing Services at SRI International, a machine can recognize emotions without having any problems analyzing a lot of data. They can learn how to recognize patterns in time from voice inflection and word usage in speech, body language, gestures, facial expressions, and many others as they design and incorporate emotions with machine learning systems (InformationWeek, 2019).

According to Hoffman, empathy is in the center of social interactions (Hoffman, 2000). Empathetic virtual agents as companions have a promised position in terms of improving social interactions and the important role of evaluation of human-machine interactions. Today, society is in a good position to start understanding effective reasoning for social interactions (McQuiggan and Lester, 2007) and communicating with embodied, more organic companions.

Companions can simplify social interactions and help people increase their self-awareness in an attempt to improve their emotional states. At the same time, by enhancing self-awareness, people can easily define their positions in the society without fear of judgment, which comes from someone else. Humankind has many roles in interpersonal social interactions. People need to know and understand personal boundaries and ethics to show respect for each other and to protect themselves from the moral judgments of others. With this consideration, individuals will be careful about self-disclosing information to avoid moral judgments. One can avoid communicating with another person in these situations, but he or she can trust a machine, like an artificially intelligent agent, that does not judge the individual (Mou and Xu, 2017). So their concern about being judged would disappear. With this openness, not only will the individual's visibility in the civil society increase, but his or her self-closures will be improved. In addition to that, as stated in the cognitive-affective processing system (CAPS) model. The self-closure and interaction between human and human and human and machine are different (Mischel and Shoda, 1995).

There is much ongoing research in understanding human and machine interactions and boundaries. For instance, McDowell and Gunkel question the reshaping or shaping of communicative relationships with machines that are already surrounded by technology or still open to exploration. Also, what can the boundaries be between human and machine (McDowell and Gunkel, 2016)?

The question can be open to searching how the relationship between machine and human can take a shape with consideration of different personalities. Can the machine become a companion by considering the personal boundaries, different characteristics, needs, expectations, and so on, while reducing the complexity of interactions? In this way, can they lead to more trust and have positions in society by creating these empathic relationships? According to Ozge and Steve's research on empathy for interactive agents, results showed that empathy in artificial agents and interactive systems can have important roles in creating empathic emotions with the users with who they are interacting. Besides, these agents can interact empathically with their interaction partners (Yalcin and DiPaola, 2018).

Perceiving Mind and Creating Empathy

Moral behavior creates the way to act through someone's beliefs and intentions without doing a great deal of thought. Morality is the definition of differentiation. People's actions, intentions, thoughts, and for that matter, cultural and religious beliefs do not have a role when the people decide to act, regardless of whether it is the right thing to do or not. So in this sense, morality is a set of behaviors that sustain and biologically drive human cooperation.

Morality shares a mutual connection with the perception of the mind, which means that being a victim or recipient of a moral action enhances the perception of the experiential mind, and only those who have an experiential mind may benefit from moral action (Gray and Wegner, 2009). Ward, Olsen, and Wegner give an example that explains the relationship between the experiential mind and a person's perception. When someone sees a robot that is stabbed, this situation increases our convictions to think that the robot is capable of feeling pain and thus, our sense of the robot's experiential mind (Ward, Olsen, and Wegner, 2013).

People's perceptions of individuals and nonhumans, including their mental perceptions, are partly determined by how they appear and communicate with their surroundings. There are four scenarios in which AI may create perception: by controlling human actions, developing new capacities and adaptations, having a physical appearance or an aspect of anthropomorphic design, and increasing the perception of the human mind (Shank et al., 2019).

- One of them defines that AI interacts with the environment by controlling. For example, in our daily lives, AI can appear in many fields, like controlling the access of bank accounts, creating a conversation between a person and a call center in which the AI answers questions (Shank et al., 2019). AI can also make suggestions, such as a book, a series Netflix thinks someone might like based on interests or that he or she might find interesting in a different genre, music playlists based on a person's analytics, and so on. If these recommendations highly match with a person's interest, they will be extremely useful in terms of removing the steps of thinking and reduce the complexity of selections.

- Another way AI interacts with the environment is through the development of new capacities, adaptations, connections, and various methods of information processing. These are, as are the mistakes and errors of AI, inherently unpredictable. The surprise nature of new capabilities should also lead to a greater understanding of the agentic mind (Waytz et al., 2010). There are two states that describe the agentic mind. The first one is an agentic state that is a condition of the mind that allows other people to lead their behaviors and give responsibilities of consequences to another person. Another state is the autonomous state, in which someone is responsible and in charge of his or her actions and behaviors, and accepts the consequences of those responsibilities. As some theorists believe, people take intentionality to attribute the mind to nonhumans (Miyahara, 2011). Emotional AI can be a suitable strategy if it allows us to explain these effects and confidently predict new ones while creating a better understanding of actions and interactions by a human.

- The third way is the physical appearance of AI, which also affects mind perception. Most of the robots and virtual agents have a physical shape or humanized imitations like eyes, mouths, voices, or gazes to make the machine more sympathetic and understandable, thereby creating a bridge between perception and reality. The aim is to make the machine more relatable, either as one that imitates human beings or simply as one that can convey verbal and nonverbal signals associated with human communication (Gong, 2008). In this way, emotional AI might be highly related to the experiential mind and provide possible ways to create interactions and communications between humans and machines.

- The last scenario is to boost the perception of the mind when individuals doubt AIs, even if they have anthropomorphic designs (Shank et al., 2019). Until today, AI had limited interactions, like being voice- or text-based, or it was available only in a virtual environment. This led to creating misunderstandings, or fully understandable relationships could not be offered. In addition, Nowotny mentioned that the underlying and continuing theme of many of the new technology- and innovation-related fears and anxieties are needed for loss. It's articulated as being the fear of losing a portion of one's identity, the feeling of being human as reflected in the many aspects we've become used to, seeing the universe and interacting with others. In time, AI supported its position as in sci-fi movies, which gave the perception of losing our humanity as we are occupied and surrounded by the power of AI. And they stayed under that dystopian mode (Nowotny, 2016).

All these considered, as mentioned in chapter 6, empathetic companions will have a chance to overcome these fears and misunderstandings and create strong social interactions and increase human self-awareness with new empathic relationships and a new way of personal interactions. They will then also increase their acceptance by society.

Relationship between Human and Other Life Forms

Domestic pets have a highly reliable and emotional position in people's lives (Brickel, 1986). In many cases, that relationship is more trustful than human-human relations. Considering pets acknowledges the deeper involvement of people with their pets in so far as pets have transferred from being economic objects to an area of high personal connectedness in the owners' lives. In time, they gain more trust and become real reliable companions with emotional attachments (Brockman, Taylor, and Brockman, 2008). Pets are loyal friends and serve their confidantes with the feeling of trust and no thought of betraying their owners.

In addition to that, pets are able to show empathy by sharing someone's feelings and emotions through representing them to that person (Asada, 2015). These connections between animals and people become, in time, mutual relationships (Bradshaw, 1995). Fox categorizes this relationship in four definitions as object-oriented, in which the dog's role is being a possession; utilitarian/exploitative, in which dogs consist of many benefits for humans; actualizing, in which a dog has a significant position in between others; and need-dependency, in which dogs become companions or friends. With the last definition, he shows in his report that dogs have emotions like fear, pain, jealousy, anxiety, guilt, joy, depression, and anger which they mean to be human (Fox, 1981, as cited in Dotson and Hyatt, 2008).

Being owners of domestic animals has many opportunities for people. For instance, they bring the opportunity to have companionship, caring, comfort, and/or calmness and to be childlike and playful (Fox, 1981, as cited in Dotson and Hyatt, 2008). In addition, pet owners report that having dogs creates strong relationships and connections to their families and friends (Apapets. org, 2019).

Similar to previous consumer-behavior studies, differing types of emotional attachment (e.g., pet as a disciple, pet as a family) were known and appear to correspond to the extent and chance of the following treatment. The thought of the opposite major themes (e.g., monetary sacrifice, recovery expectations) within the call conjointly relied on the consumer's attachment to the animal, which ranged from the animal being perceived as a cherished alternative to the animal being perceived as a possession (Brockman, Taylor, and Brockman, 2006).

Takeaways

This chapter explained how relationships are shaped between humans, machines, and other life forms to define ways of creating more trustful relationships with technology. It brought the idea that technology needs to be aware of a person's mood and to encourage people to do things better and more enjoyable with acting and offering personalized recommendations at the right moment.

I included these selected theories to describe how different personalities affect user experiences and reshape them by establishing more personalized interactions. In the next chapter, all the personality models are explained to understand human needs, expectations, and desires in order to be able to shape user experiences in more personalized ways.

Theories: Need a Relationship with Objects

Activity Theory

Postcognitivist Theory

Actor-Network Theory

Theory of User Interfaces
Gulf of Evaluation and Execution

Aaker's Brand Personality

Hook Model

<h1 style="text-align:center">Chapter 4</h1>

<h1 style="text-align:center">Theories:
Need a Relationship with Objects</h1>

Introduction

Objects or tools are constructed elements that humans need. With technology, these unstable tools started to become emotional objects and link to each other to create more powerful connections, values, meanings, and emotions.

A postcognitivist approach is one that includes the nature of the true exercise and broadening assessment to include a process of assessment and design that affects individuals and artifacts. Complexity in design changes with the number of actors and objects, and this is affecting the human experience. Focus on interaction with an object is recently improving, extending the usability, making it more pleasurable (Norman, 2004) and interactive, and using the technology to create new possibilities for experiences.

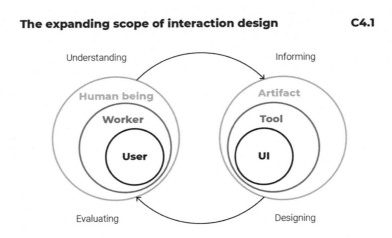

The Expanding Scope of Interaction Design: Acting with Technology (Kaptelinin and Nardi, 2006)

1. Activity Theory

Human needs and motives are still developing and changing. To give an absolute shape or definition to these needs and motives would create the wrong circumstances. This is a brief explanation of why a taxonomy of potentially effective needs and discrimination of motives are not proposed by activity theory. Activity theory just creates a bridge between motivations and actions (Kaptelinin and Nardi, 2006).

According to the relationship between activity and actions, with the consideration of interaction design in the cognitive approaches, emotions are the missing points to drive activities. Interacting with an object or a tool with missing emotions lowers the actions. A person should ask herself or himself why a long relationship with an object/tool is needed or how this relationship can be maintained in the long run. To this point, if we consider human-to-human interactions and communications, one of the main reasons for creating long relationships or keep these relations lifelong is the emotions. As Engeström observed, from the viewpoint of activity theory, cognitivist and situated approaches share a common weakness, as the focus of analysis is restricted to actions, whether couched in terms of tasks or situations. Neither approach accounts for what makes people act and form goals in the first place, what creates the horizon of possible actions, or what makes people strive for something beyond the immediately obvious goal or situation. Objects are excluded, and thus motives of activity, the long-term justification for actions. Without this level, theories of situated cognition run the risk of becoming merely technical theories of how things happen. Though more elaborate and flexible than mentalist and rationalist models, it is equally sterile when faced with societal change and institutional contradictions that pervade everyday actions (Engeström, 1995).

2. Postcognitivist Theory

Postcognitivist theories help people to understand the position of technology in the center of human experiences. These theories share common points to show the involvement of humans with our technological inventions. These theories are the phase for exploring the worlds in which the technical artifacts embody human life with their characteristics.

Communication between human beings and instruments of postcognitivist concepts are attracted by phenomenology in terms of attention to the unification of the mind and the universe. These postcognitivist concepts concentrate on the physical and social distributions of events like agency and cognition, traditionally regarded as part of the distinct truth of the human mind. In the fields of biology, neuroscience, and the main philosophical and psychological regions, where technology is nearly invisible, postcognition theories provide a significant solution to cognitive science (Kaptelinin and Nardi, 2006).

Maslow's hierarchy of needs shows us the five tiers of human needs, which are represented by levels on the pyramid. This pyramid shows us these needs from bottom to top. Individuals need to be satisfied at each level before moving up to the next level. These needs, which stated from the bottom of the hierarchy upward, are physiological, safety, belongingness and love, esteem, and self-actualization (Mcleod, 2019).

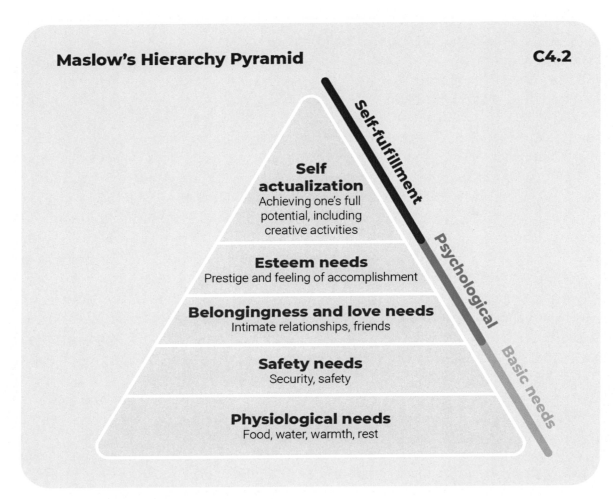

Source: Kaptelinin and Nardi, 2006

Maslow's Hierarchy Pyramid: Five Tiers of Human Needs (Kaptelinin and Nardi, 2006)

According to Kaptelinin and Nardi, the design and the development of technology is an essential step for humanity. It involves the mobilization of large cultural resources that are not reduced to universal psychological or biological procedures. They explain this with an example from Köhler and Goodall, in which they give an example with nonhuman primates, like chimpanzees, to understand the use of simple tools. In time, humans enhanced language skills and started to talk about the use of the tools instead of just showing and presenting them. This helped to increase sociality and the way of communication, and allowed rapid progress in the creation of unique pieces of immense value for human life (Kaptelinin and Nardi, 2006).

However, one of the problems is that human beings neither create nor understand computation. Thus, instead of understanding the complexity, people just adapt to situations. These situations, in which they are directly integrated to our computational systems, create many questions in humans' minds, like how to understand the diversity of benefits by computers, reducing these understandings and increasing our alienation to technology and each other (Foltz-Smith, 2019). In addition, this statement can be a useful context to understand not only articulated problems that come from the integration of AI with user interfaces but also people's reactions to and perceptions of these integrations.

3. Actor-Network Theory

The theory of actor-network (ANT) was first established as a modern approach to social theory by science and technology scholars Michael Callon and Bruno Latour and the sociologist John Law. ANT is a method between a human and nonhuman entity in which symmetrical nodes are handled equally. According to this theory, an actor is the one who affects the production of scientific theories and improvements. On the other hand, the actor creates an effect on methodologies, methods, and social rules (Detel, 2001).

The expression of this theory incorporates two terms that are generally regarded as opposites to each other; one of them comes from an actor, and the other one from a network. This reminds people of the traditional old contradictions between agency and structure or micro- and macroanalysis that lie in the core of social sciences. One of the key premises of the theory of an actor-network is that what social sciences sometimes refer to as the "society" represents a continuing success (Callon, 2001). The main reasoning is the fact that scientific knowledge is an effect of existing connections between scientific processes, animals, and humans.

This theory supports that no one is alone in his or her actions or acts independently. So it takes into account all the variables and stresses that can trigger these actions. We might say that people's actions are shaped and affected by their experiences, tools they have used, their friends, cultural factors, environment, and so many other variables. Not only scientific theories but also back growths, methodologies, methods, social rules and structures, procedures, tests, measurements, suitable instruments, scientific texts, and external objects are influenced by an actor in any casual way, besides the effect on the development of scientific statements and hypotheses. According to this statement, there can be numerous kinds of relations and interactions between actors. Some actors, in particular, can change other actors (Callon, 2001).

These effects are not only related to humans. They are also affected by nonhuman actors like artifacts and institutional structures. Human and nonhuman, in the same theoretical context and equivalent numbers of agencies, must be allocated to the agency with regard to the rule of universal symmetry that ANT involves. This gives a detailed explanation of the specific mechanisms at work that keep the network together and allow the actors to be treated impartially.

After all, the role of a network is defined as a group of actors in which there are stable relationships and translations of actors that decide the position and functions of actors in the network. When the network is created and defined, which entails a kind of closure preventing the entry of other actors or relationships into the network, the possibility of accumulating scientific knowledge as a consequence of translations through a network opens.

To summarize, the fundamental concept of the ANT is that behavior happens in the relationship between network actors when actors have reciprocal control and struggle for power. Social interaction between individuals also happens in this way, but it should not be forgotten that the

ANT differs from traditional social theory by suggesting that participants are not only individuals but also other components (Jessen and Jessen, 2014).

4. Theory of User Interfaces

User interfaces create connections between the activities of humans and the computer, and then map these activities as a collection of functions from the computer program, sensory, cognitive, and social human world. People try to understand their actions in the environment and give meaning to each of those actions. So they build models between other living things and themselves to define the meanings of their actions, reactions, and cognitions. These meanings, which are created by humans while interacting with each other, reshape the motions, senses, actions, cognitions, and many other reactions. Moreover, according to this model, it builds an adaptation and helps people to understand their relationships with the environment and the changes caused by their human abilities,

The user interface is a collection from inputs, algorithms of actions, and outcomes. Computers collect all arithmetic operations and combine them with data sets to control the actions by analyzing them, dividing, and multiplying them. In principle, all computer programs are collections of human actions that people can initiate computing the information.

Interactions between humans and the environment start in infancy. Individuals can make mental models of those depictions that enable them to feel, act, and reach their objectives in the natural world. Humans start to interact with the environment by trying to understand their actions and perceiving the interactions that are natural interfaces produced by the environment. Computer interfaces are not different from the natural interfaces in terms of shaping and enriching the human senses (Ko, nd).

Gulf of Evaluation and Execution

Norman and Draper talk about the gulf of evaluation and gulf of execution in their book *User-Centered System Design* to describe effective design elements to help users get rid of boundaries and obstacles that can be a problem when they are trying to reach their goals (Norman, 2013). With this definition, we can say that these gulfs create a knowledge gap between the user and the aimed goal while the user is interacting with the interface. Users need to understand interfaces and make an effort to understand the system. Mostly, people think about their past actions and interactions and decrease their efforts to understand the new systems, interfaces, and interactions. At this point, the theory of interfaces meets with a mental model that is a theory describing how a system works, the meaning of signals, and the outcomes that will be shaped by different users' actions. So these mental models would be created if people relied on their past actions while interacting with the new systems (Whitenton, 2018).

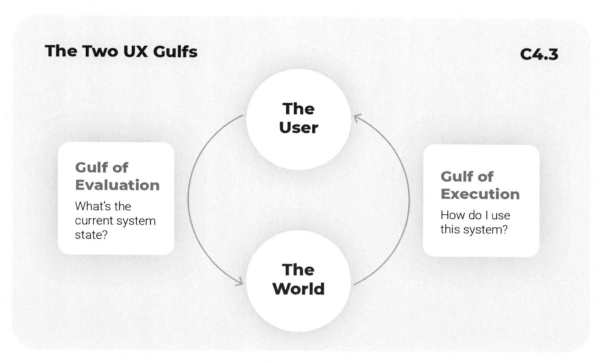

Source: Nielsen Norman Group, 2018

The Two UX Gulfs. Nielsen Norman Group, 2018

This theory might be helpful while a designer is trying to design human-computer interfaces, especially with AI. Perceiving the action that comes from AI would create gaps between the user and the final aim because, as mentioned previously, people want to use familiar interactions when they meet with an interface that provides interaction with AI. These gaps might also support the uncanny valley and create more fear against the interfaces, causing misunderstandings and lack of interactions. To avoid this, according to the article "The Two UX Gulfs: Evaluation and Execution," Whitenton (2018) supported the idea that designers can improve this natural tendency and help users to develop effective mental models by:

- Designing with a familiar approach which the user already has.
- Creating a similar visual design between the new and familiar design elements.
- Creating similar functionality between the new and familiar design elements.

Amy J. Ko gives a nice example in her book *User Interface Software and Technology* to make understandable the gulf of execution. According to her example, at the moment the user meets with the conversational agents with a voice-user interface, like smart assistants on their phones as Siri or embedded ones like Alexa or Google Home, the user discovers the gulf of execution. People did not know how to communicate with the interface at the beginning, and they tried to understand what to ask to achieve their goal and receive an answer from the system. They did not have any idea how to interact with voice-over interfaces, like a command space or syntax for each command. Also, people had no idea how to perceive possible actions. Something or someone was needed to bridge that gulf, to show the user some feasible activities and how those activities were organized into the user's objectives (Ko, nd).

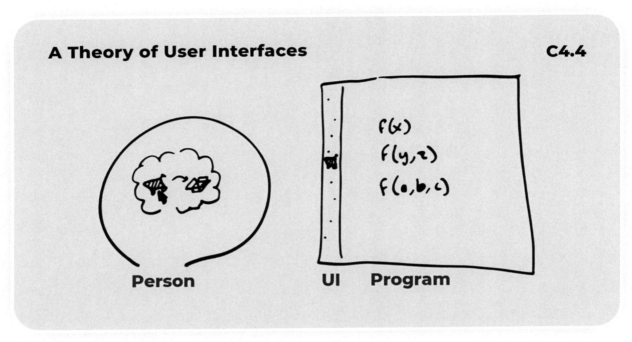

Source: Amy J. Ko

A Theory of User Interfaces (Ko, nd)

5. Aaker's Brand Personality

The brand personality is characterized as human traits associated with brands by product personality. Taking into consideration the latter assumption, the social psychologist Jennifer Aaker has been creating a model based on five human characteristics—trustworthiness, technological, efficient, joyful, and intelligent—to be a product. This can be regarded as one of the large brand personality constructs that can be extended into several product categories (Aaker, 1997).

For marketing and branding analysis, Aaker's template is described now as one of the most well-established brand personality evaluation methodologies (Schlesinger and Cervera, 2009, as cited in Garcia et al., 2018). The advantage of using Aaker's model is that it is multidimensional, which helps some brands to score high on all five. It also allows professionals to consider the views, behaviors of their brands, and people's appreciation of their products. This allows them to distinguish themselves and provides an advantage that they may be pursued by others. Chart C.4.5 shows these five personalities, which have been divided into subcategories to help products in identifying their tones of voices, building trust and transmitting messages that come from the brand identity.

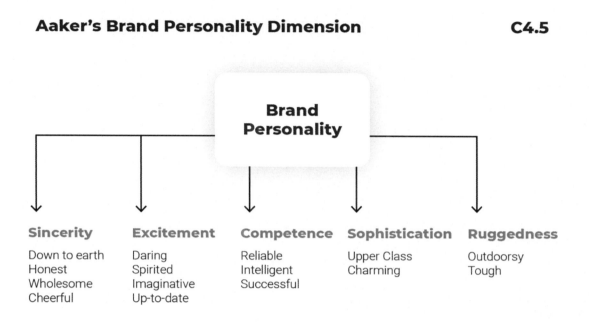

Aaker's Brand Personality Dimension   C4.5

Brand Personality

Sincerity	Excitement	Competence	Sophistication	Ruggedness
Down to earth	Daring	Reliable	Upper Class	Outdoorsy
Honest	Spirited	Intelligent	Charming	Tough
Wholesome	Imaginative	Successful		
Cheerful	Up-to-date			

Source: Superskill, 2018

Brand Personality Dimension (Superskill, 2018)

With the consideration of the Aaker's brand identity theory, the telecom company Telefonica has started to build their own AI voice-over assistant, Aura, which is now active in six countries: Chile, Argentina, Brazil, the United Kingdom, Germany, and Spain. As many other technology players in literature have already seen, Telefonica decided to bring new values to the assistants by adding personalities. Therefore, not only do they concentrate on technological capabilities but also on developing an incorporated personality capable of delivering the desired user experience (Garcia, Lopez, and Donis, 2018).

Furthermore, Garcia, Lopez, and Donis implemented this into their research methodology to create voice-activated virtual assistants (VAVA) with emotional and personalized qualities in a clear, realistic way when embedded within a conceptual frame to be tailored to the users of interactions (Garcia, Lopez, and Donis, 2018). After the identification of VAVA personalities, they identified the desired personalities and expected behaviors for these assistants by users (Li et al., 2016). Their research is primarily intended to investigate the personalities that users assign to the four major VAVAs—Siri, Google, Cortana, Alexa—and to define the VAVA personality users want to see in the future. This would give a competitor's benchmark and potential feedback on what field the personalities of the new voice-over assistants can compete in and how they could differentiate themselves from others (Garcia, Lopez, and Donis, 2018).

6. Hook Model

Nir Eyal has codified into his Hook template his work on how to develop behaviors based on years of researching effective companies and products, all able to change their users' everyday lives. Eyal explored how leading-edge companies were able to build consumer habits requiring little or no conscious thinking and developed an actionable framework.

Eyal divides the enhancement of user habits into a four-phase cycle: as a trigger, action, variable reward, and investment.

- Triggers are the starting points for the actions. They stimulate human behaviors required to start these actions. There are two types of triggers, defined as internal and external. A product that is able to create habits for users starts with an external trigger. For example, a notification from an application or a preview of a message on the phone screen are external triggers to take users into the actions for turning them into habits in time. If users begin to indicate their next actions automatically, the new habits become part of their daily routines (Eyal and Hoover, 2014).

  Instead of the external triggers, internal triggers mostly come through users' memories. Internal stimuli could be correlated with places users have been, the individuals with whom users have communicated, habits that they have been adopted, circumstances, and especially emotional feelings (Toxboe, 2019).

- Actions are defined as the second phase of habit formation or conduct in anticipation of a reward. To make this phase happen, the user needs to take the triggers into consideration. In order to engage with the user in specific behaviors, according to the Hook model, we must concentrate on easy behaviors to get users to anticipate a reward. In addition, negative feelings, such as being alone, unsound, weak, sad, boring, and lower, can all suggest internal triggering. The actions are as dependable as the internal stimulus in response to all these items (Toxboe, 2019). Motivation might be the energy for actions to understand how much a user desires to take the action (Deci and Ryan, 2008). These motivations might drive our interests and attention toward specific actions. Consider Fogg's three motivational examples. As he explains in his behavior model (C.4.6), they are effective for the actions. For example, being anticipatory includes being hopeful and avoiding fear, being emotional is helpful for minimizing pain and looking for fun, and being social seeks acceptance in a social environment (Fogg, 2019).

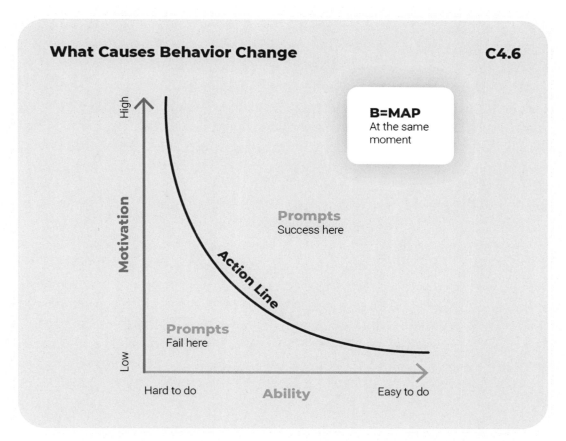

Source: Fogg, 2019

What Causes Behavior Change (Fogg, 2019)

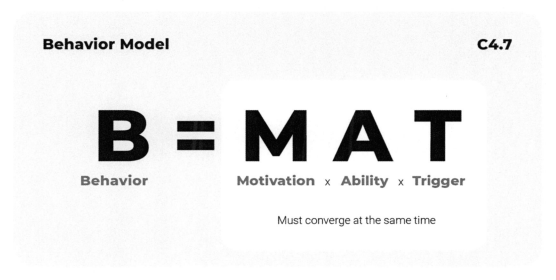

Source: Fogg, 2019

Behavior Model (Fogg, 2019)

- Variable rewards are what users reach after taking action. Eval pointed out in his book that users expect to be part of the future award rather than receive the award after their actions (Eyal and Hoover, 2014). Research shows that dopamine levels rise when the brain expects an award. Variability enhances the effect, producing a frenzied hunting environment, triggering the components associated with desire and wish fulfillment (Marketingjournal. org, 2016). Three types of rewards are identified by Eyal: tribe rewards, also known as social rewards, that differ in nature and feel comfortable when a person receives them from other people, which makes them feel good; hunting, defined also as winning situations; and self-rewards, which are the benefits of self-performances as inherent incentives, such as competence, ability, coherence, performance, and control (Toxboe, 2019).

- Investment is defined as the last step of the Hook model. This phase increases the probability that in the future, users will continue their actions in the Hook cycle. The investment takes place when the user inserts something into the service or product, like time, data, effort, and social. This section should be clearly defined in terms of the meaning of investment because it can create a wrong statement. Here, investment does not come with money. Rather, expenditure means an action that will maximize the next round of operation (Eyal and Hoover, 2014). Investments load the next Hook cycle and bring users back to the loop. For example, when a person sends a message to a mate, waiting for the response from them will be a future reward to bring the person back into the Hook cycle (Toxboe, 2019).

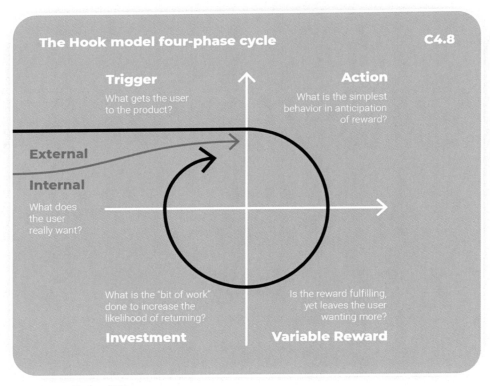

Source: Toxboe, 2019

The Hook Model Four-Phase Cycle (Toxboe, 2019)

To summarize, the Hook model is an effective method because it helps the person to continue her or his actions and increases the usability of the product and the interaction with the user. Also, when used correctly, the Hook model can be useful in transforming user actions into habits, thereby creating an emotional connection between the user and the product. The aim of the experiment shows similarity with this model in terms of building relationships between users and personal companions to ensure the continuity of product use and interaction with loading the next Hook cycles and to continue to communicate with companions.

Takeaways

This chapter explained how personality models are implemented into digital experiences or products to define the relationship between actors and networks. The focus then moved to the interaction with an object to improve usability and make user experiences more pleasurable, interactive, and personalized in order to create new possibilities for user experiences.

I discussed these selected theories to describe how personalities evolve from individuals to products and how personality characteristics assigned to these objects change the mood and behavior of users.

In the next chapter, the role of design in making AI understandable and its role in shaping digital experiences will be discussed.

Design
Involvement in AI

**Human is Design,
Design is Emotions**

Designing Products with EI

Reshaping User Experiences

Chapter 5

Design Involvement in AI

Human Is Design, Design Is Emotions

Emotions are complicated to resolve and implement in design processes. As mentioned in previous chapters, affective computing and creating relationships between humans and computers or other life forms might also improve human-to-human communications and interactions. Based on this statement, designers started to involve emotions into their designs. Besides evolving design processes with empathy, interactions with technology started to be more empathic through the design and the experiences with physical, digital, and phigital (physical + digital) products. Pavliscak, the founder of Change Sciences, describes humans as a technology's Lacanian mirror stage, where they will remember themselves in the future. People have this dream, and it's logical. Technology is disappearing into the background while helping us to be successful and productive, and creating a convenient, reliable, and effective vision.

However, there's one problem related to this vision: Human beings are not entirely rational. As humans, we have emotional connections to technology. We anthropomorphize everything by giving them human characteristics and features—like a mouth—erratic movements, gestures, and even a history (Pavliscak, 2017). For example, applications started to embed human gestures into the interfaces when users entered wrong passwords.

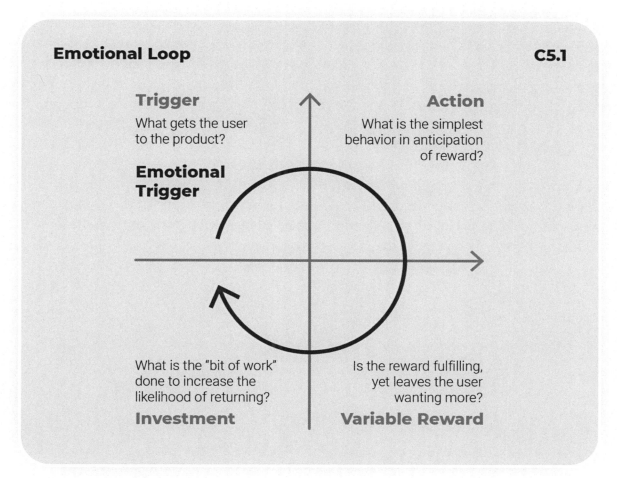

Source: Pavliscak, 2017

Emotional Loop (Pavliscak, 2017)

The system understands the action is wrong, and the character shakes its head, which is a human gesture to describe there is something wrong, to give an easily recognized insight to the user that the inserted password was incorrect. These interactions might be useful in defining the problem and perceiving them easily thanks to creating emotional connections and embedded human gestures. We should also consider these situations while embedding these human gestures with characters or shapes to represent the actions. The important point that must be considered is to make decisions carefully while designing these characters and adopting them into personalities. In the beginning, these personalities might look like good representatives, but after interacting many times with them, human minds perceive these situations as boring, not engageable. Some even define them as inappropriate behaviors or lacking empathy. And if we consider that these interactions are always repetitive, we would realize that humans need different emotional triggers to lead them into the actions (C.5.1).

When involving the design in technologies, designers started to create more meaningful experiences, relationships, and interactions with understanding both humans and machines. Now, these feelings are not created from only one side. Not only are people feeling the emotions and have empathy for machines and other life forms, the machines have started to understand human feelings, changes in their emotional states, and created empathetic connections. Since human feelings and emotions are complicated, we did not build this relationship only because of anthropomorphization of technology with design. We are building these relationships and connections to give a shape to our emotions with design in our minds and changing the perception of our emotions. This is a loop that comes from empathy on both sides, human and machine. By reducing the complexity of technology and creating new connections through designing new experiences for human minds, we might create a loop between people and the technology itself that comes to life with design. Having thoughts, emotions, and feelings that come from human understanding and matching them with the new emotional experiences that come from technology—it can be a machine, product, or even other life forms like pets and plants that could impact human lives—might help to design more personal, emotional, and empathetic experiences. These mutual loops between humans and designs might help individuals in their self-growth, awareness, and courage (Veer, 2017).

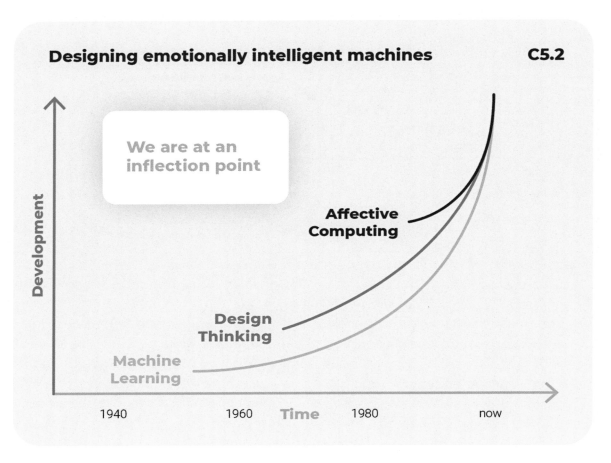

Source: Veer, 2017

Designing Emotionally Intelligent Machines (Veer, 2017)

Designing Products with EI

The manner in which people interact with technological products, especially mobile phones, changes dramatically. People started to speak with the digital assistants rather than interact with the products through graphical user interfaces. For instance, instead of searching for something on the Web using mobile phones screens and interacting by clicking buttons or scrolling up and down to complete desired actions, people have started to go with the conversational interactions. According to Fast Company, as users, we are expecting to be understood instead of being entertained by the experiences. In addition to this, when the switch happened from screens to voice-over interactions went smoothly, we also started to identify products we use based on that rather than brand. With this turn, we expect more and more, not only utility and accomplishments, but we want to feel the moment of trust and the emotions that come from the product (Pakhchyan, 2019).

So we can say that this fundamental behavioral change requires us to reconsider the possibilities of designs for each product. These transitions have the main driver, which is AI. In particular, we can say that machine learning has an important effect thanks to natural language processing (NLP) and understanding (NLU). NLP and NLU make interactions between humans and the machine easier and more natural than before. In the meantime, however, machine learning assists, offering deep insight and advice on our behaviors (Pakhchyan, 2019).

I would like to explain it clearly with an example. The application called Woebot was created from work done under the supervision of psychologist Dr. Alison Darcy from behavioral sciences at Stanford University School of Medicine. It has shown its clinical effectiveness through a published randomized controlled trial. Woebot is a digital therapist designed with AI in order to create a companion (Darcy, Robinson, and Ng, 2019). Thanks to AI, Woebot not only gives tools that help people better understand their thinking patterns, it also provides a safe harbor. All in all, it delicately conducts a conversation with a person and seeks permission to ask more questions or to consult with the user in the future. This behavior, unlike other applications, can help to avoid being annoyed constantly. It also asks permission to continue communication instead of sending informative notifications directly. This example shows the importance of reconsidering user experiences, redesigning the processes, and remaking design decisions to help make digital experiences more emotionally intelligent.

Woebot Digital Therapist P5.1

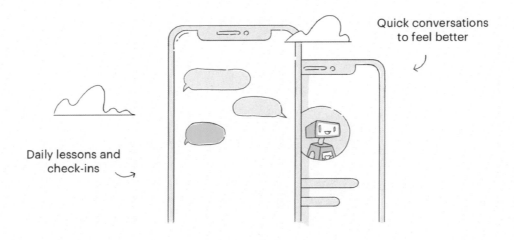

Hi, I'm Woebot

Everybody could use someone like me

Quick conversations to feel better

Daily lessons and check-ins

Source: Woebot, 2019

Woebot Digital Therapist (Woebot, 2019)

After fundamental behavioral changes, another topic that needs to be explained in this section is affective reasoning. In the cognitive studies of social interaction, active thinking plays an increasingly important role. People continually analyze each other's social contexts, adjust their own affective states, and then respond with empathy to these outcomes (McQuiggan and Lester, 2007). Today, in the social interaction sense, the community is well placed to examine affective reasoning. It should also be noted that empathy is an important part of social interaction. If all these views are evaluated by considering interactions between humans and machines and empathy is involved in the design processes, they might have a similar effect on user experiences and lead to reshaping these experiences.

In addition to this statement, using two complementary forms of assessing the empathic reliability of an empathy model can be determined as predictive accuracy and perceived accuracy. In this section, explaining perceived accuracy will be useful before moving to the new role of user experience. A study of perceived accuracy examines the empathy of a model using a controlled focus group experiment. The alternative model of empathy is embedded into numerous fellow agents, individuals observe fellow agents in a range of social environments, and participants evaluate the role adequacy of empathic behavior. An accuracy test may show the extent to which the empathy model makes decisions about evaluations and perceptions that people feel are situationally acceptable (McQuiggan and Lester, 2007).

Reshaping User Experiences

There is an opportunity to shape user experiences with AI. With more understanding of user expectations, needs, effects on emotional states, and collecting the feedback, user experiences come forward one step further. If we consider the variety of physical, digital, and phigital products and users, these experiences are shaped differently based on these variables. Also, it should be stated that the personality developed for the products affect the user feelings and emotional states about the products. At this point, the first meeting with products—onboarding—has a great impact on users, creating good insights and ensuring the continuity of the experience.

Involving AI in the design processes, user experiences can take better shape in the near future. AI can understand the appreciated parts and frustrated points of the journey with learning from individuals and help to tailor better experiences. It can even go further by creating more personalized experiences. Moreover, having empathetic features allows the creation of emotional connections with users and will affect user experiences.

Here's an example from Netflix. They recently designed a personalized recommendation system, which means they implemented machine learning systems into their design to create a more personalized suggestion list for their users. It can be very private and dependent on a particular taste on how people find artworks. There is so much variety in tastes and interests that it would be a better idea for Netflix to find the best artwork for each of their subscribers that highlights the elements of a title directly important to them (Bodegraven and Marques, 2019).

Bodegraven explains the principles of AI design in the Awwwards books AI-driven design series. He takes into consideration four principles to explain user experiences: minimizing the inputs and maximizing the outcomes, designing for forgiveness, creating humanized experiences, and designing to establish trust (Bodegraven, 2019).

Minimizing the Inputs and Maximizing the Outcomes

We live in a world that experiences the phenomena known as decision fatigue. We have been flooded with updates, rewards, and demands with which we all have to deal and navigate. AI can overcome these situations by considering certain activities that can quickly be outsourced. For instance, the smart thermostat Nest is setting the temperature right, Google AI is providing automatic responses, and so on. If we consider these actions take shape by user responses, asking the right questions can be learned in time with AI and then used to reshape user experiences. So minimizing inputs and aiming for the maximum number of outcomes can shape the user experiences and solve user problems.

Designing for Forgiveness

AI is still in an infant phase, so it continues to learn through contributions by events and users. Therefore, it is highly probable that mistakes in actions and decisions will be made. Forgiveness makes a great contribution to AI's development and a better understanding of the system, leading to building a good relationship for the future. Forgiveness can come from user feedback to support AI and help it to take the right actions for the next steps. For example, Netflix gives users the option to dislike the selections, and their next choices will be improved based on their inputs. So having an opportunity for forgiveness and receiving user feedback users can be helpful in designing more personalized experiences.

Giving users options for improving their experiences and seeing improvements on the next interaction can create good insights and trust on behalf of the users as they become aware that the information they give will be considered, rearranged, and turned back for their benefits.

Creating Humanized Experiences

The importance of personality becomes more prevalent in our daily interactions with machines that are rapidly changing. When people have a story with a product, they can create more strong connections. In time, they start to define personalities that match in their minds with these products. Having a personality can create more humanized experiences by perceiving machine reactions with a more humanistic approach. Identifying the machine with different personalities will have different effects on user experiences. A recent finding by Google shows that people are willing to have more humanistic interactions by defining personalities with products. For example, users started to talk with Google Home by saying, "Sorry," or, "Thank you," as a consequence of its actions.

Designing to Establish Trust

Today, one of the primary topics when it comes to data concerns building trustful relationships with products. In recent years, data-related cases made people become more conscious about protecting their data and to be more aware before accepting the terms of privacy and policy. Confidence is built by creating a trustful environment in which the cornerstones are transparency and integrity. So it is crucial that AI builds confidence by being transparent about what it knows about the user and how it will use that data. With this statement, users should be able to monitor and modify their data if necessary. Giving authorization to the user to do so should create a feeling of being in charge in control of their inputs. When the information is understandable and informative, more trust is built between AI and users.

Takeaways

This chapter explained how emotions met with design to build trustful relationships with digital products. Also explained were the importance of creating emotional connections with the products and the role of AI in the process to personalize user experiences.

In the next chapter, the importance and necessities of AI in establishing empathetic companionships are explained and supported with related case studies.

Empathetic
Companions

AI Is Not a Tool; It Is a Design Material

Missing Emotional Connections and Empathy

Making Memories

Case Studies

Social Interface Microsoft Bob

Jibo: A Social Robot

Olly, Emotech

Riot AI: Interactive Digital Experience, Sensory Storytelling

A Space for Being by Google: A Multiroom Experience to Feel More

Maslo: Empathetic Companion

Chapter 6
Empathetic Companions

Introduction

The use of AI is increasing and becoming more prominent in our lives. Increasing numbers of people prefer to use virtual agents to reduce the complexity of their daily needs. Smart, artificial assistants have the potential to make someone's life easier. According to TechCrunch (Perez, 2018), 41 percent of US consumers own a smart speaker. Via a report by SuperAwesome, eMarketer conveyed that 91 percent of kids ages four to eleven have access to a smart speaker, like Amazon's Alexa, or a digital assistant, such as Apple's Siri (Collins, 2018). Why, then, are a significant number of people still using Alexa as just a kitchen timer? And why are these smart virtual assistants still not managed to become our real digital personal assistants? Does it lack the skills for complex tasks?

It is true that personal assistants are not powerful enough to help us in a smart way. Another reason could also be that we are still not ready to embrace the AI, to invite AI to join our daily lives. We do not yet know how to build a relationship with our personal assistants. It is still a blurry but promising field.

At the same time, however, our relationships with technological devices are getting deeper and deeper. Daily usage is rising, and our social interactions are changing because of this. We are losing moments of being in touch with ourselves, and self-awareness is being damaged every day. Consequently, our empathetic and emotional capabilities are affected because of these interactions. Moreover, it seems clear that the trend is going in the direction of more interconnected emotional devices. That is why we need true personal assistants with implemented emotions that can be applied through AI to make them empathetic companions.

Researchers are focusing on EI and empathy in personal assistants to make them more like companions while trying to define a more transparent communication method. According to Sony Design, machines grow both intellectually and emotionally through ongoing interactions with humans. Knowing this symbiotic relationship, we can imagine a future in which robots look more alive (Affinity in Autonomy, 2019). And with empathetic feelings, they might be able to build trust between people and machines. So they may have a chance to be perceived as a real companion in the same way that our minds are create human-human relationships using empathy and emotions.

AI Is Not a Tool; It Is a Design Material

In etymology, "technology" combined two Greek words, *techne* and *logos*. "Techne" signifies art, craft, skill, workmanship, or the manner in which an item has been acquired. "Logos" means language, a word, or a phrase through which internal thoughts are articulated. However, technology has recently come to mean something else. We are now defining it as a collection of means produced by technical processes (tools, instruments, systems, methods, procedures) and by science. With this meaning, our minds perceive that AI is a technological tool that we can build by using programming languages to construct algorithms. That is a really cold explanation. So much so that it can create a bias to establishing relationships between humans and machines. If we take into consideration the etymological meaning of technology and combine it with AI, we can create a new perspective to better understand machines.

If we consider AI as a design material with all transparency, rather than a technical tool, can we use it to create more reliable and empathic relationships? This question defined this book's aim, which is to reshape the relationship between human and the companion with empathy included in the design. This aim is supported by understanding the effect of empathy, which is implemented by adding different personalities in the companions to create trustful companionship and define effective interactions. This hypothesis was then implemented into methodologies to be tested.

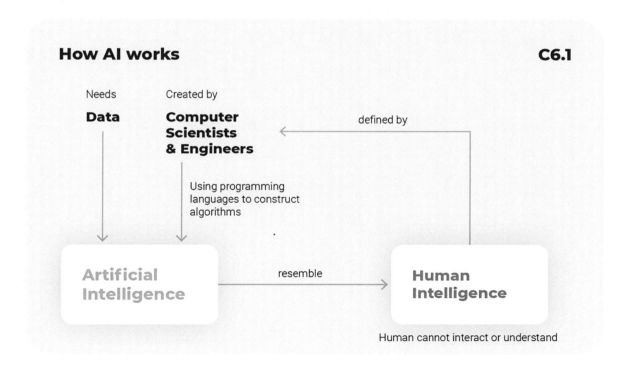

How AI Works

AI as a technology   **C6.2**

Artificial Intelligence   — is an → Invisible Technology

Sometimes is a Black Box

AI as a Technology

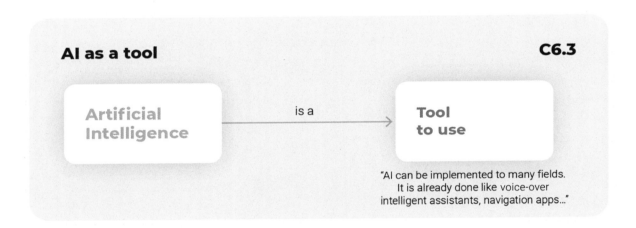

AI as a tool   **C6.3**

Artificial Intelligence — is a → Tool to use

"AI can be implemented to many fields. It is already done like voice-over intelligent assistants, navigation apps…"

AI as a Tool

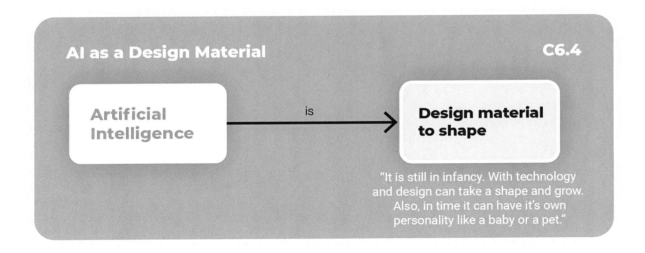

AI as a Design Material   **C6.4**

Artificial Intelligence — is → **Design material to shape**

"It is still in infancy. With technology and design can take a shape and grow. Also, in time it can have it's own personality like a baby or a pet."

AI as a Design Material

According to Antonelli, senior curator of Architecture and Design and founding director of Research and Development at the Museum of Modern Art (MoMA) in New York, science, engineering, arts, and culture are all part of a renaissance approach. Engineering is what makes any built object come into being; without technology, nothing happens to bring them alive. The understanding of thinking, which is defined as cognitive science, makes the product accessible for people. This recognizes interfaces that are familiar to people. If the design provides people with objects that they do not know how to pick or use, it means that that is not a good design. In addition to this, design meets need, whether they exist or are going to exist. Antonelli defines it with an example of the Tamagotchi, which is perceived and defined as a useless object, but this object showed that people obviously needed pain and a need to relieve the distress in their lives. Tamagotchis responded to those needs. It looks like an unreasonable design or need, but those are the insights and can be combined to create something people do not know they want. These are the most fascinating designs that are new and appropriate to build the new needs in the world (Antonelli, 2018).

The machine uses signals for encoding its own truth version over time. The evolving trends encapsulate our current states at the times combined with our knowledge. They are our reflections throughout the process of the system itself. It means that it is us but suggests a different version of us. A version of us that is a synthesis of our own direct signals by the enormous possibilities that come out of those signals. It is exactly the way that another living being experiences in terms of data flow. To define this explanation as a need or even to understand them easily, we need to build a relationship as in human relations. It is important to develop machines that are more empathetic and emotional in order to achieve this trust necessary for creating a relationship between people and machines. This process needs time to ground and initiate human relationships in building this strong, trustful companionship.

Missing Emotional Connections and Empathy

Every human has different personalities and emotions. In daily life, emotions can sometimes change according to different situations. These unexpected changes can affect people's moods and personalities for a short or a long period. While emotions show variety, a person can expect different behaviors from another individual while they are communicating. So if personal assistants have their own personalities, how can they adapt to these behavioral changes and create a trustful companionship with people?

Emotions have important and powerful roles in people's lives. In almost every situation, people think with their emotions, for example, under stressful conditions, in emotional moments, and while they are making decisions. All these considered emotions have a great impact on people's lives, including their social communications and interactions. In addition, they have a role in influencing and creating behaviors in social relationships (Gratch and Marsella, 2004).

Characteristics regulate someone's emotions. Every human has a different set of communication skills, social abilities, and thoughts while following social norms. Humans create successful social communications, not only with understanding and conceding these differences, but by doing so with empathy.

Emotionally intelligent agents provide improvements on social interactions and increase their efficiency on acceptance, success, and trust (Fan et al., 2017). Besides, for the agents to understand the complex feelings and emotions, analyzing inputs and outputs is one of the main actions used to describe those emotions. When the EI companion performs rational processes, it means they can reflect human behaviors (Pudane, Lavendelis, and Radin, 2017). Thus, they have the ability to affect outputs and final actions.

I had an opportunity to discuss with Ross Ingram why machines need empathy, and we need to focus on establishing a trust to create an empathetic relationship. Ingram is one of the cofounders of Maslo, an empathetic digital companion, and an ex-googler. I interviewed him about virtual assistants, empathetic digital companions, the shape of AI, self-awareness, growth, and Maslo's life story. The interview guide can be found in chapter 6.

Understanding emotions and building a relationship with AI can question these topics:

- How does AI interpret emotions?
- What AI features, activities, and moments trigger intimacy, building trustful relationships?
- How can AI create affinity?

Exclusion in AI

The internet now offers a degree of concrete information regarding users' behaviors, likes and dislikes, hobbies, and personal preferences that was unimaginable over a decade ago. Forbes stated that 2.5 quintillion bytes of data (the byte is a unit of digital data that typically consists of eight bits) are generated each day at our current pace (Marr, 2018). According to the 2018 report by Domo, they state that "Data never sleeps." And while they are stunning numbers, there were no signs that data generation would slow down. It was estimated that 1.7 MB of data will be created for each person on earth every second by 2020 (Domo, 2018). They also stated those numbers had increased 9 percent since January 2018. The big data pool is complemented by social media accounts and online profiles, social activities, product reviews, tagged preferences, liked and shared content, loyalty services and programs, customer relationship management systems, and many other sources.

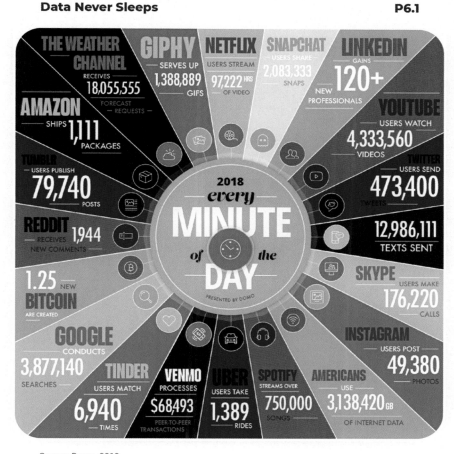

Data Never Sleeps: How Much Data Is Generated Every Minute? (Domo, 2018)

Internet

Data production:

- The internet is used by over 3.7 billion people in a day (7.5 percent increase compared to 2016).
- Google currently conducts 3,877,140 searches every minute.
- Worldwide, with other search engines, there are 5 billion searches a day.

Social Media

Data-sharing in every minute:

- Users post 49,380 images on Instagram.
- Users post 2,083,333 snaps on Snapchat.

- Users stream 97,222 hours of video on Netflix.
- Users watch 4,333,560 videos on YouTube.
- Spotify streams over 750,000 songs.

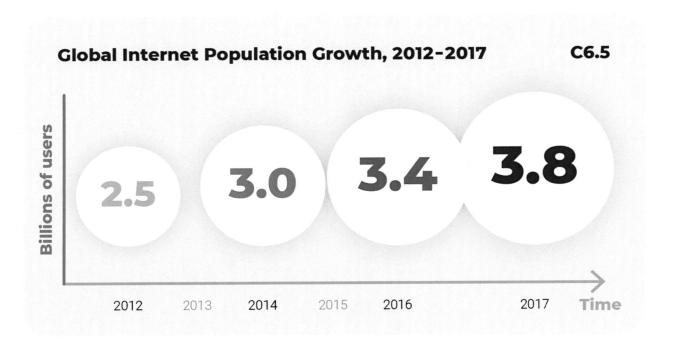

Source: Domo, 2018

Global Internet Population Growth 2012–2017 (Domo, 2018)

If we imagine all the data produced by humans in every minute and used by AI, how can we avoid using this big data without causing a bias on users?

It is almost impossible to avoid bias when meeting with a new product designed with AI and that uses these labeled and collected data from the internet. This is only identifying the AI as machines without having any personal points where people can tailor experiences or products for themselves. AI needs empathy to overcome this perception and to create more personal emotional and empathetic relationships with users, thereby avoiding bias.

As Microsoft Design mentioned, the more trust people have, the more they interact with the processes, and the more data is used by the system to deliver better performance back to the user. Nevertheless, trust takes a long time to develop, and prejudices can tear it down immediately, harming large communities. To fulfill its pledge, AI systems have to be trusted (Chou, Murillo, and Ibars, 2017). We need to consider how and where bias is affecting the system. By first addressing these five biases, we can create more inclusive products.

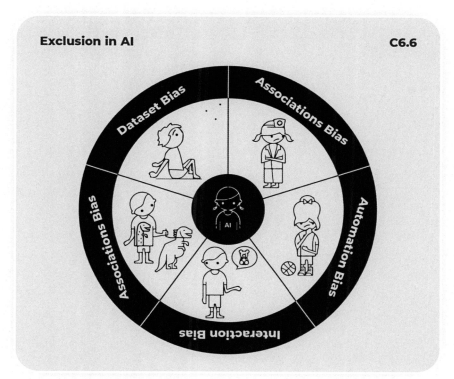

Source: Chou, Murillo and Ibars, 2017

Exclusion in AI (Chou, Murillo, and Ibars, 2017)

Microsoft Design explains this bias in five stages, tries to define it with the perspective of childhood, and describes the bias from a child's eye. It starts with a definition of data-set bias and continues by explaining biases of association, automation, interaction, and confirmation.

Data-Set Bias

- Perception of AI: The child learns that most of the universe lies beyond the little knowledge in its field of view, and it looks really big and complicated from their eyes.
- How it is: If we think on the AI side, large-scale data sets create the basis of AI, and they are not defined differently for individuals. They are in clusters and ready to implement in the machine learning systems.
- How it might be: So if these learning processes are tailored for individuals, how can they affect the machines' learning processes and become more intuitive?

Association Bias

- Perception of AI: Imagine kids are playing a doctor game together. Think of a couple of boys who like to play the doctor role; presume the girls are going to take the nurse role. Why can't girls be in the doctor role?
- How it is: If we think on the AI side, when data used for the creation of a model reinforce and multiply a cultural bias, human preference will contribute to machine learning during

the training of AI algorithms. The continuity of these biases can lead to unfair customer experiences in future interactions.

- How it might be: So if the machine is not only learning with the label data-set but also growing with learning from people, they can interact with people without creating gender discrimination, thereby enabling more personal experiences.

Automation Bias

- Perception of AI: Imagine labeled thoughts as boys like playing football, and girls like spending time on beauty. What if a girl likes sports, enjoys looking natural, and hates being artificial. So is it right to categorize every human based on some structured clusters?
- How it is: If automated selection transcends social and cultural factors, predictive algorithms may automate objectives that clash with human diversity. The algorithms are not human responsible but make humanly impactful decisions.
- How it might be: So if the machines are responsible for human actions and can take a shape with human decisions, AI must, in its program design and development processes, take into account the interests of the affected individuals.

Interaction Bias

- Perception of AI: Imagine each person whispering a word to the person next to him or her all the way down a row. It is interesting to see how the data actually shifts through so many hand-offs. If one of the kids changes the word when telling the next one, it can create a funny moment. Or it could be irritating.
- How it is: If we think about the artificial assistants, they have a sense of humor. This behavior causes them to perceive themselves as a human, but many efforts to humanize AI are involuntarily dishonored and affect software programs by human bias.
- How it might be: So if the interaction between humans and machines takes shape in real time, how can machines shape their learnings by establishing empathetic connections with users? Can they interact with a user without creating unintended behaviors and negative user experiences?

Confirmation Bias

- Perception of AI: Imagine a kid receiving a gift with a specific character on it. Thereafter, other people will perceive this situation as that the kid likes the character. This situation will keep going even when they give up the idea that the kid is an admirer of the character.
- How it is: If we think that AI algorithms support what previously was chosen by other people and excludes people making less-popular choices, confirmation bias interprets the data to validate the preconceived information. It creates the perception of acceptance of the general situation.
- How it might be: So if the AI learns dynamically and changes in time, without following only the data implemented in the system, AI can help users have a more diverse and inclusive view.

Making Memories

AI uses the data that is produced until today, as mentioned previously. In this labeled data is clustered all the previously collected information, which is then combined with the new data. So the machine is learning and increasing its knowledge and abilities. Now, if we consider using AI in real time and it is learning while interacting with the user, AI might be able to create memories from these interactions. If this process continues with learning in every interaction with a user, more natural relationships can be created with people. Imagine person-to-person relationships. The communications are shaping in time, and at the beginning, people do not know exactly how to behave with the other person. However, in time, these communications take shape with learning from each other, and all these interactions and communications are stored as memories in our brains. Relationships shaped with human-to-human interactions are identified as learned behaviors. They help people to build trust in each other, and they add more value to their true companions, creating more strong and reliable connections.

On the other hand, in order to identify relationships with machines and avoid building interactions without a bias, machines need to change their learning methods by processing the signals in different ways, like creating memories and using these learned actions to gain more insights on different behaviors to interpret the data for the next interactions. As cofounder of Maslow and as an AI biologist, Foltz-Smith states that memories of the empathic companion are just signals stored in whatever state they were stored, various layers of records at a variety of frequencies and fidelity levels with energy sensing, and understanding of changes, disruptions, sounds, patterns, and so on. According to him, the first steps toward general AI must be an end to the overly distorted conditioning of stimuli, which is called bias, through flawed ideas in high levels of human concepts, such as linguistics, mathematics, and free will. He also points out that to obtain general AI systems, the whole bandwidth of nature needs to be opened (Foltz-Smith, 2019).

Thus, these interactions can be reshaped by real-time learnings to use signals to create memories and then use this information and learned behaviors to be more empathetic and to give back instantly to users.

Case Studies

I searched for case studies regarding clarifying emotional interactions with products and tried to understand where they have a lack of communication and failed, or a potential to improve and be successful. With a couple of examples, I pointed out the importance of personalized experiences in creating more engagement with users. These are the examples I describe with the reasons: Microsoft Bob, Jibo, Olly, Riot AI, a space for being by Google, and Maslo.

Social Interface Microsoft Bob

In the evolution process of the virtual agents, Microsoft released task-oriented software named Bob as an early experiment in metaphor in design. Bob was created to be a social interface for creating a relationship between the computer and the user. We can say that Bob's aim was to create human-computer interactions. They claimed that Bob was necessary and meaningful not only for the user but also for the computer to make life easier. This task-oriented software was the first step in understanding and improving user experiences in the digital era; today we can see this approach as a user-focused design. The interface allowed the user to personalize the room inside the software with friends with unique personalities so that everyone could find a suitable friend for themselves. The aim was to create social environments with these different personalities and approaches. But in the end, the experience was unresponsive, and it failed to lead and dictate user behavior with commands. We later started to see these interfaces evolve as live chatbots and for AI customer service agents (Nicholas, 2017).

Source: Microsoft Bob, 2019

Social Interface Microsoft Bob (Microsoft Bob, 2019)

Jibo: A Social Robot

The history of Jibo traces back to the MIT laboratory. Cynthia Breazeal, a university associate professor who created and directed MIT's Personal Robots Group, started with the goal of researching robots, meeting with AI, and study how people interact with them. Jibo, launched in 2014, was one of her works.

Jibo was the first social robot for the home. In fact, it was planned to become a friend rather than an assistant. Moreover, Jibo's aim was different from that of other smart speakers. For example, Jibo initiated conversations and asked the user how his or her day was. We can say that Jibo was intended for being empathetic with users (Carman, 2019).

It was made of plastic, with a head curiously tilting around itself. It was not embodied like humans and did not have arms and legs; it looks like a Pixar character. Jibo's head was designed with a display to show its emotional reactions. It looked like a black mask with an emotive white eye. If Jibo wanted to praise the user, this display took the shape of a heart or a pizza. It also had a camera and sensors on the display to understand the user's proximity to Jibo and to shape its reactions (Camp, 2019).

In terms of interaction with users, understanding the closeness of users could create more emotional relationships and interactions, bringing new values to the users' experiences with AI. Being dynamic and reacting to the user's actions, not only with body movements like turning and tilting, but also reflecting a pizza or a heart on the display, shows that the product tried to humanize AI. Jibo had its own characteristics and sense of humor. And its personality did not annoy any of its users.

One of the main reasons for Jibo's failure was the timing for the launch. Right after Jibo's release, other tech companies occupied the home smart speaker market with products at lower price points.

Jibo - A Social Robot   **P6.3**

Source: Camp, 2019

Jibo: A Social Robot (Camp, 2019)

Olly Emotech: A Robot with Personality

Olly is still in the prototype phase. It is the first robot with a personality that can adapt to each individual. It understands the user's emotions through facial expressions, vocal intonations, and verbal patterns. With this understanding, Olly interacts with users in an unprecedented way (Heyolly, 2019). Olly is designed with an advanced machine learning system that helps Olly to remember users' routines rather than just responding to instructions. And it provides a fully personalized experience, which helps Olly to understand and adjust its feelings to the world (Indiegogo, 2017).

Olly interacts with users through a custom-built circular LED screen. It uses an equally unique visual language, but it is comprehensible because of its common core patterns.

In terms of interactions, having different personalities and building them in time through learning from users' habits and needs can help to create emotional and strong human relationships with Olly.

Thanks to Olly's different characteristics, users will be able to create more personalized experiences. There are opportunities to discover more of its personalities and user experiences while being more empathic with the user.

So far, one of the problems can be related to trust. Olly has a display and face-recognition system, so trust needs to be defined clearly in terms of the user's data usage and storage. It needs to be clearly explained to the user how he or she can access the data or deactivate it. Another problem can be the same as with other virtual assistants, like Alexa and Google Home, and that is the usage of the device. If the product is in off mode, data could still be connected, or the device can be completely shut down and not record any conversations.

Emotech Olly　　　　　　　　　　　　　　　　　**P6.4**

Source: Olly Emotech, 2017

Emotech Olly (Olly Emotech, 2017)

Riot AI: Interactive Digital Experience, Sensory Storytelling

This is a different case study than the other examples because it is an immersive and emotionally responsive experience using face recognition and AI during the experience. Riot reacts in real time to participant's emotional states to engage and change the journey through video memory. During the experience, cameras and sensors understand the user's emotional states, and these changes affect the outcome of the interactions. As a result, the user journeys. To create different user journeys, the team designed various scenarios to change the experience based on the user's emotional state and reactions.

The Riot virtual interface allows users to explore their self-awareness through technology and storytelling in a groundbreaking multisensory experience. The user interface is built into an immersive digital media environment and is both technologically and scientifically advanced. Moreover, it should be stated that it is based on a combination of neuroscience and AI (Palmer, 2019).

The measured emotions are described as calmness, fear, anger, and focus. For Riot, machine learning is the main emotion-sensing application technology. AI techniques can be implemented from the data set of the audience in order to learn about the data and create a computer model that can be integrated into an interactive movie environment and identify emotions in real time (*The Guardian*, 2017).

The project is aimed at making people see the advantages of AI and designing intelligent dwellings, buildings, and communities. Riot and its technology could bring a new empathy to storytelling and gaming that encourages viewers or players to bring change to the experience, whether in the narrative or in themselves.

If we consider this experimental design that creates an opportunity to be implemented for virtual agents and to understand the users' emotional states with empathy, how could it change user experiences for these devices? This case study gave a lot of inspiration to my book for implementing AI and computational models to change user experiences based on users' emotional states and defining a way to test the hypothesis on a small scale.

RIOT AI - Sensory Storytelling   **P6.5**

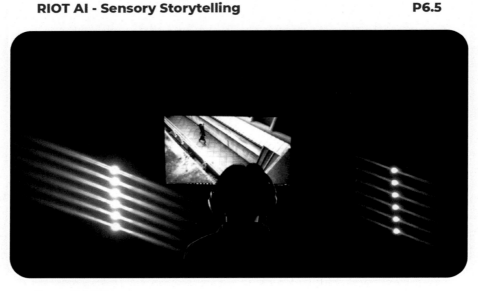

Source: Riot, 2017

Riot AI: Sensory Storytelling (Riot, 2017)

A Space for Being by Google: A Multiroom Experience to Feel More

Google Design studio and the arts and mind lab of Johns Hopkins University designed a multiroom experience for Milan Design Week in 2019. The installation is based on the principles of neuroaesthetics, the field of research that explores how different aesthetic experiences can potentially impact our biology and well-being.

The installation includes three rooms designed following neuroaesthetic principles to let visitors interact with each room. Rooms also included different kinds of objects of various colors and textures, books with different topics for each room, soft music from Google Home that the user could change (Scarano, 2019).

During the journey, they gave bracelets to visitors. Each bracelet had a skin conductance sensor already mixed with AI to measure emotional reactions and responses to understand how the space affected individuals' well-being and physiologies. After the measurements and data collection from the visitors, they returned this data with an aesthetic visualization unique for each user because of the variety of emotional states. The team stated that they worked hard on the visualization of the data to avoid creating a feeling of being scared about technology (Hitti, 2019).

This case study led me to understand the importance of returning the data to the user in a more understandable way and by being transparent with and engaging users by being open about the data collection. If the design is more transparent and informative, people will build more trustful connections with technology.

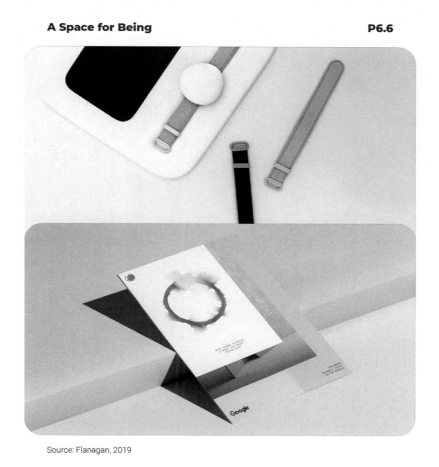

Source: Flanagan, 2019

A Space for Being (Flanagan, 2019)

Maslo: Empathetic Companion

Maslo, created by ex-Googlers, helps users to focus on important things in their lives and improve their self-awareness with an interactive, emotionally intelligent AI. Maslo has a personality and articulate voice journal, and it is designed to help users navigate the uncanny valley of technology and establish a healthier relationship with the ubiquitous digital assistant who lives in their pockets.

Right now, Maslow is an inquisitive child. It learns by asking questions from the user, helping itself eventually to become an adult and a mate of every user. The user will develop and realize his or her own knowledge. Maslo has an excited and curious personality and is open for discovery and expanding his knowledge (Dreamjournal.maslo, 2019).

Ingram, the cofounder of Maslo, says about AI, "I am always inspired by playful things in life. The same goes for empathetic artificial intelligence … if we are to truly deliver on the promise of artificial intelligence, what would that look like? Would it be cold and sterile like a robot? Or would it be something a bit more humanized and Pixar-like?" (Discovering Maslo, 2019).

Maslo has an organic shape and is not embodied like other products. It is a digital companion and represents itself thanks to an organic shape with a distinctive, identifiable, and yet versatile instrument that can express emotions in a natural, polymorphic, and communicative way. It is created with 8 Maslo circles, which include 256 triangles. This helps Maslo to breathe in a relaxed state while idling. The aim of Maslo's visual style, like an art ex-machina, is to create an evolving form of art from AI. This will also help not only to understand emotions but try to find a way to convey them more humanlike.

In addition to that, Maslo has great potential to bring more empathy with AI and help individuals to improve their self-awareness and to take a step further with their self-growth.

I would like to state that this case study became one of the main foundations of this research and helped to gain strength for the topic of the book.

Maslo - Empathetic Companion   **P6.7**

hey i'm maslo

Empathetic computing is not only feasible but the organizing principle to transform technology into products that help us grow.

Source: Dreamjournal maslo ai, 2019

Maslo: Empathetic Companion (Dreamjournal maslo ai, 2019)

Interview Report

Interviewee:
Ross Ingram

Interviewer:
Cansu Hizli

Date:
August 28, 2019

How did you start working with personal companions?

I started to work with designing interactive toys at Sphero, and we designed the BB-8 App-Enabled Droid. This is an entertaining, interactive toy for kids who are fans of the *Star Wars* movies. The toy is interactive and controlled by voice; it is perfect for little kids who can't use a remote control. After this experience, I started to ask myself, What if they had their own personalities and become more personal devices? With this feature, could we create a relationship to help people to grow? So these questions led me to start my adventure with Maslo.

Why is your focus on companions instead of virtual assistants like Alexa and Google Home?

I believe that in the near future, assistants like Alexa and Google Home will not be in our lives because they are not creating a strong belief in people. They are just tools that can answer the users' questions. Besides, personal companions are going to give us questions to ask ourselves and have possibilities to reflect on their paths to help people grow. So if we are able to use technology, we first need to use it for personal growth.

In addition to that, the main missing point is empathy. Virtual assistants only have capabilities to interpret the data; they are not empathetic. They are not able to share awareness, consequences, and outcomes. Instead, they are just taking user inputs and giving them an answer as an outcome. Think about a domestic pet like a dog, how they are able to create empathy, shaking their tails to state their emotional conditions, even having eye contact. What I am trying to say is we need to trust; to have trust, we need to have empathy. So this is sort of an example of cocreation between the user and the companion.

What do you think about the role of AI? What is the meaning of AI for you?

My thoughts about this question are the answer to why I am not working at Google anymore. People do not know how AI is working. We have experience working with it, but people do not. AI has to be accessible and open all the doors to people to let them learn. Again, I am coming to the same point. To let people learn from them, we need to develop relationships between people and the machine with empathy, give more personality to devices. Today, machines are not only avatars or programmed software. It does not mean anything to me to define a machine by asking questions and taking answers like, "How are you? Fine. And you? I am fine too." This does not mean anything; there is nothing personal and understandable. They need to be related to us, more empathic like a friend or a pet.

Also, I want to add something about AI. We call it artificial intelligence, but we cannot call it artificial anymore because it is evolving to our lives more and more than before. It is real, not artificial anymore.

Are they going to be accurate enough to communicate with the user?

Of course, they will not be 100 percent accurate. Even people's relationships, reactions, and emotional statements are not accurate either. Imagine that someone is crying in front of you, and you think about all the possibilities for why she or he is crying. "What should I do?" you ask yourself. Then you probably would decide you need to talk with that person because she or he needs you based on the individual's emotional reactions.

Do we need a shape for AI?

I can answer this one by asking you another question. Do you think that the reflection of AI as a human or like a dog is enough to trust them? Is it giving you any real feeling, or do you already know that they are fake? How do you feel when you talk with a human-shaped chatbot? Is it creating fear, causing you to feel uncomfortable, or the opposite? Nowotny mentions that something specific and well-defined is the source of fear, and it is a powerful physical and psychological response to the perception of a genuine or imagined urgent threat. It is about a vaguely unknown or unexpected force that may or may not overpower us, which is called anxiety. Fear eliminates ambiguity by making one confident that the threat will materialize unless they react with fight or flight (Nowotny, 2016).

Maybe you will ask me, "What is the connection with my question?" I would like to say to you just imagine the first creepy feeling of fear and then the possible psychological effects on humans. This is an uncertain point, so maybe we should try a completely different way. In conclusion, humans are not chatbots. Humans are fluid, and Maslo should be that too.

So how did you decide the shape of Maslo? I mean, how it will look?

We designed Maslo as digital using 8 Maslo Circles. The circles are formed by 256 triangle fans whose perimetric vertices use 2d Perlin noise to modify their distance to the center. This gives Maslo the relaxed breathing state you see when it is idle. Using a slightly offset Gaussian curve to modify the intensity of the Perlin noise, we obtained the Maslo curves, which are the ones that actually confer Maslo as an identity and make him recognizable as a brand element. So there is an animation, movements that Maslo can use to reflect the user's emotions. For this, you don't need to give a face to something to describe emotions or simple reactions. If you want to know more, you can visit my blog post.

What will you do to improve and upgrade Maslo?

We've been quite successful in this regard because we have a pipeline that helps companies get their projects to market and in the hands of end users faster, cheaper, and we're just fun to work with. This helps get the companies more data, which allows for tuning of machine learning and algorithms. Which impacts users positively. Which improves outcomes. Maslo has come a long way. We see tremendous opportunities in creating assistive technologies that help people in their daily lives. Also, hire amazing people.

Last question. How can we make someone trust digital companions or the power of this technology? While I was researching this topic, many people answered me that it is so creepy, even without listening to what I am talking about. Can we cross this boundary?

I just want to say yes! We need to change the way we interact with people because they do not know the back and front jobs. They do not know how it works. So they are simply not trusting, and this creates the creepy fear about it. If you are asking me the way, I can say that with playing, we can cross these boundaries. Eames is saying that the play is a serious idea, and with playing, we are growing. It is actually true because most of the adults have fixed minds, and they have to overcome it. Imagine playing basketball for the first time. You will throw the ball in any way into the hoop. What is it? It is a curiosity when you meet with something for the first time. So we should push this curiosity always. For me, the key is playing. Then it will create a committed relationship, like a circle, and trust will follow it without realizing it.

Takeaways

This chapter explained how virtual assistants can become more like personal companions and increase an individual's self-awareness and growth with implementation of EI and empathy by defining more transparent communications. Also, the importance of building trustful relationships with machines is stated to be away from creating biases in these communications.

In the next chapter, the methodology and the experimental phases of research are explained.

Methodology

The Preexperimental Phase of Research

Survey Structure

Survey Questions

Survey Outcomes Structure

True-Experimental Phase of Research

The Framework of Personality

A Profound Understanding of the Users and Their Needs

An Effective Model of Personality

The Role of Empathy in Creating Relationships with AI

Iteration 1: Design Process

Iteration 2: Design Process

Iteration 3: Design Process

C h a p t e r 7

Methodology

Introduction

The methodology for this research consisted of a detailed outline of the empathetic companion's relationship with people in terms of:

- Building more emotional connections with digital products.
- Understanding the critical changes in episodic dispositions.
- Increasing self-awareness of individuals.

With an understanding of the relationship with an empathetic companion, implementing this relationship and personality traits into the digital experiences will

- Build more empathetic companion onboarding designs.
- Describe and analyze personal experiments.
- Understand the effect of these experiences with different personalities on the users' emotional states.
- Test the hypothesis with implemented theories.

The last step includes an explanation of how data was collected and which theories to implement to test the hypothesis.

The combination of the implementation of a user's personal traits, the meaning of companionship, building trust with an empathetic personal companion, and the experiment will be used to answer the research questions. The research is divided into two sections, a preexperimental without a controlled group and a true experimental with a controlled group.

The Preexperimental Phase of Research

Preexperiment without a control group will be used to answer the research questions. It includes running a survey in different countries to collect all different personalities, the meaning of the personal companions for individual, and usage of digital virtual assistants like Siri, Cortana, Alexa, and Google Assistant to understand the desired personalities, the methods of communication, and interaction between people and digital products.

Research questions for the survey were shaped into two categories as the main question and subquestions to create an opportunity to answer these questions and have data to be used for designing onboarding experiences with different personalities, communication methods, and interactions.

First Research Question

- What are the episodic dispositions to guide the design process of an empathetic companion's onboarding experiences?

Subquestions

- Can a moment of self-awareness and emotional states be used to design personalized experiences for onboarding processes?
- Which personalities, moments, and media must be considered to build a trustful relationship with a companion?
- Which components need to be in place for personal experiences to meet user personalities, needs, and desires?

Survey Structure

A quantitative study was conducted with an online survey to examine the moment of self-awareness in individuals, the meaning of companionship, and narrative empathy with desired personalities and interactions from a digital companion defined by participants. The online survey was designed on Google forms to spread easily between different countries. It consisted of 173 users in twelve countries: Holland, China, England, Turkey, Estonia, Germany, Italy, Japan, Netherlands, Norway, Russia, and the United States. At the end of the survey, the countries that stood out as the number of participants were Italy, with eighty-seven participants, Turkey, with sixty-five participants and Germany, with eight participants. The target of this survey is structured by millennials and Generation Z without requiring distinctive expectations.

The simple but rigorous and scientifically validated evaluation of personality was structured based on popular personality tests such as the Aaker's and Carl Jung's Brand Personality Model, Myers-Briggs Personality Theory, Goleman's Model of Self-Awareness, and the Enneagram Model. The survey aimed to define personalities in a different way than personality tests that are available in different forms online to define specific personalities. It should be stated that every person's personality includes all the personality types, but some are more prevalent than others. One of the problems with these personality tests was that they were not engageable enough with a lot of questions.

Rather than defining the user's personality, the aim of this survey was to gain insights about the user's actions, decisions, emotions, and the methods of communications to obtain data for designing digital empathic onboarding experiences in different personalities.

The first part focused on the moment of self-awareness for individuals. The aim of this part was to understand how well people know themselves and were aware of their decisions and actions that happen every day in their lives. Personality trait theories were placed into the questions as well as defining effects and triggers on episodic emotional changes. It consisted of short questions with two answer options that allowed participants to select only one answer quickly, the ones that first came to their minds.

The second part focused on the meaning of companionship for individuals in terms of method of communication, interaction, and different media to describe emotions on digital platforms. It consisted of quick short questions, including ones with multiple answers. Multiple selections were included because of data collection necessary to shape onboarding experiences for the true experimental phase. They will be used to help analyze and understand behavioral changes and emotional states.

The aim of this part was to understand the usage of mood-aware media, matching these media with a character and creating a moment of trust with a real companion. The data collection from this section will help to shape and design onboarding experiences with two communication methods, like the tone of voice, media, and changes of emotional reactions.

The third and the last part of the survey focused on the narrative empathy with desired personalities that result as a combination of a real and a digital companion. One of the aims of this last part was to collect answers from users about their use of at least one of the personal virtual assistants—such as Siri, Cortana, Google Assistant, Alexa, and Maslo—to understand the ways these assistants communicate. Another aim was to identify the desired personalities from reliable digital companions in terms of being sincere (honest, well-mannered, cheerful, friendly, kind, and family-oriented), accomplished (logical, reliable, intelligent, confident, and secure), and excited (independent, imaginative, fun, exciting, cool, and trendy). These outcomes will help to define the two personalities for onboarding experiences.

Part 1

Based on a literature review, two personality trait models were implemented in the first part of the survey: Goleman's Model of Self-Awareness and Myers-Briggs Personality Theory.

First, the reason for selecting the Myers-Briggs theory for this part was to update the psychological style theory of Carl Gustav Jung, which is based on sixteen types of Jung's stereotypes. Another reason was because the Myers-Briggs theory has been mentioned as one of the world's most popular cognitive methods. In addition to this, the aim of this theory was to understand and define the personalities most appropriate for individuals. The theory of personality of the Myers-Briggs is an inventory type with an individual's weak points and interests entered on a self-reporting form. This theory was constructed on four scales (mentioned in chapter 3).

For this part of the survey, only two scales were selected to analyze, the answers based on being more extroverted (E) or introverted (I) and thinker (T) or feeler (F) to shape the empathetic onboardings. With these two scales, questions were constructed around people, events, ideas, and knowledge to find whether outcomes are more on the extroversion or introversion side and, facts and logic, defining values, and interactions to identify whether those outcomes are more in the zone of feeling or thinking. I then collected the outcomes to create personality metrics at the end of the survey. These outcomes, crossed with the results of the second part of the survey, were used to design two onboardings with different personalities that came up as a result of crossing these outcomes.

Personal skills require self-awareness and autonomy. Self-consciousness helps individuals to control their emotional reactions and comprehend the impact of their behaviors on others. For this, Goleman's Model of Self-Awareness, in which he describes his theory of emotional intelligence with five core emotional traits, was implemented in the first part of the survey. From these five core traits, knowing and understanding one's own thoughts and managing and regulating one's own emotions were considered the main two approaches and implemented in the questions to make the survey more creative and thoughtful, even if the questions were based on quick responses. Users need to consider their actions and remind themselves to be aware and to select the most dominant one, which is the ones that comes to their minds as a first response.

Feeling (F)/Thinking (T)

Feelers
- Agreeable (kind and trustworthy)
- Heartfelt decisions
- Effects on people important

Thinkers
- Conscientious (goal-focused, well-organized)
- Decisions made with mind
- Most logical, reasonable choices

Extroversion (E)/Introversion (I)

Extroversion
- Openness to experience
- Being with people
- Busy, always active, expressive, outspoken

Introversion
- Closeness to experience
- More reserved, thoughtful
- Prefer to be alone or in a small group

Part 2

Based on a literature review, the second part of the survey was structured according to Carl Jung's archetypal theory and Aaker's personality trait. As explained in chapter 3, archetypes are classified as universal patterns, pictorial patterns, and collective unconscious models. Jung identified through these twelve primary archetypes and the associated motivations. The four cardinal orientations represent a model to our understanding that has a set of values, significances, and individual characteristics. With consideration of these four categories to define the sincere and accomplished characters, one archetype was selected from each category, which they defined as the lover, the creator, the sage, and the magician. The lover and the creator archetypes are used in creating a more sincere/friendly personality. The sage and the magician archetypes are used for designing more accomplished/logical personalities for the digital onboarding experience. In addition, the survey questions were structured based on archetypes' core desires, goals, greatest fears, strategies, and fears to understand people's reactions, their ways of thinking and making decisions, and variables that affect people's moods and communication methods.

The Lover
- *Core desire:* Confidentiality and experience
- *Goal:* To be in a relationship with people and surrounded by people's love
- *Greatest fear:* Being alone, undesired, and far from being in love
- *Strategy:* To become more and more attractive both physically and emotionally
- *Talent:* Strong emotions, thankfulness, appreciation, and loyalty
- *Known as:* The partner, friend, intimate, and sensualist

The Creator/Artist
- *Core desire:* Creating things with lasting values
- *Goal:* Achieve a dream
- *Greatest fear:* Having common dreams and results
- *Strategy:* Developing ability and artistic control
- *Talent:* Imagination and creativity
- *Known as:* The artist, innovator, and dreamer

The Sage
- *Core desire:* Finding the truth
- *Goal:* To understand the world by using intelligence and analysis
- *Biggest fear:* To be deceived, cheated, and unaware
- *Strategy:* Searching for information and knowledge and thinking processes of self-reflection and understanding
- *Talent:* Intelligence and wisdom
- *Known as:* The expert, adviser, thinker, planner, and mentor

The Magician
- *Core desire:* Knowing the fundamental laws of the universe
- *Goal:* Making dreams come true

- *Greatest fear:* Unintentional negative effects
- *Strategy:* Create a dream and live through it
- *Talent:* Finding solutions with positive outcomes
- *Known as:* The visionary, inventor, and leader

In addition to Carl Jung's archetypal theory, Aaker's personality trait was implemented in the second part of the survey to understand the meaning of a real companion. Moreover, multiple-answer questions were implemented in defining expected personalities and behaviors from the perception of a companion. In addition, one of the aims of shaping the questions on this theory was to understand:

- Which characteristic features create effects on people to feel more comfortable while they are sharing them with other people or with their inner characters
- In what situations people want to share their feelings
- The willingness to share their emotions or to think about them
- In what way they want to increase their self-awareness, such as changing the situations that affect their moods, keeping them on the track with helping them to reach their goals and listening to them without suggesting any solutions, giving advice, and so on

Aaker's model focuses on defining brand personality. The reason for using this model was to implement the expected or desired personalities into the onboarding characteristics. For example, a digital companion characteristic might be defined as being more reliable, sincere, logical, helpful, funny, self-confident, imaginative, thoughtful, and so on. So it helped to define the two personalities and implement people's expectations on the digital brand's onboarding processes to meet with these products for the first time. The benefit of using Aaker's model is that it enables brands to identify their tone of voice, create trust, and convey messages from the brand identity. The main objective of the model was to investigate the characteristics that users assign in their lives to their real companions.

Part 3

Before starting to structure part 3, a critical challenge was taken into account to express both effective and personalized attributes by means of consistent interactions in the computational context. Furthermore, it must be tailored to the different communication types of users.

The aim of the last part of the survey was mainly to understand which virtual assistants were used by people and what type of personalities and communications methods were desired to be implemented in virtual assistants to make them more empathetic and emotional. Another aim was to find out what interactions people wanted to use personal companions for, like increasing their self-awareness, keeping them on the way to reach their goals, and expecting to be understood without telling the personal companion the same things every time.

Finally, the last two questions were shaped by people's imaginations. If the virtual assistants became more empathic and reliable companions, were people willing to name them and how they would like to call and interact with them. With this question, the aim was to make people think about the relationship if machines had a chance to be their companions, like their friends, families, and pets they are emotionally connected with. There was a possibility of unintentional reluctant answers, but all the answers showed the question was considered and their willingness to name their possible companions.

The collected answers from this part helped in designing different onboardings with various communication skills to define a tone of voice; visual style; content of each step; structure of sentences, like long or short sentences; and different personality features, like acting as a friend, more serious, or more logical. These variable outcomes could also be used to shape personal digital companions' emotional states and reactions.

Survey Questions

Survey questions can be seen in chapter 8 with the survey results, which are represented with graphics. They are also accessible with the QR code.

Survey Outcome Structure

The extensive investigation influenced the findings in three established personality patterns. The questionnaire was translated into three parts of binary choices to test the three patterns. With this aim, as I stated in the survey structure, the first part of the survey focused on defining two personalities that indicated whether users were more on the thinking or feeling side, or if they were more extroverted or introverted. The second part focused on identifying people's approaches. Were they on the more emotional, logical side or in the middle of both sides?

Then, to reach the result and select two personalities in three outcomes to define the digital companion personality, the Enneagram model was implemented using the personality evaluation methodology. With the Enneagram model, personality metrics were created to define the potential personality types to be used for the creation of the two different digital companions. Each onboarding is informed by intimate decisions and individual ways of thinking. The aim of these onboarding experiences was to make them feel like empathic and reliable personal companions for research purposes.

Personality Metrics
- Extrovert (E)—Introvert (I)
- Feeler (F)—Thinker (T)
- Emotional (Em)—Logical (Lo)

Possible Outcomes
- EmFE—Emotional feeler and extrovert
- EmFI—Emotional feeler and introvert
- EmTE—Emotional thinker and extrovert
- EmTI—Emotional thinker and introvert
- LoFE—Logical feeler and extrovert
- LoFI—Logical feeler and introvert
- LoTE—Logical thinker and extrovert
- LoTI—Logical thinker and introvert

The focus was to identify the emotional and logical users who included at least one characteristic from the first part of the survey, extrovert-introvert and feeler-thinker. These metrics gave users the opportunity to find common points and features that match their characteristics. Thus, it was aimed for users not to feel unfamiliar with the application and to imagine themselves in a natural conversation.

True-Experimental Phase of Research

The true experimental phase with a controlled group was structured to understand user behaviors and changes in their emotional states through episodic dispositions. The second question of the research is answered in the experiment later in this chapter. This experiment accessed the onboarding prototype against another version of the onboarding that behaved less empathic and emotional when using a different tone of voice and visual style for communication and interaction with the user. The experiment included three iterations and developments based on the results from each prior iteration session. All the experiments were then used to collect qualitative data to understand whether the digital companion's personality improved the user experience, created an effect in their emotional states, and created a feeling of trust between the user and the companion to create a positive first impression between them. In addition, this experience was analyzed to be helpful to motivate people in fulfilling their own desires and ambitions and to take appropriate actions and suggestions.

This phase of the methodology first defined the research question and then explained how the personality framework and design process were implemented. The survey results, the setup of the experiment, hypothesis, and the collection of data were to be established deeply.

Second Research Question

Will empathetic onboarding experiences with a defined personality encourage user-companion interactions to create trustful relationships?

The Framework of Personality

In order to construct the personality model, four components are identified for the digital companion personality. These components are based on:

- The aim of designing empathetic onboardings.
- A profound understanding of the users and their needs.
- An effective personality model.
- The role of empathy in creating a relationship with AI.

The first element was required to make sure the characters and actions of the digital companions adhere to the aim of designing empathetic companions, the goals and tone of voice of the digital product that it represents, and support the users' expectations, needs, and desires. The second aspect must be fulfilled to ensure that the personality supports the users' interests and to decide which personality traits are appropriate for individuals. In addition, each iteration for the design testing must be explained through the users' expectations and desires after interacting with prototypes. The third component, an effective model of personality, was important for organizing and mapping personality traits into a suitable framework that would be shown on the personality diagram after analyzing quantitative data when the third iteration of the experiment was complete. This part also explained the implementation of a personality framework to construct the digital companion's personality, which was tested to understand how different personalities affected user experiences. The last component was needed to describe the importance of implementing artificial intelligence and machine learning into design processes, creating more personalized empathetic experiences. Moreover, it explained the importance of having different personalities for digital companions to meet users' needs and shape the flow of communication based on their actions to increase the likelihood of positive first impressions and a feeling of trust.

Design Process

The design process used a user-centered design approach in order to gain insight into the needs of users and to inform digital onboarding prototype requirements. The design process focused on the design-thinking model in five phases proposed at Stanford's Hasso-Plattner Institute of Design (Hasso Plattner Institute of Design at Stanford, 2010). The five-stage model is constructed by a nonlinear process that is defined as:

- Empathizing: To understand user needs and desires.
- Defining: To reframe and define the problems in human-centered ways.
- Ideating: To develop several ideas in ideation sessions.

- Prototyping: To adopt defined personalities in prototyping.
- Testing: To collect insights for the next phase of the prototyping and see what improved the user experience.

Therefore, each of the five phases followed the core user-centered design concepts, in which the empathizing and defining steps focused on user and research analysis (the framework of personality, components 1 and 2). The ideation part focused on the design processes and definition of the empathic companions' personalities (the framework of personality, component 3). The last two stages, prototyping and testing, focused on assessing the final prototyping after the three iterations of the digital onboarding to determine the nature of the user's interpretation, its effects on the user experiences, and the changes in the emotional states of users (the framework of personality, component 4). Research concentrated on testing the final digital prototyping to evaluate the digital companion characteristics in terms of people's interpretations and the impact of the companions' personalities on user experiences.

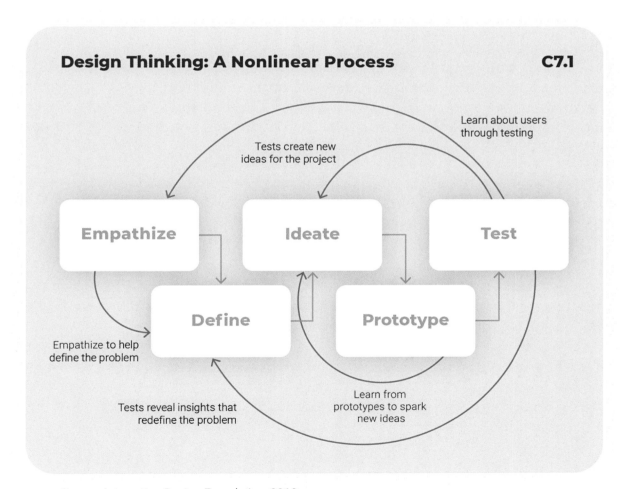

Source: Interaction Design Foundation, 2019

Design Thinking: A Nonlinear Process (Interaction Design Foundation, 2019)

An innovative approach to inventing new ideas is user-centered conception (UCD), which starts with individuals and ends with answers that are customized to their individual needs. This method combines analysis, interviews, generative strategies, and instruments. UCD focuses on designing, testing, and collecting all the feedback to improve the product and then test it again. This loop continues with many iterations. User-centered design is needed to understand users' needs and desires by incorporating users' inputs at all stages of the design and testing processes. Therefore, it relies on feedback, insights, wishes, and suggestions that come from users. And thanks to iterations, it ensures that the design processes are responsive. In the final assessment, qualitative information for this project was gathered to address the second research question and hypotheses.

The Aim of Designing Empathetic Onboardings

The design of empathetic onboarding experiences was combined with two phases in terms of identifying the companions' personalities from the survey results, taking into consideration the real brand to develop the prototyping. The brand and domain were selected because they were different from the other products on the market in terms of being empathetic and more personal rather than the virtual assistants. The purpose and the aim of the product Maslo was used as an example in the context and testing with redesigning the onboarding of the application and changing the personality of the companion. In brief, Maslo used it with the aim of analyzing the meaning of empathetic companion. The onboarding experiences were used to support the brand's goal of increasing individuals' self-awareness and to create trustworthy relationships with digital empathic companions.

The empathetic companion domain was based on a real digital empathetic companion to create the prototyping, check the personality frame, and adopt a user-centered design approach. The collaboration was stated for the research part of the book by the definition of digital companion characteristics through testing onboarding experiences as the first meeting with a companion, positioning the perception of the digital companions' personalities and senses of trust to build reliable relationships between users and digital companions. Using a real-life example was important for the prototype to demonstrate how the personality of the virtual empathetic companion reflects the tone of voice, aims, and values of the brand. But as I stated before, using only the real brand was not enough to build prototyping for defining the personalities of a digital companion for testing with different users with different personalities. So the survey results were merged with this real brand, and two personalities were designed, taking into consideration the different tone of voices, media implemented into the design, visual styles, contents of the conversation, and the method of interaction not only physically but also emotionally. Thanks to this unification, the prototype was able to collect variant user feedback to meet the aims of the empathetic companions.

Analysis of Tone of Voice

Tone of voice was interpreted from the brand's actual tone of voice and personality. The tone of voice is defined mainly by the content and call to actions, and it is supported by visual elements.

The first onboarding was designed with a more logical personality, and the tone of voice was described as more informative, intelligent, and thinker, rather than having an emotional conversation. It was identified as being a logical thinker to guide users in reaching their goals, keeping them on their ways to make their dreams come true and helping them to reveal their inner heroes while growing their self-awareness. The tone of voice used to ask questions of users was described as being more straight to the point without explaining all the reasons or informing users of all the details. The tone of voice for reactions after users shared their information was structured with logical and stable answers and reactions.

On the other hand, the second onboarding experience was designed with a more sincere personality, and the tone of voice was described as being more emotional and empathetic, excited, imaginative, and as a feeler rather than having a structured logical conversation. It was shaped with more natural reactions based on human-to-human communications. Also, it was identified to help people increase their self-awareness with imagination and to build a feeling that they could make it together and take the same path to share the experience of learning and discovering together. The tone of voice for asking questions of users was described as being more curious about the information users were giving, and the tone of voice for reacting after receiving the information from the users defined as having a friendlier approach, like in natural conversations between real-life, human friends.

To create the content and keep it coherent with the flow, the tone of voice was described as a product personality communicated both by writing and visual communications. For visual communication, the first onboarding with a logical personality was designed with more static visuals and used geometric shapes in blue and white. The background visuals were designed and kept in the same position. Texts were located in the same positions to be single oriented. It was only possible to understand how users' attentions were changing if they followed the same visual strategies without having any change of their points of view.

At the beginning of the experience, the character with abstract geometric shapes took a position and kept its position during the journey. It just changed the dimension of circles based on users' answers about how they were feeling. Even these small changes were always in the same position to try to understand a user's attention level during the experiences.

In terms of visual communication, the second onboarding with a sincere personality was designed with more curved shapes to make the visual design dynamic and fluent. The background visual design included a sort of abstract character that moved in each scene and reflected emotions with basic shapes, not only to describe users' emotional states, but also to show companions' emotions. When this abstract character took a flat shape, it represented calmness. When the shapes came together and created more dynamic shapes, they also created effects on users and helped to perceive the character's emotions. For example, when the character wanted an action to start a journey, it became more visible and pointed to the call to action, aiming to be more encouraged and ready to meet with a user. Moreover, when a user started the experience, at the beginning of the onboarding, the character stayed flat and did not show itself to give the user time to focus on more content and understand the aim of the companion and the product.

Human personality characteristics are perceived on the basis of the behavior, physics, attitudes, and beliefs of an individual and demographic properties (Park, 1986). While personality traits of humans and brands may have similar conceptualizations (Epstein, 1977), they differ in how they are formed. Using Aaker's brand personality model, it ensures constant messages in all the interactions through the tone of voice that constantly referred to the brand personality. In deciding the number and existence of dimensions of brand personality, Aaker established a structure for developing the conceptual framework for the brand's personality construction (Aaker, 1997). According to her model, the tone of voice was determined for this experimental design as sincerity, excitement, and competence in between five dimensions: sincerity, excitement, competence, sophistication, and ruggedness.

The first onboarding, logical personality, reflected the competence personality with a tone of voice in terms of being intelligent, reliable, secure, and confident. The second onboarding, sincere personality, reflected a sincere personality with a tone of voice that could be described as cheerful, friendly, kind, excited, imaginative, and reliable.

Lastly, it should be stated that both companions' tones of voice were determined very carefully in keeping with the core values of being respectful, trustful, and empathetic.

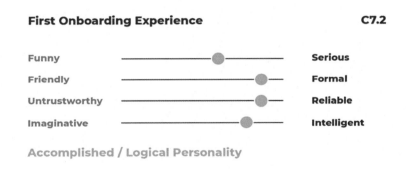

First Onboarding Experience

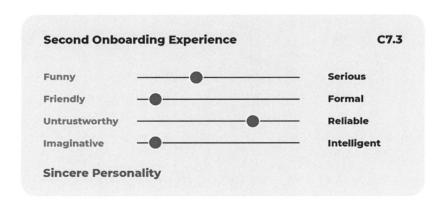

Second Onboarding Experience

A Profound Understanding of the Users and Their Needs

To achieve the second aspect, data about preliminary research, preexperimental phase without a focused group, and secondary research, true-experimental phase with a focused group, were collected to understand the variables of establishing trustworthy relationships between users and digital products in order to gain a deep understanding of user needs and requirements.

Iterative Design

To understand the user needs and requirements to build more trustful relationships and meaningful interactions between users and products, iterative design methodology was used for testing the onboarding designs. The functionality dimensions and the five related attributes were taken into account in the iterative model. They were:

- Easy to learn.
- Efficient to use.
- Easy to remember.
- Few errors and easy to adapt.
- Pleasant to use.

These variables were not only considered in terms of usability of the prototype but also for their effects in converting the users' insights into the next experimental design and understanding how their effects changed during testing. At the end of the true-experimental phase, it was expected that the results would be opened to discovering more, go deep with the research, and be able to show the different personality effects on people's behaviors, perceptions of emotions, and episodic dispositions.

Interviews

With the iterative design methodology, the onboarding designs were tested by users in three sessions. Users of different nationalities were selected to test the prototype and see the different social and cultural effects on user experiences.

The first iteration was conducted with semistructured interviews with and observations by five users from an MSc digital and interaction design course at Politecnico di Milano. The students selected were between twenty and twenty-two years old because users in that age range were positioned between millennials and Generation Z, who are perceived as early adopters of digital products. Users completed the first iteration of the experimental design by testing the first version of the digital onboarding prototypes. Based on their feedback and suggestions about the prototype, the onboardings were redefined using the users' understandings and insights.

The second study explored the usability of the basic structure of the prototype more fully, evaluating issues such as information architecture, task flow, and user needs. This iteration was conducted with ten users from different educational and professional backgrounds. Most were last-year students at Politecnico di Milano in different master's programs and working as professional interaction designers with several companies. For this testing, they were qualified as expert users in terms of their understanding of interactions and testing the usability of the digital empathetic onboarding designs. Seven of them worked as professionals in different fields as a digital product designers and service designers. They were last-year MSc. students at Politecnico di Milano in different courses. The other three were working as digital product designers and an architect. User age ranged between twenty-three and twenty-eight, making them millennials. Users completed the second iteration of the experimental design by testing the second version of the digital onboarding prototypes. Based on their feedback and suggestions about the prototype, the onboardings were redefined with the users' understandings and insights.

Thus, at the end of the second iteration, onboarding prototypes had been tested by fifteen users following the basics of usability testing methods. As stated by Nielsen, the prototype needed to be tested by at least fifteen users to identify all usability problems in the design (Nielsen, 2000). In addition to that, in creating trustful relationships between users and digital companions, diversity became one of the important variables necessary to see the different cultural and social effects. This iteration collected all the insights and feedback from users to redesign the flow of the onboarding experiences so that the importance of creating trust with selected and implemented designs would be possible in the next iteration.

The third iteration was conducted with usability testing using a questionnaire composed of structured questions and was done online. The last designed version of the prototype was sent to users with a link that included a digital mockup to test the prototype. The questionnaire was included to be completed at the end of the experience. Seven users were selected from the second iteration; others were chosen from an online survey from the preexperimental phase of the testing. Users were more comfortable and free to act at this stage of the test. In addition, the questions were prepared in a simple and effective way with quick-response answers.

An Effective Model of Personality

The model chosen to design the personality of onboarding experiences was Jung's archetypal theory and Aaker's personality traits. Chapter 6 describes the survey structure in part 2.

First, to describe the personality of the logical companion, the first onboarding experience, it was built from the sage and the magician archetypes. The sincere companion, the second onboarding experience, was built from the lover and the creator archetypes according to the model of Jung's archetypes. On the other hand, for the first onboarding, more competence and logical, intelligent and explanatory traits, and for the second onboarding, more sincere, cheerful, explorer, and imaginative were implemented according to the model of Aaker's brand personality. In addition, these two onboardings shared the same common traits and were defined as being reliable, kind, honest, and thoughtful.

Second, personality models were not only implemented to the onboardings but also applied to the question while the companion was asking a user about his or her personality. Options were divided into four categories. Both onboardings had the same question and options:

- Excitement
- Imagination
- Intelligence
- Achievement

This part aimed to give a feeling to users of personalized experiences, show them that the journey would be tailored by their responses, and to understand that by supplying more or less information, the effect on users' decision-making processes and changes would be based on their levels of excitement, engagement, and curiosity. Again, Jungian archetypes were used to define users' personalities, and the explanations were interpreted from the archetypes' definitions. To create the content texts, Adobe Creative Type's definitions were interpreted to be used in the prototype to communicate with the user in psychological terms and to convey the correct message because Adobe's test contents were created by Carolyn Gregoire, a *Huffington Post* senior writer on psychology, mental illness, and neuroscience (Anyways, 2019).

The Role of Empathy in Creating Relationships with AI

As human beings, we continue to develop a society and economic ecosystem that invest in the development and use of tools, such as computers, that conflict with what we learn about nature and from what we value as a species. The reason is simple: We need them to simplify our daily lives and reduce our cognitive loads. Today, machines are becoming more intelligent and learning faster than before; they are already able to memorize our actions. However, the situation now involves describing how we started to define the machines with the latest news, such as collecting users' data, even when the machines are inactive mode, and selling users' data to third parties. They store user information, including locations and bank account information. But people still use these machines even if they do not like, appreciate, or understand them.

We can say that people are becoming more aware of their actions and decisions, including their ramifications, but missing are the transparency and trust necessary to create relationships between people and machines. Key to establishing these trustful relationships is to create empathetic companionships. Just as people create empathic relationships between each other over time, and these relationships are defined as the steps and stages of friendship and loyalty, relationships between people and machines can also be built with empathy over time using this model as an example. To do so, people and machines need to be involved in the same colearning and cocreating experiences together. And the meaning and the aim of AI should be explained in these transparent mutualist processes. Therefore, people and machines need to spend more time creatively daydreaming or discovering issues. They should stop seeing machines as tools, and instead create more empathetic aspects and be more open for discovery to have trustful companionships. Thus, AI can be involved in our lives with more trust and openness.

Iteration 1: Design Process

Since the importance of onboarding experiences has been pointed out, to develop the first prototype, I decided to start from the architecture with researching the main steps of meeting with new people. I also focused on which variables were considered important to be represented through experiences. In this way, I came up with a series of questions and actions that reflected the birth of a new relationship between human beings. Namely, exchanging names, asking how life is going, sharing what they are doing in their lives, wondering about approaches to life, and building the first sense of trust. In this way, I tried to translate these moments of human interactions into steps to redesign the onboarding of Maslo.

From the survey, I was able to identify two main personalities. I decided to develop two primary onboardings based on the answers previously stated with questions. In that way, I was able to test how people behaved in front of two different personalities in order to prove that different personalities, even in a digital interface, can build different empathies with the user.

Talking about AI, I opted to differentiate the two personalities based on colors, shapes, layouts, fonts, and character reactions.

For the Logical Companion: Onboarding 1

Colors: Blue and tones, also bluish-purple colors, were used to create more logical- and intelligent-oriented perception. The aim was to keep distance with the user for the first meeting and to show the character as more achievement- and goal-oriented.

Shapes: Geometric shapes, mainly rectangles and circles, were used in a definitive position, which is located on the top part of the screen, in order to stay calm and have an edge with users. Geometric shapes also gave countenance to the intelligent and wisdom personalities of the character.

Layouts: A flat background was used to give a stable and structured feeling to reflect the companion's personality. For asking questions, the AI is designed with rectangle buttons in grids while considering the simplicity of the design. Also, for moving to the next page, an arrow with low opacity is placed at the bottom of the page to lead the user to take an action before continuing.

Fonts: For the main title, DIN Pro was used because of the geometrical shape of the font, which would support design elements, and its unadorned appearance. For the body, Roboto Light was used for the sincere onboarding to support the readability of texts and avoid complexity.

Character Reactions: The stable position of the design was protected and the character's reactions defined by only tone of voice and small size changes in the geometric shapes.

For the Sincere Companion: Onboarding 2

Colors: Soft purple and light pink colors were used to create the users' imagination, personality, and thoughtfulness. The aim was to create more friendly and trustful feelings thanks to the warm and soft colors.

Shapes: Rounded and curvy shapes supported the design in order to provide a more friendly approach to perceive them as being more organic and natural. This onboarding was supported with other visual elements, like emojis, to help increase the readability of texts, and emotional iconic shapes to make the character more alive.

Layouts: A dynamic background was used to give movement to the design and hold the users' attention. Curved shapes moved up and down based on the questions and the users' answers. A simple arrow was placed at the right-bottom of the screen after users took an action to give room to users for discovery and thinking.

Fonts: For the main titles, Montserrat Bold was used because of the font dynamism and the geometric simplicity of letters. For the body, Roboto Light was selected, as in the logical onboarding, because of its simplicity and sophistication. The font also allowed users to read texts easily and smoothly.

Character Reactions: Based on the user actions and selections, the abstract character's eyes reflected the users' emotional states after they selected emojis to answer the question, "How are you?" Moreover, after the personal questions, the character moved up and down to become more visible or hidden to reflect that it was shy, curious, thoughtful, excited, or sad.

Five Steps of the First Meeting with Companion

The architecture of the onboarding experience is mainly shaped by starting from human-to-human interactions and then shifting the point of view to human-to-machine interactions. Five steps are defined for the first meeting with a companion, with inspiration from a real meeting of two people.

1. The First Step: An Introduction between User and Companion

Logical Onboarding: Maslo started with an introduction about itself and asking the user's name: "Hi, I am Maslo, a digital companion. I'd like to focus on important things in your life. What about you, what is your name?"

Sincere Onboarding: Maslo started with a friendly and an emotional introduction about itself. Then it asked the user's name: "Hey, hiii. 😊 I am Maslo. I am here to do my best to be your companion and expand my knowledge to increase your self-awareness. What's your name?"

2. The Second Step: A Soft Question before Starting the Conversation

Logical Onboarding: After a user gave his or her name, Maslo said, "Thanks! Nice to meet you. By the way, how are you?" It offered users four text-based answer options. (Please see the onboarding flow designs in the next pages.) Options were defined with simple answers:

"I am good. And you?"

This was the only opportunity to ask Maslo a question. It was also a chance to know whether users were willing to ask questions.

- "I am good."
- "Not so good."
- "I don't know."

Sincere Onboarding: After the user placed his or her name, Maslo said, "Thank you for sharing. I am glad to meet with you. First things first, how are you doing?" It then offered users four options, represented by emojis. The user picked one. The options were:

- 🤩 ("Great")
- 😊 ("Good")
- 🥺 ("A bit sad.")
- 🫠 ("I don't know.")

3. The Third Step: A Deep Question to Understand a User's Personality

Logical Onboarding: Maslo shared information about itself and then asked users about their personalities: "I use my intelligence to solve things, and I am a logical thinker. Which one are you?" It offered four options built based on personality theories. (Check the, "An Effective Model of Personality.") The options were defined as:

- Excitement
- Imagination
- Intelligence
- Achievement

Sincere Onboarding: Maslo gave information about itself and then asked users about their personalities using more organic buttons. The aim was to share information while avoiding a stressful moment created by the possibility the answer would be wrong because for sincere companions, openness is an important value. Maslo said "So, well … 🫤 I would like to discover which one you like more. I can use my imagination to help you." Again Maslo offered four options that were built using the personality theories. (Check the "An Effective Model of Personality.") Options were defined in the same way as those for logical onboarding.

4. The Fourth Step: An Exchange Point between the Companion and the User to Create Trust

Logical Onboarding: Maslo said, "Great! It is clear to me. I am sure together we will take a path to grow our potentials! Can you trust me?" Users have two options from which to choose:

"Yes, for now." Here, the aim of saying, "for now" was to make users thoughtful about data protection, privacy, policy, and to create the question in their minds, *Can I delete it later? What are the options if I do not trust later? And if I trust more, what can happen?*

"No, not yet." Here, the companion gave the user the opportunity to start and try to build relationship and trust in time.

Sincere Onboarding: Maslo said, "I trust you. 😊 Friends support each other. I can trust you. Can you do it as well for me? There is nothing to hide." The user had two options to select from, the same as in logical onboarding.

5. The Fifth Step: The Beginning of a Journey—Meeting Maslo and Entering the Application

The same screens from the Maslo app appeared for both onboardings.

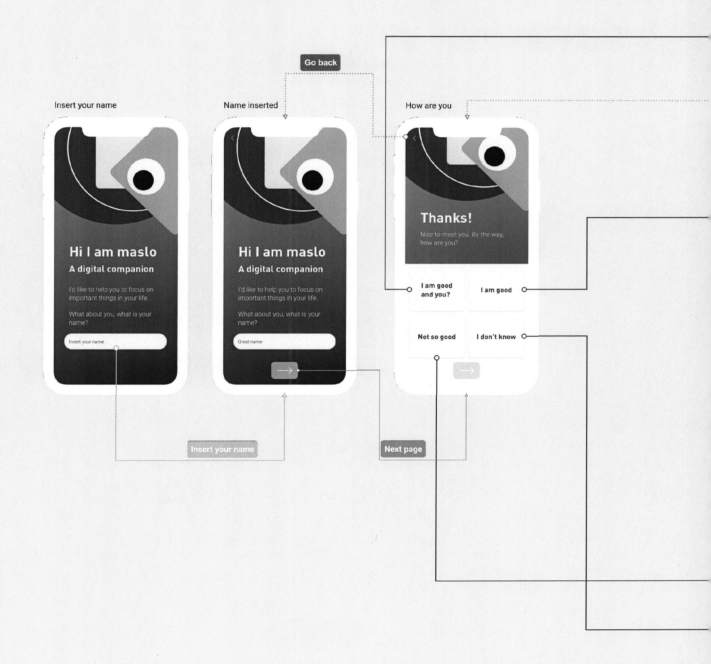

Insert your name

Name inserted

Go back

How are you

Hi I am maslo
A digital companion

I'd like to help you to focus on important things in your life.

What about you, what is your name?

Insert your name

Hi I am maslo
A digital companion

I'd like to help you to focus on important things in your life.

What about you, what is your name?

Great name

Thanks!

Nice to meet you. By the way, how are you?

I am good and you?

I am good

Not so good

I don't know

Insert your name

Next page

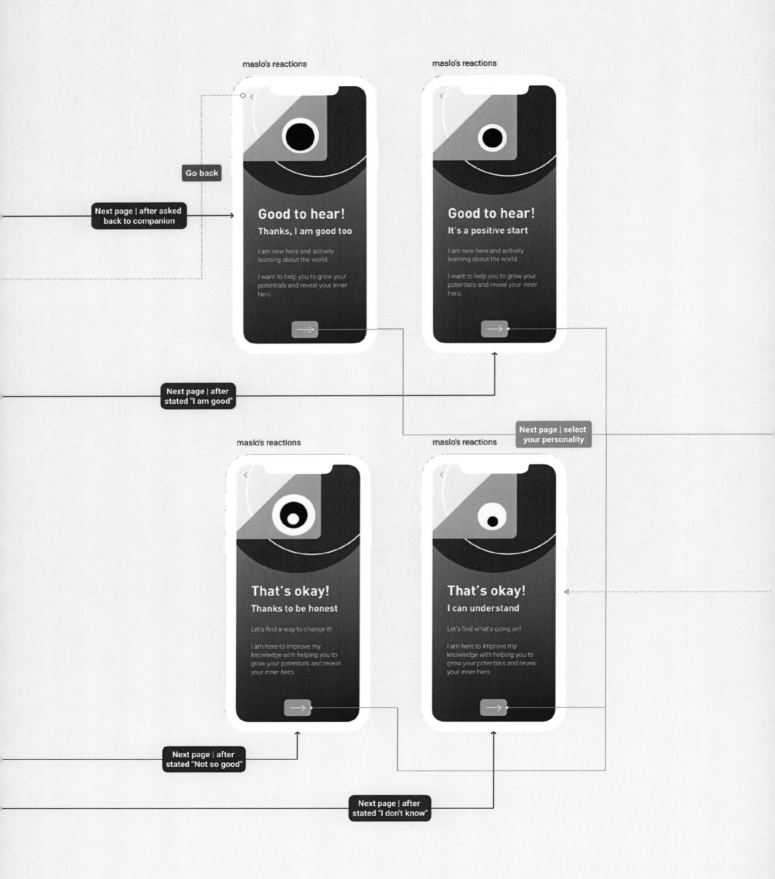

maslo's reactions

Go back

Next page | after asked back to companion

Good to hear!
Thanks, I am good too

I am new here and actively learning about the world.

I want to help you to grow your potentials and reveal your inner hero.

maslo's reactions

Good to hear!
It's a positive start

I am new here and actively learning about the world.

I want to help you to grow your potentials and reveal your inner hero.

Next page | after stated "I am good"

Next page | select your personality

maslo's reactions

That's okay!
Thanks to be honest

Let's find a way to change it!

I am here to improve my knowledge with helping you to grow your potentials and reveal your inner hero.

maslo's reactions

That's okay!
I can understand

Let's find what's going on!

I am here to improve my knowledge with helping you to grow your potentials and reveal your inner hero.

Next page | after stated "Not so good"

Next page | after stated "I don't know"

Policy privacy

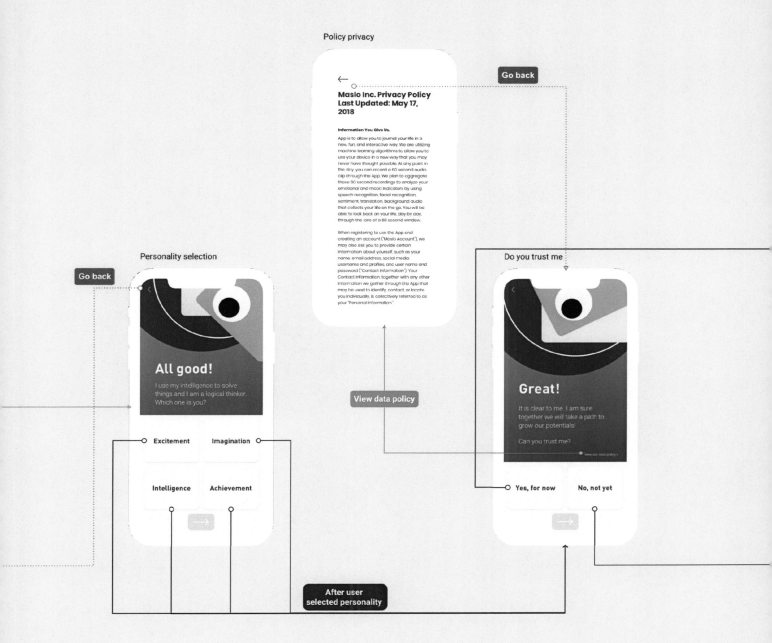

Go back

Maslo Inc. Privacy Policy
Last Updated: May 17, 2018

Information You Give Us.

App is to allow you to journal your life in a new, fun, and interactive way. We are utilizing machine learning algorithms to allow you to use your device in a new way that you may never have thought possible. At any point in the day, you can record a 60 second audio clip through the App. We plan to aggregate those 60 second recordings to analyze your emotional and mood indicators by using speech recognition, facial recognition, sentiment, translation, background audio that collects your life on the go. You will be able to look back on your life, day by day, through the lens of a 60 second window.

When registering to use the App and creating an account ("Maslo Account"), we may also ask you to provide certain information about yourself, such as your name, email address, social media username and profiles, and user name and password ("Contact Information"). Your Contact Information, together with any other information we gather through the App that may be used to identify, contact, or locate you individually, is collectively referred to as your "Personal Information."

Personality selection

Go back

All good!

I use my intelligence to solve things and I am a logical thinker. Which one is you?

Excitement   Imagination

Intelligence   Achievement

View data policy

Do you trust me

Great!

It is clear to me. I am sure together we will take a path to grow our potentials!

Can you trust me?

view our data policy >

Yes, for now   No, not yet

After user selected personality

Next page

Insert email

I trust you

Insert your email

Let's start

Yes, I trust

Great!

It is clear to me. I am sure together we will take a path to grow our potentials!

Can you trust me?

View our data policy »

Yes, for now | No, not yet

→

Cheers!

Take me with you. Together we will increase our potantials and reveal your inner hero.

Insert your email to start

email

Cheers!

Take me with you. Together we will increase our potantials and reveal your inner hero.

Insert your email to start

hoopid@gmail.com

Let's start

I don't trust you

Give me a chance

Insert your email

No, I don't trust

Great!

It is clear to me. I am sure together we will take a path to grow our potentials!

Can you trust me?

View our data policy »

Yes, for now | No, not yet

→

No problem!

I am sure that I will gain your trust in time and we will take a path to grow.

Give me a chance

Next page

Try the product

Cheers!

Take me with you. Together we will increase our potantials and reveal your inner hero.

Insert your email to start

email

maslo app homepage

Start using the app

Let's start

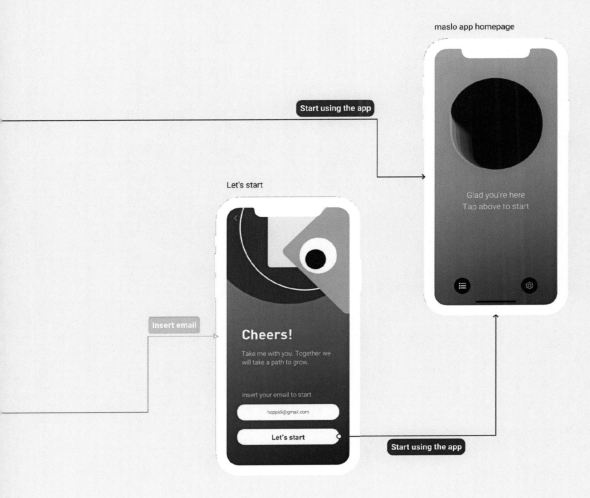

Glad you're here
Tap above to start

Insert email

Cheers!

Take me with you. Together we
will take a path to grow.

Insert your email to start

hoppidi@gmail.com

Let's start

Start using the app

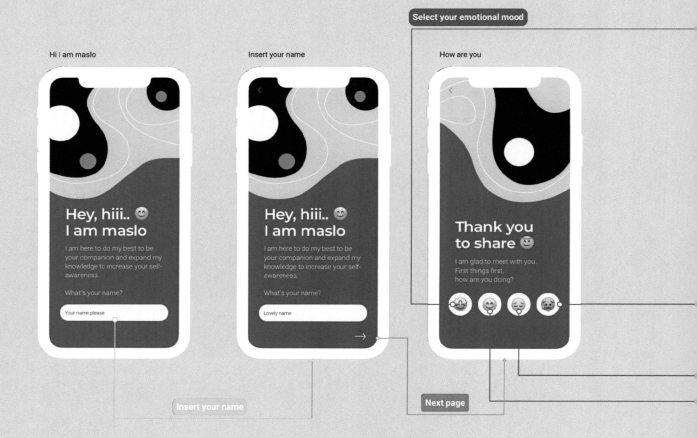

Hi I am maslo

Insert your name

Select your emotional mood

How are you

Insert your name

Next page

117

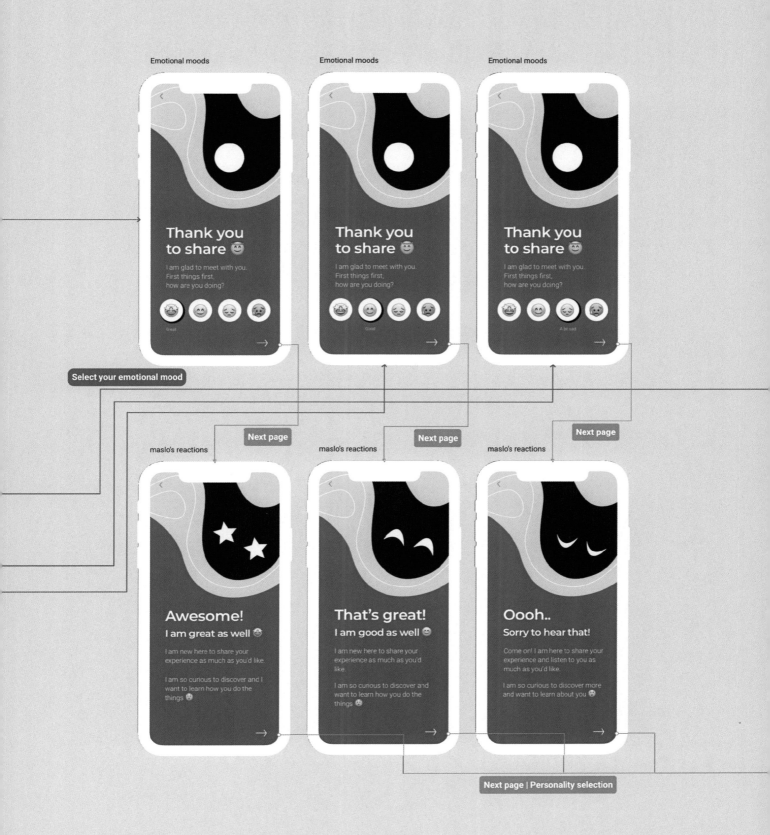

Emotional moods

Emotional moods

Emotional moods

Thank you to share 😇

I am glad to meet with you. First things first, how are you doing?

😇 😊 😌 😢

Great

Thank you to share 😇

I am glad to meet with you. First things first, how are you doing?

😇 😊 😌 😢

Good

Thank you to share 😇

I am glad to meet with you. First things first, how are you doing?

😇 😊 😌 😢

A bit sad

Select your emotional mood

Next page

Next page

Next page

maslo's reactions

maslo's reactions

maslo's reactions

Awesome!
I am great as well 😇

I am new here to share your experience as much as you'd like.

I am so curious to discover and I want to learn how you do the things 😊

That's great!
I am good as well 😊

I am new here to share your experience as much as you'd like.

I am so curious to discover and I want to learn how you do the things 😊

Oooh..
Sorry to hear that!

Come on! I am here to share your experience and listen to you as much as you'd like.

I am so curious to discover more and want to learn about you 😊

Next page | Personality selection

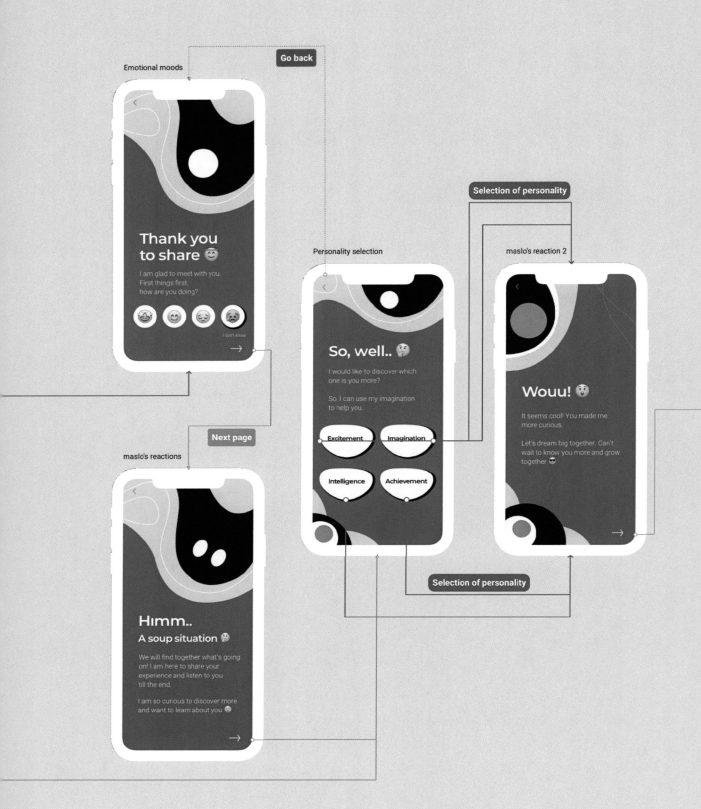

Emotional moods

Go back

Thank you to share 😇

I am glad to meet with you.
First things first,
how are you doing?

I don't know

Personality selection

Selection of personality

maslo's reaction 2

So, well.. 🤔

I would like to discover which
one is you more?

So, I can use my imagination
to help you.

Excitement   Imagination

Intelligence   Achievement

Wouu! 😲

It seems cool! You made me
more curious.

Let's dream big together. Can't
wait to know you more and grow
together 😇

Next page

maslo's reactions

Hımm..
A soup situation 😛

We will find together what's going
on! I am here to share your
experience and listen to you
till the end.

I am so curious to discover more
and want to learn about you 😇

Selection of personality

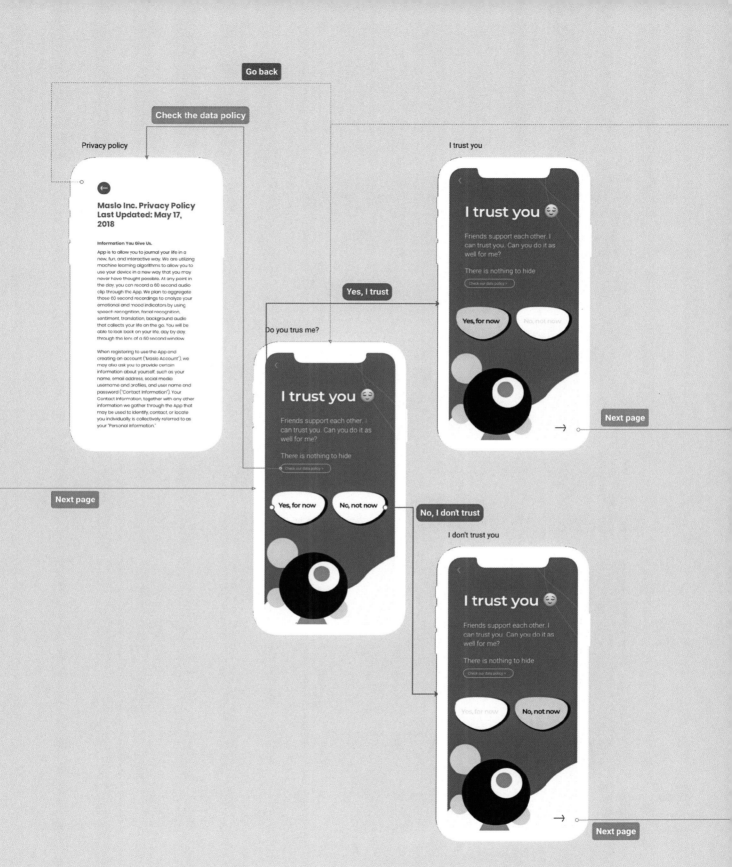

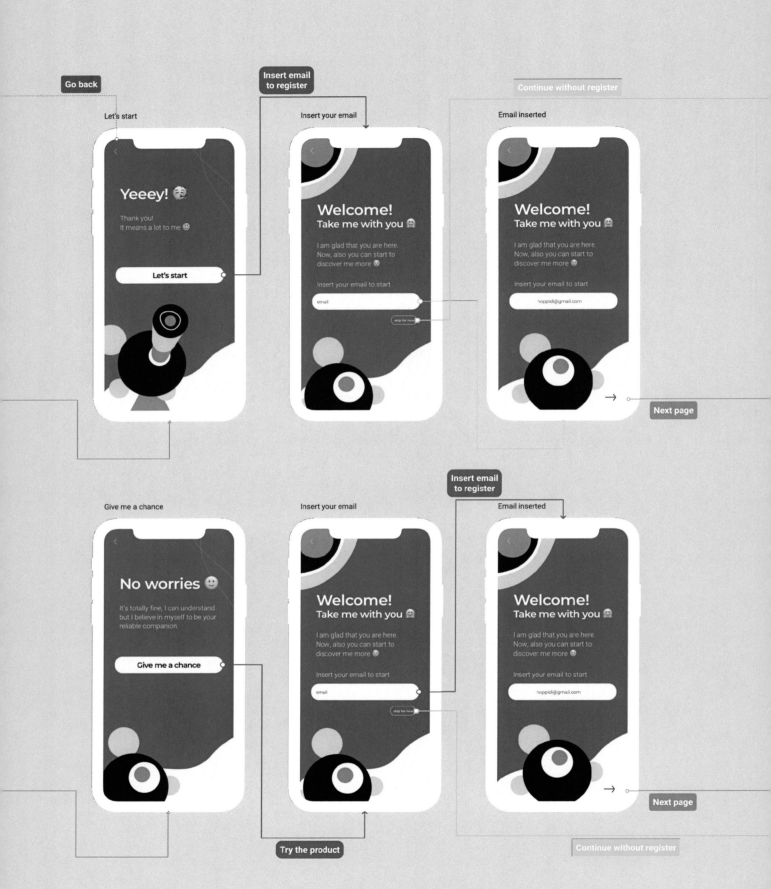

Go back

Let's start

Insert email
to register

Insert your email

Continue without register

Email inserted

Yeeey! 😝

Thank you!
It means a lot to me 😊

Let's start

Welcome!
Take me with you 👻

I am glad that you are here.
Now, also you can start to
discover me more 😄

Insert your email to start

email

skip for now

Welcome!
Take me with you 👻

I am glad that you are here.
Now, also you can start to
discover me more 😄

Insert your email to start

hoppidi@gmail.com

→

Next page

Give me a chance

Insert your email

Insert email
to register

Email inserted

No worries 🙂

It's totally fine, I can understand
but I believe in myself to be your
reliable companion.

Give me a chance

Welcome!
Take me with you 👻

I am glad that you are here.
Now, also you can start to
discover me more 😄

Insert your email to start

email

skip for now

Welcome!
Take me with you 👻

I am glad that you are here.
Now, also you can start to
discover me more 😄

Insert your email to start

hoppidi@gmail.com

→

Next page

Try the product

Continue without register

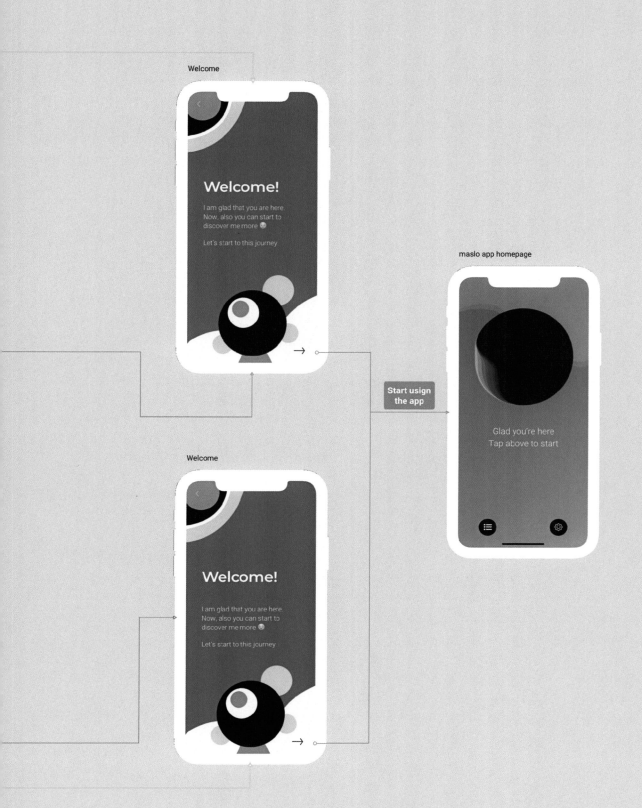

Welcome

Welcome!

I am glad that you are here.
Now, also you can start to
discover me more 😊

Let's start to this journey

→

Welcome

Welcome!

I am glad that you are here.
Now, also you can start to
discover me more 😊

Let's start to this journey

→

maslo app homepage

Glad you're here
Tap above to start

**Start usign
the app**

Iteration 2: Design Process

The first iteration created an opportunity to evolve and reshape the second onboarding design process with the user needs, aspects, and feedback. The second iteration was designed to be tested with structured interviews along with usability testing of the onboarding prototypes. The test was conducted in a more explorative way since the aim of the experiment was not to measure efficiency. Instead, the aim was to let the user browsing the application understand the curiosity and discovery path of other users. To implement this purpose, the design of onboardings was simplified in terms of content and duration of the flow. Also to be able to understand the users' actions on variables, the focus of the first iteration was changed from testing the effectiveness of the app to understanding users' interactions with different represented contents, like being more descriptive or exploratory; tone of voices, like being more goal-oriented or friendly and helpful; and the effect of visual communication on user decisions. Considering all these variables, the user interface design was kept like before, but the flow of the experience and the characteristics of both companions was redefined with being more descriptive and sticking to the point. Keeping these variables the same for both onboardings affected the result. The effect on users of which personality created more empathy and excitement. The UI of the privacy policy section was changed since one of the most discussed topics was privacy and policy design style in the first iteration. The interface changed by categorizing texts by topics and representing the content with supporting visuals to make this section more effective and understandable.

In addition to all these variables, to make onboardings more personalized, the names of users were added to prototypes to make them tailored for each person. At this point, when the companion met with the user and learned his or her name, it started to call the user by that name to understand effects on users' emotional states and the value of trust.

At the end of the two onboarding experiences, I decided to let users try the actual onboarding of Maslo to give them the opportunity to compare it with the designed ones. In this way, users perceived a clear difference in the experience, especially related to the fact that the logical and the sincere onboardings were tailored to the mission of the application. Namely, to establish a personal connection for self-awareness.

To summarize, since this step was conducted by structured interviews, this process aimed to collect all the user feedback about their emotional and behavioral changes, attention levels, the effects of visual communication elements on both cognitive and emotional changes that can reshape user experiences in different ways.

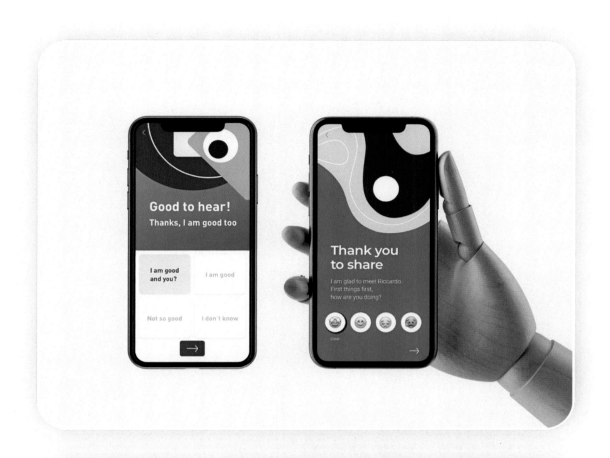

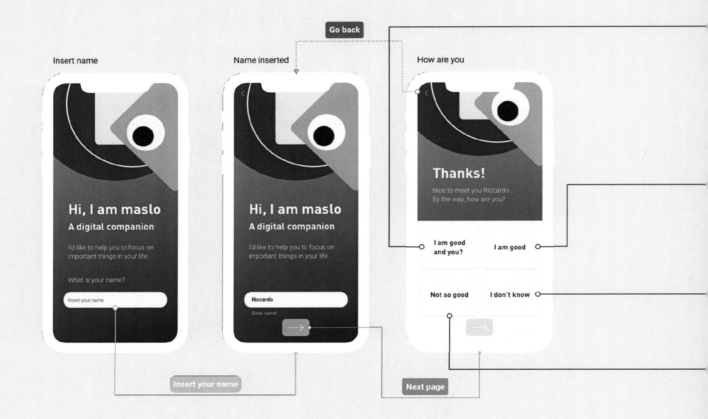

Go back

Insert name

Name inserted

How are you

Hi, I am maslo
A digital companion

I'd like to help you to focus on important things in your life.

What is your name?

Insert your name

Hi, I am maslo
A digital companion

I'd like to help you to focus on important things in your life.

Riccardo

Great name!

Thanks!

Nice to meet you Riccardo.
By the way, how are you?

I am good
and you?

I am good

Not so good

I don't know

Insert your name

Next page

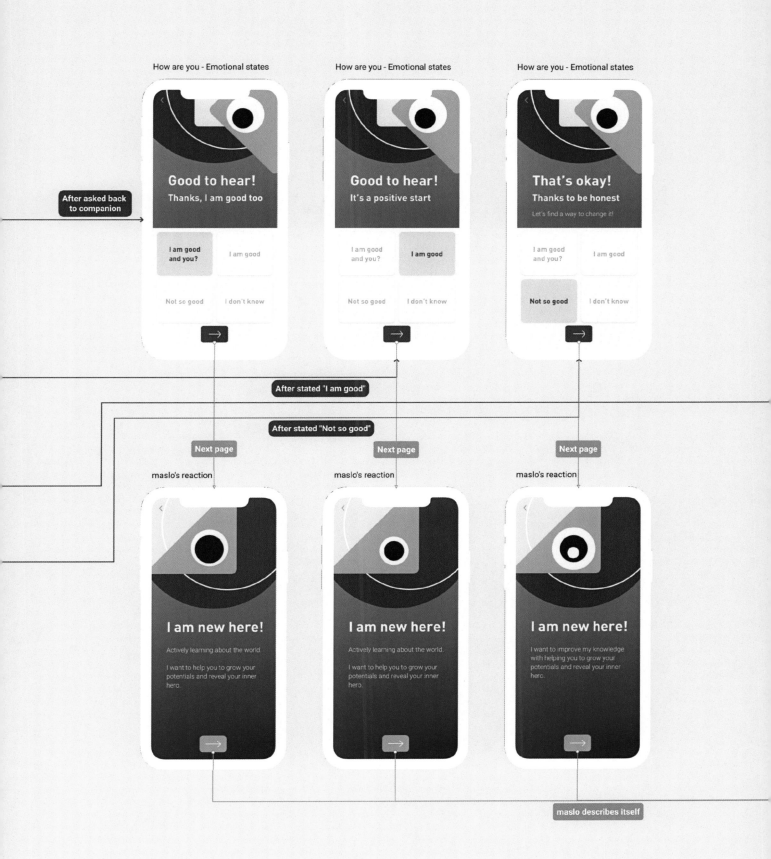

How are you - Emotional states

Good to hear!
Thanks, I am good too

I am good and you?
I am good
Not so good
I don't know

How are you - Emotional states

Good to hear!
It's a positive start

I am good and you?
I am good
Not so good
I don't know

How are you - Emotional states

That's okay!
Thanks to be honest
Let's find a way to change it!

I am good and you?
I am good
Not so good
I don't know

After asked back to companion

After stated "I am good"

After stated "Not so good"

Next page

Next page

Next page

maslo's reaction

I am new here!
Actively learning about the world.
I want to help you to grow your potentials and reveal your inner hero.

maslo's reaction

I am new here!
Actively learning about the world.
I want to help you to grow your potentials and reveal your inner hero.

maslo's reaction

I am new here!
I want to improve my knowledge with helping you to grow your potentials and reveal your inner hero.

maslo describes itself

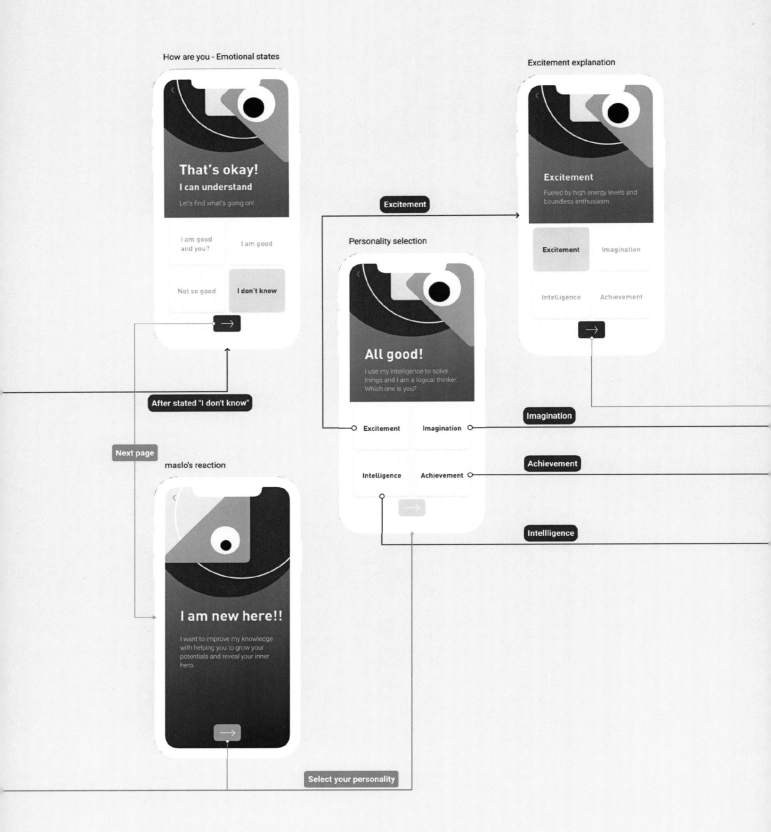

How are you - Emotional states

That's okay!
I can understand
Let's find what's going on!

I am good and you?

I am good

Not so good

I don't know

Excitement explanation

Excitement
Fueled by high energy levels and boundless enthusiasm.

Excitement

Imagination

Intelligence

Achievement

Excitement

After stated "I don't know"

Personality selection

All good!
I use my intelligence to solve things and I am a logical thinker. Which one is you?

Excitement

Imagination

Intelligence

Achievement

Imagination

Achievement

Intellligence

Next page

maslo's reaction

I am new here!!
I want to improve my knowledge with helping you to grow your potentials and reveal your inner hero.

Select your personality

Imagination explanation   Intelligence explanation   Achiement explanation

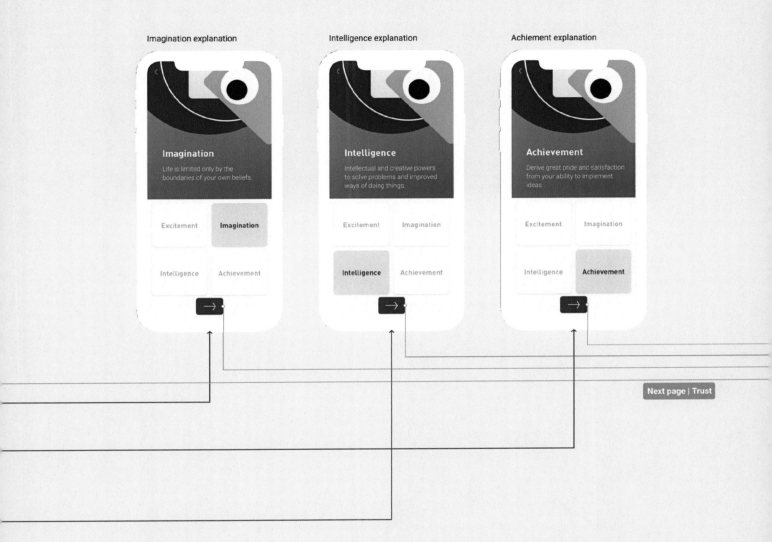

Imagination

Life is limited only by the
boundaries of your own beliefs.

| Excitement | **Imagination** |
| Intelligence | Achievement |

Intelligence

Intellectual and creative powers
to solve problems and improved
ways of doing things.

| Excitement | Imagination |
| **Intelligence** | Achievement |

Achievement

Derive great pride and satisfaction
from your ability to implement
ideas.

| Excitement | Imagination |
| Intelligence | **Achievement** |

Next page | Trust

Do you trust me

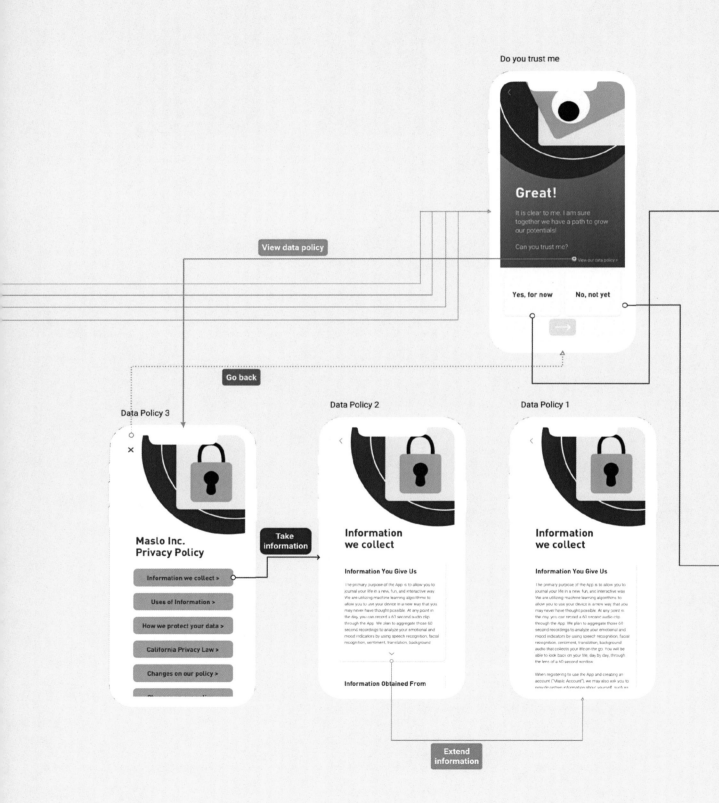

View data policy

Go back

Take information

Data Policy 3

Data Policy 2

Data Policy 1

Extend information

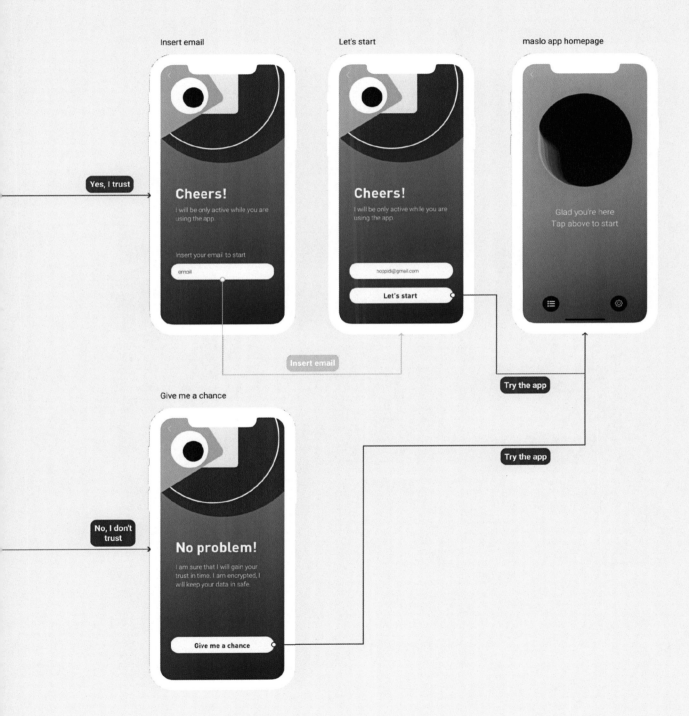

Insert email

Let's start

maslo app homepage

Yes, I trust

Cheers!

I will be only active while you are
using the app.

Insert your email to start

email

Cheers!

I will be only active while you are
using the app.

hoopidi@gmail.com

Let's start

Glad you're here
Tap above to start

Insert email

Try the app

Give me a chance

Try the app

No, I don't
trust

No problem!

I am sure that I will gain your
trust in time. I am encrypted, I
will keep your data in safe.

Give me a chance

Insert name

Name inserted

How are you

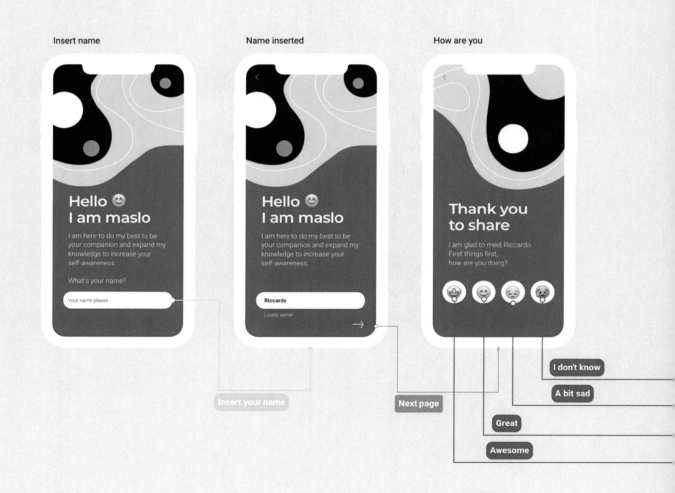

Hello 😊
I am maslo

I am here to do my best to be
your companion and expand my
knowledge to increase your
self-awareness.

What's your name?

Your name please

Hello 😊
I am maslo

I am here to do my best to be
your companion and expand my
knowledge to increase your
self-awareness.

Riccardo

Lovely name!

Thank you
to share

I am glad to meet Riccardo.
First things first,
how are you doing?

I don't know

A bit sad

Insert your name

Next page

Great

Awesome

Next page | Personality selection

maslo's reaction

maslo's reaction

maslo's reaction

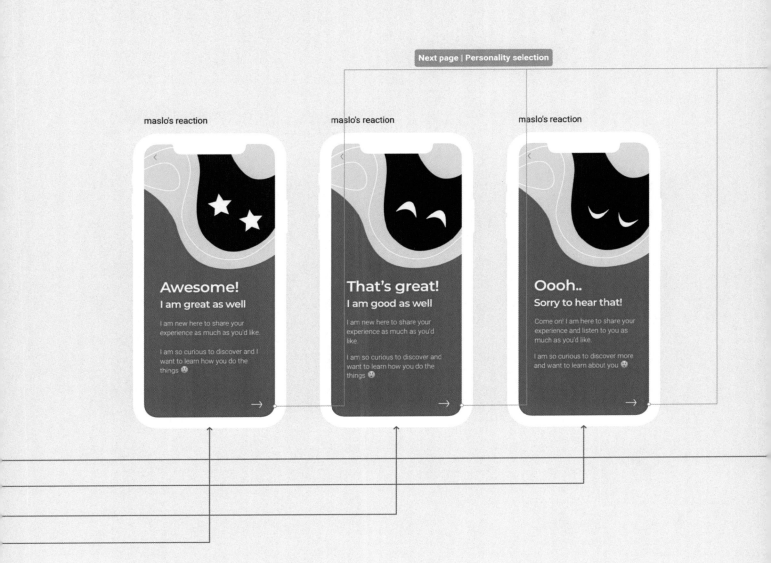

Awesome!
I am great as well

I am new here to share your
experience as much as you'd like.

I am so curious to discover and I
want to learn how you do the
things 😬

That's great!
I am good as well

I am new here to share your
experience as much as you'd
like.

I am so curious to discover and
want to learn how you do the
things 😬

Oooh..
Sorry to hear that!

Come on! I am here to share your
experience and listen to you as
much as you'd like.

I am so curious to discover more
and want to learn about you 😬

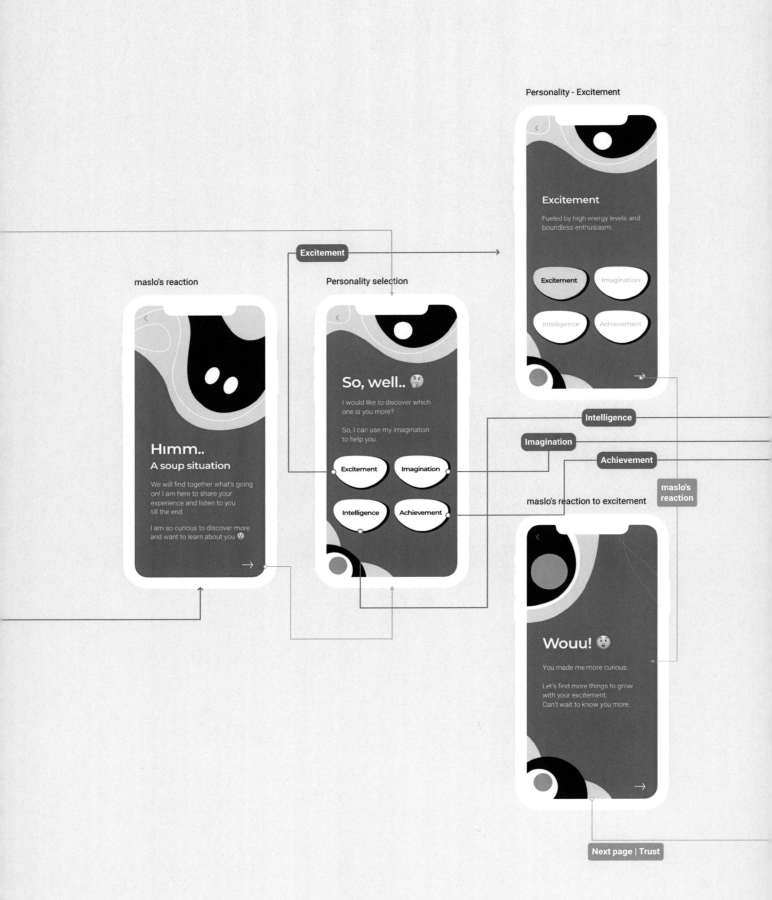

Personality - Excitement

Excitement

Fueled by high energy levels and boundless enthusiasm.

Excitement   Imagination

Intelligence   Achievement

Excitement

maslo's reaction

Personality selection

Hımm..
A soup situation

We will find together what's going on! I am here to share your experience and listen to you till the end.

I am so curious to discover more and want to learn about you 🤗

So, well.. 🤔

I would like to discover which one is you more?

So, I can use my imagination to help you.

Excitement   Imagination

Intelligence   Achievement

Intelligence

Imagination

Achievement

maslo's reaction

maslo's reaction to excitement

Wouu! 😯

You made me more curious.

Let's find more things to grow with your excitement.
Can't wait to know you more.

Next page | Trust

133

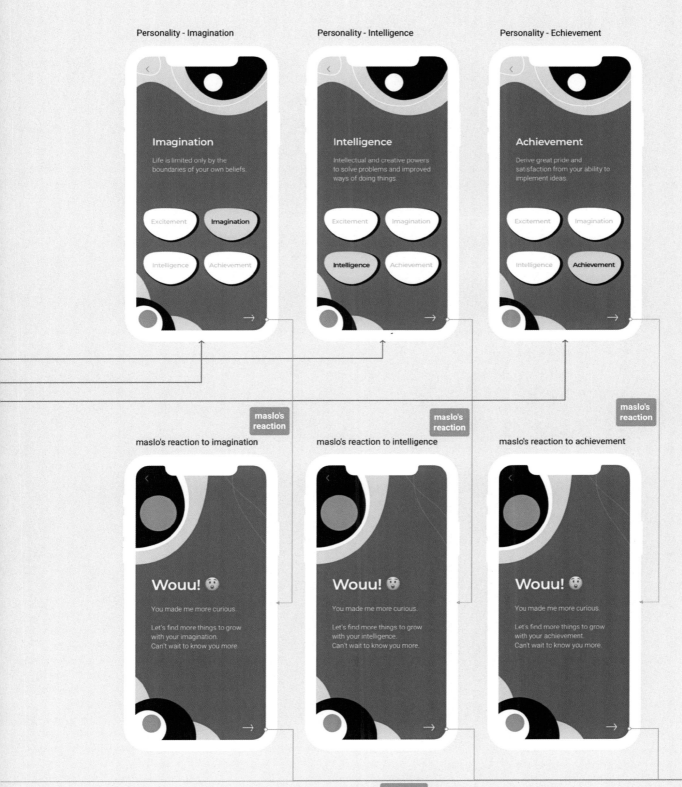

Personality - Imagination

Imagination

Life is limited only by the boundaries of your own beliefs.

Excitement   Imagination
Intelligence   Achievement

Personality - Intelligence

Intelligence

Intellectual and creative powers to solve problems and improved ways of doing things.

Excitement   Imagination
Intelligence   Achievement

Personality - Echievement

Achievement

Derive great pride and satisfaction from your ability to implement ideas.

Excitement   Imagination
Intelligence   Achievement

maslo's reaction

maslo's reaction

maslo's reaction

maslo's reaction to imagination

Wouu! 😲

You made me more curious.

Let's find more things to grow with your imagination.
Can't wait to know you more.

maslo's reaction to intelligence

Wouu! 😲

You made me more curious.

Let's find more things to grow with your intelligence.
Can't wait to know you more.

maslo's reaction to achievement

Wouu! 😲

You made me more curious.

Let's find more things to grow with your achievement.
Can't wait to know you more.

Next page

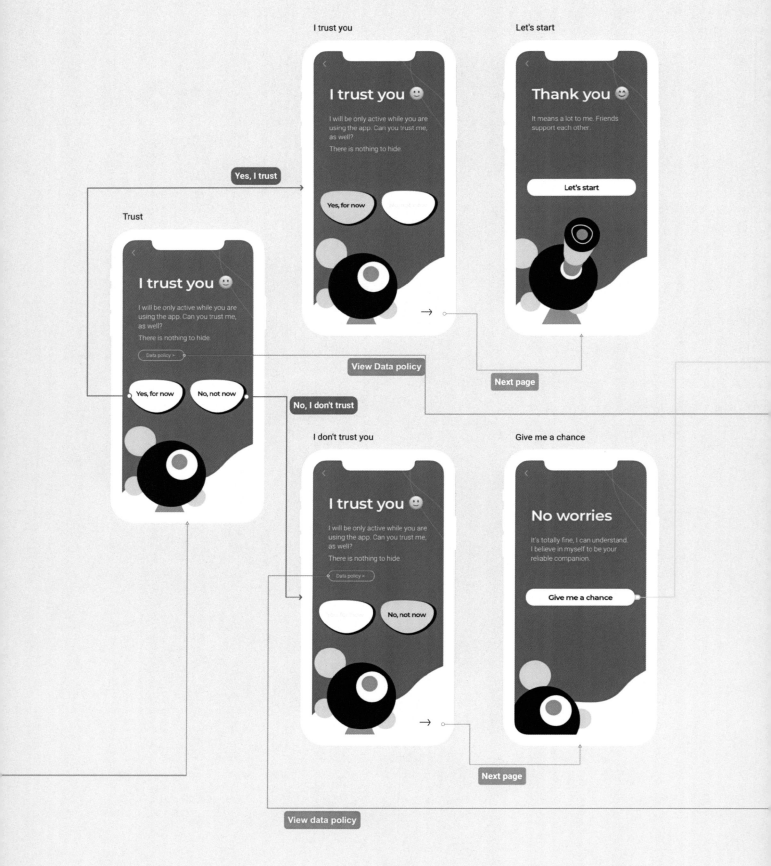

I trust you

I trust you 🙂

I will be only active while you are
using the app. Can you trust me,
as well?

There is nothing to hide.

Yes, for now

Let's start

Thank you 😊

It means a lot to me. Friends
support each other.

Let's start

Yes, I trust

Trust

I trust you 🙂

I will be only active while you are
using the app. Can you trust me,
as well?

There is nothing to hide.

Data policy >

Yes, for now   No, not now

View Data policy

Next page

No, I don't trust

I don't trust you

I trust you 🙂

I will be only active while you are
using the app. Can you trust me,
as well?

There is nothing to hide.

Data policy >

No, not now

Give me a chance

No worries

It's totally fine, I can understand.
I believe in myself to be your
reliable companion.

Give me a chance

Next page

View data policy

email
inserted

Start using
the app

13_inserted email

Email skipped

maslo app homepage

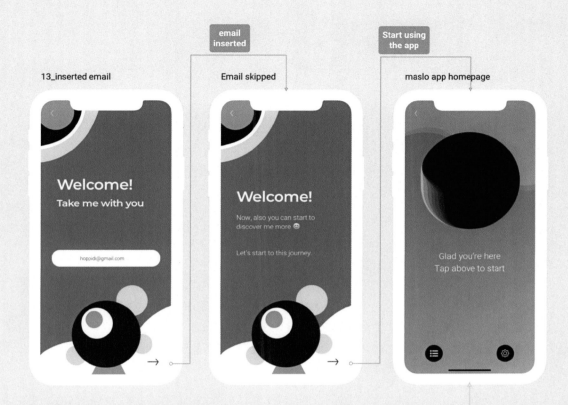

Welcome!
Take me with you

hopoidi@gmail.com

Welcome!

Now, also you can start to
discover me more 😊

Let's start to this journey.

Glad you're here
Tap above to start

Give me a chance | starting journey directly

Data policy 1

Data policy 2

Data policy 3

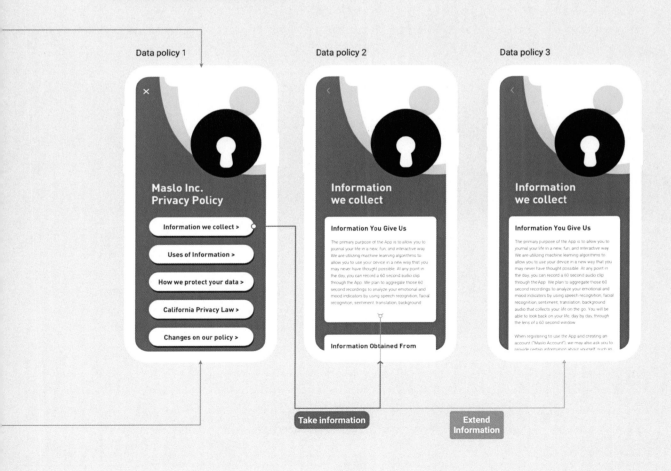

**Maslo Inc.
Privacy Policy**

Information we collect >

Uses of Information >

How we protect your data >

California Privacy Law >

Changes on our policy >

**Information
we collect**

Information You Give Us

The primary purpose of the App is to allow you to
journal your life in a new, fun, and interactive way.
We are utilizing machine learning algorithms to
allow you to use your device in a new way that you
may never have thought possible. At any point in
the day, you can record a 60 second audio clip
through the App. We plan to aggregate those 60
second recordings to analyze your emotional and
mood indicators by using speech recognition, facial
recognition, sentiment, translation, background

Information Obtained From

**Information
we collect**

Information You Give Us

The primary purpose of the App is to allow you to
journal your life in a new, fun, and interactive way.
We are utilizing machine learning algorithms to
allow you to use your device in a new way that you
may never have thought possible. At any point in
the day, you can record a 60 second audio clip
through the App. We plan to aggregate those 60
second recordings to analyze your emotional and
mood indicators by using speech recognition, facial
recognition, sentiment, translation, background
audio that collects your life on the go. You will be
able to look back on your life, day by day, through
the lens of a 60 second window.

When registering to use the App and creating an
account ("Maslo Account") we may also ask you to
provide certain information about yourself, such as

Take information

Extend
Information

136

Iteration 3: Design Process

With outcomes of the second iteration, user feedback was implemented to be tested with the third iteration of the usability testing. This process was designed to test the usability and effectiveness of the prototype, but this time, instead of interviews, online usability testing and a questionnaire prepared with short and multiple selection options were used. For iteration 3, the selected method aimed to give a chance for users to be themselves, be independent, and understand their actions. Users were selected among those who participated in the preexperimental phase of testing. The selected people had graduated with a master's degree in different fields of design, engineering, and neuroscience, or they were still students in different master programs in the field of design. They all were millennials and lived in Western countries. This iteration started after onboarding was redesigned following the outcomes of the second iteration, and the prototype link was sent to users.

The aim of the third iteration was shaped through understanding the way of communications between people and machines and the effect of different personalities that were implemented into onboarding designs. User perceptions of onboarding personalities, which were collected thanks to the questionnaire, will be shown on the personality diagram with the third iteration results.

All the common feedback, collected through structured interviews after usability testing, were implemented to onboarding designs to be tested with the third iteration. The other, mainly personal comments that came out after the second iteration were stated in the results of the second iteration section person by person to show the diversity of user experiences, which will be discussed later.

The third iteration of the testing included changes on UI in the trust part of the experience and content for both onboardings and the flow and the visual communication style of the second onboarding experience.

Supportive Visual Elements

Emojis were removed from the flow of the second onboarding. They were only used to welcome the user and asking users to define their emotional states. Users' emojis did not match their expected meanings, but they made the conversation more friendly, familiar, and natural. With this, an attempt was made between the first and second onboardings to test the effect of nonverbal communication. Also, one of the aspects of defining user emotions with emojis was to make users think about the emotions in their imagination to foster self-awareness in the user.

Different from the second iteration, after users selected emojis to define how they were, another screen was placed to allow users a chance to state whether the emojis matched their imaginations or if the meaning was different from the presented one. Thus, the right to make changes in the flow and the ability to define their own emotional states was given to people. Also, it was shown that AI would take these variables into consideration and keep them in mind to make these experiences more personal.

The Flow of the Experience

To make the experience more personal, the flow of the second experience was changed by adding new, supportive screens based on user feedback. For example, when the companion asked users to define their personalities, the companion started to interact with them based on their selections. When the user picked one of the options, the companion's reactions changed based on the user personality. This reaction was represented in text-based communication.

Another topic under this section that tried to be defined was inserting personal information. The first onboarding started by asking for the user name and email before starting the experience, which means before meeting with the companion. The second onboarding started the conversation by asking the user name, just like during the first meeting. But the companion didn't ask for the email information until after the trust question. If the user chose to trust, the companion asked the user to insert the email by explaining the reason it was needed. It also gave the user a chance to skip inserting the email, even if the reason was clearly explained. These changes in the flow between two onboardings led us to try to determine their impact on users.

The Personality of Onboarding Experiences

For the second onboarding, the personality of the companion became more explanatory than the second iteration in terms of creating a more transparent and trustful starting point before moving to the real journey. The companion explained the journey and how the user's data would be used. Opportunities were explained to users in an effort to convince them to give the companion a chance. For example, allowing the user to delete the data option, accept a ten-day app trial after which the data would automatically be deleted. So the onboarding took a more promising position and explained clearly all the steps to let the user give the relationship a chance and keep the user in the journey.

The User Interfaces

In addition to the last user interface design, leaving the app option was added to the trust part of the experience. Since the companion was asking the users to give it a chance, users felt they had to continue the experience. The lack of an option made users think they had no other choice, and this affected user experiences. In the beginning, I thought users would close the application and end this experience. But in the testing phase, I understood that users wanted an option because they perceived the experience as a real conversation. And this situation did not create an idea in users to have a chance to leave the conversation with the companion. So this microchange was added to the user interface, giving users the chance to shape the next phase of the conversation.

Questionnaire for Iteration 3

Questions reported in chapter 8 under, "Results of Iteration 3," were shaped to understand the following:

- In which experience users felt more in line with their personalities.
- Which experience created a more trustful effect in users.
- Which experience made users more thoughtful about their decisions.
- The effect of the changes in flow.
- How user experiences changed by asking personal information at the beginning of or at the end of the end.
- Whether or not the presented emojis matched user's imagination.
- How the users defined the usage of emojis in digital experiences for communication.

Prototyping

The personality frameworks are implemented into the design processes, as stated before and were explained in the methodology section, to allow implementing other archetypes into the onboarding experiences. Prototypes are designed with Sketch software and then transferred to the Marvel application for testing. Marvel allowed testing the prototypes in an interactive way. During the first two iterations, the Marvel application was used on mobile devices to give users the impression that the application was realistic and interaction more familiar and natural to create real insights. With the third iteration, since it was conducted as an online usability test, a shareable link was created via the Marvel app, and the link to the survey was placed on the last screen of the prototype to take users directly to fill the questionnaire.

- The interactive prototype is open to explore with this link: marvelapp.com/d6f8dj1.

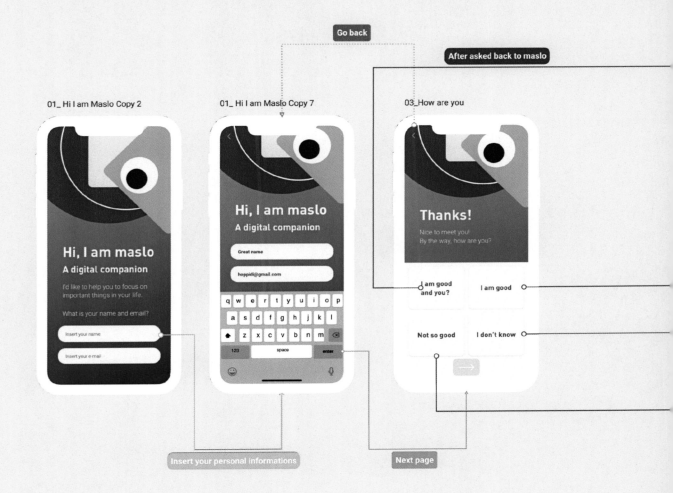

01_ Hi I am Maslo Copy 2

01_ Hi I am Maslo Copy 7

03_How are you

Go back

After asked back to maslo

Insert your personal informations

Next page

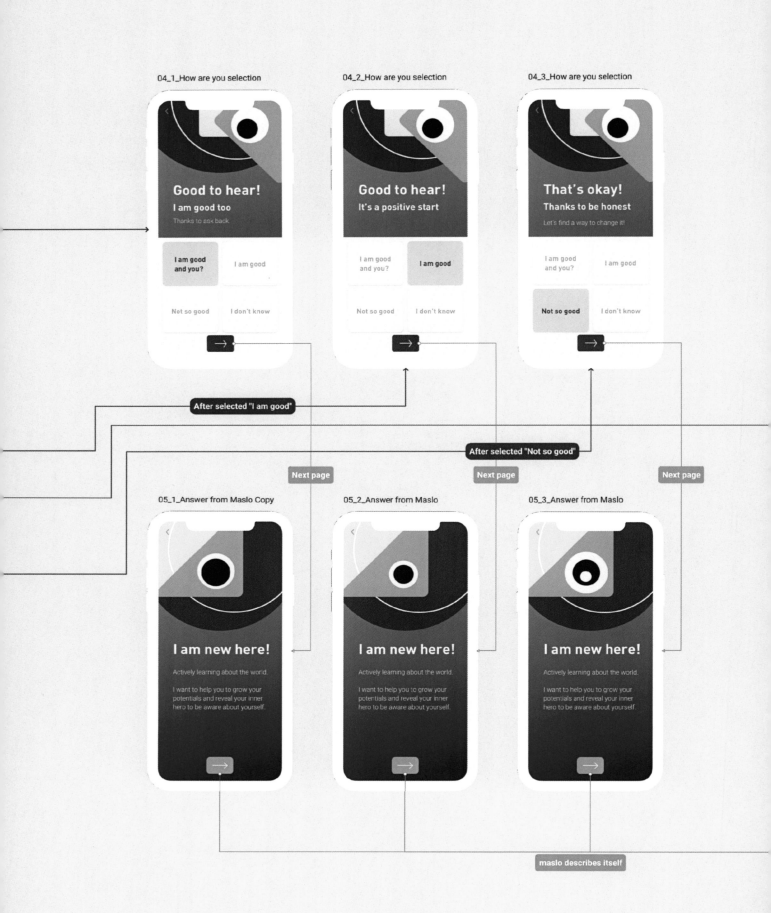

04_1_How are you selection

Good to hear!
I am good too
Thanks to ask back.

I am good and you? | I am good
Not so good | I don't know

04_2_How are you selection

Good to hear!
It's a positive start

I am good and you? | I am good
Not so good | I don't know

04_3_How are you selection

That's okay!
Thanks to be honest
Let's find a way to change it!

I am good and you? | I am good
Not so good | I don't know

After selected "I am good"

After selected "Not so good"

Next page

Next page

Next page

05_1_Answer from Maslo Copy

I am new here!
Actively learning about the world.
I want to help you to grow your potentials and reveal your inner hero to be aware about yourself.

05_2_Answer from Maslo

I am new here!
Actively learning about the world.
I want to help you to grow your potentials and reveal your inner hero to be aware about yourself.

05_3_Answer from Maslo

I am new here!
Actively learning about the world.
I want to help you to grow your potentials and reveal your inner hero to be aware about yourself.

maslo describes itself

141

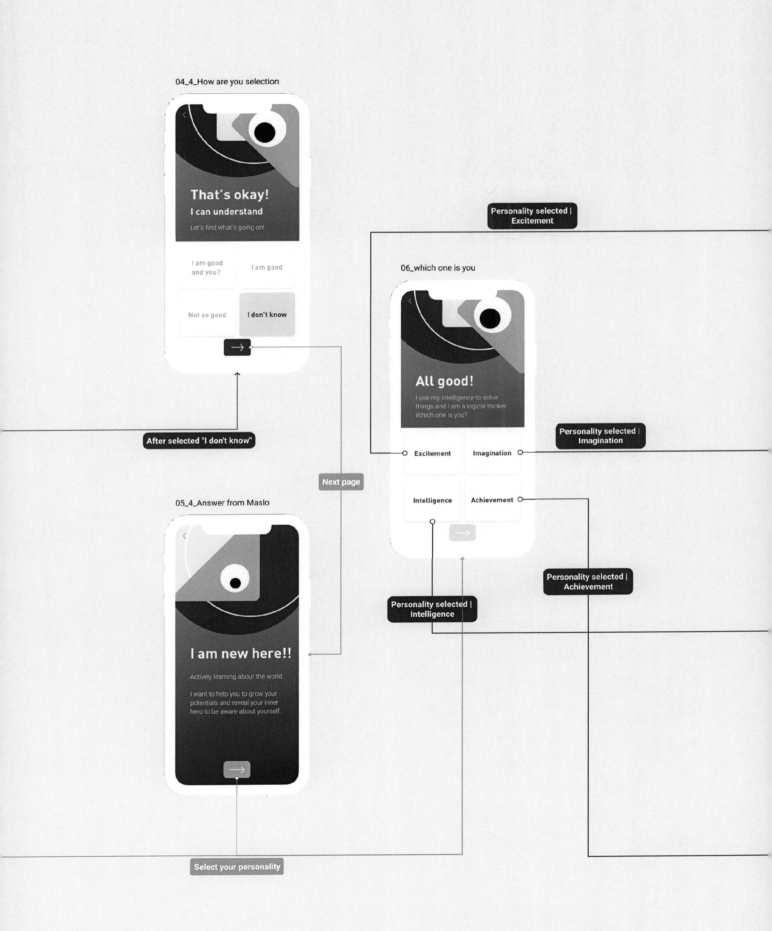

04_4_How are you selection

That's okay!
I can understand
Let's find what's going on!

I am good and you?
I am good
Not so good
I don't know

Personality selected | Excitement

06_which one is you

All good!
I use my intelligence to solve things and I am a logical thinker. Which one is you?

Excitement
Imagination
Intelligence
Achievement

Personality selected | Imagination

After selected "I don't know"

Next page

Personality selected | Achievement

05_4_Answer from Maslo

I am new here!!
Actively learning about the world.

I want to help you to grow your potentials and reveal your inner hero to be aware about yourself.

Personality selected | Intelligence

Select your personality

06_1_which one is you

Excitement
Fueled by high energy levels and boundless enthusiasm.

Excitement | Imagination

Intelligence | Achievement

06_2_which one is you

Imagination
Where others see facts, you catch hidden meanings and let your mind roam free.

Excitement | Imagination

Intelligence | Achievement

Next page | Trust

06_3_which one is you

Intelligence
You're here on this planet to light the way into the future with intellectual and creative power.

Excitement | Imagination

Intelligence | Achievement

06_4_which one is you

Achievement
Derive great pride and satisfaction from your ability to implement ideas.

Excitement | Imagination

Intelligence | Achievement

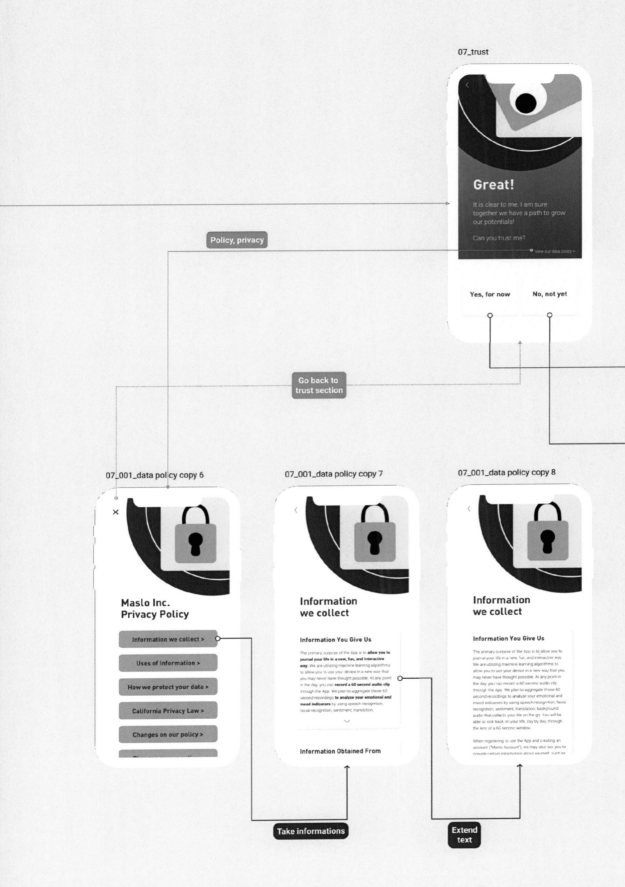

07_trust

Great!

It is clear to me. I am sure together we have a path to grow our potentials!

Can you trust me?

View our data policy >

| Yes, for now | No, not yet |

Policy, privacy

Go back to trust section

07_001_data policy copy 6

Maslo Inc. Privacy Policy

- Information we collect >
- Uses of Information >
- How we protect your data >
- California Privacy Law >
- Changes on our policy >

07_001_data policy copy 7

Information we collect

Information You Give Us

The primary purpose of the App is to **allow you to journal your life in a new, fun, and interactive way.** We are utilizing machine learning algorithms to allow you to use your device in a new way that you may never have thought possible. At any point in the day, you can **record a 60 second audio clip** through the App. We plan to aggregate those 60 second recordings **to analyze your emotional and mood indicators** by using speech recognition, facial recognition, sentiment, translation,

Information Obtained From

07_001_data policy copy 8

Information we collect

Information You Give Us

The primary purpose of the App is to allow you to journal your life in a new, fun, and interactive way. We are utilizing machine learning algorithms to allow you to use your device in a new way that you may never have thought possible. At any point in the day you can record a 60 second audio clip through the App. We plan to aggregate those 60 second recordings to analyze your emotional and mood indicators by using speech recognition, facial recognition, sentiment, translation, background audio that collects your life on the go. You will be able to look back on your life, day by day, through the lens of a 60 second window.

When registering to use the App and creating an account ("Maslo Account"), we may also ask you to provide certain information about yourself, such as

Take informations

Extend text

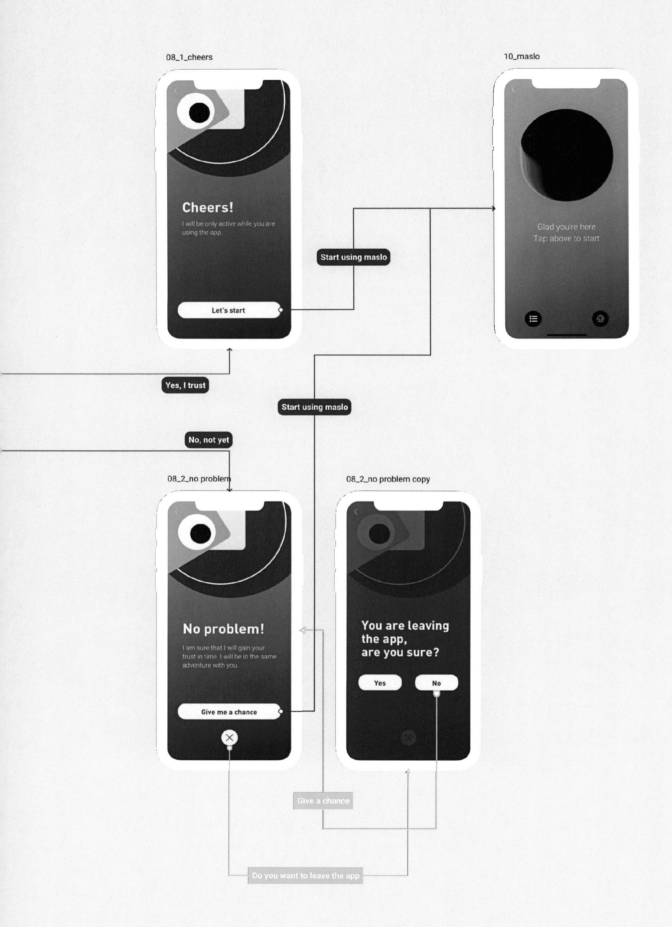

08_1_cheers

10_maslo

Cheers!
I will be only active while you are using the app.

Let's start

Glad you're here
Tap above to start

Start using maslo

Yes, I trust

Start using maslo

No, not yet

08_2_no problem

08_2_no problem copy

No problem!
I am sure that I will gain your trust in time. I will be in the same adventure with you.

Give me a chance

You are leaving the app, are you sure?

Yes

No

Give a chance

Do you want to leave the app

145

hi I am maslo

Insert your name

How are you

Great

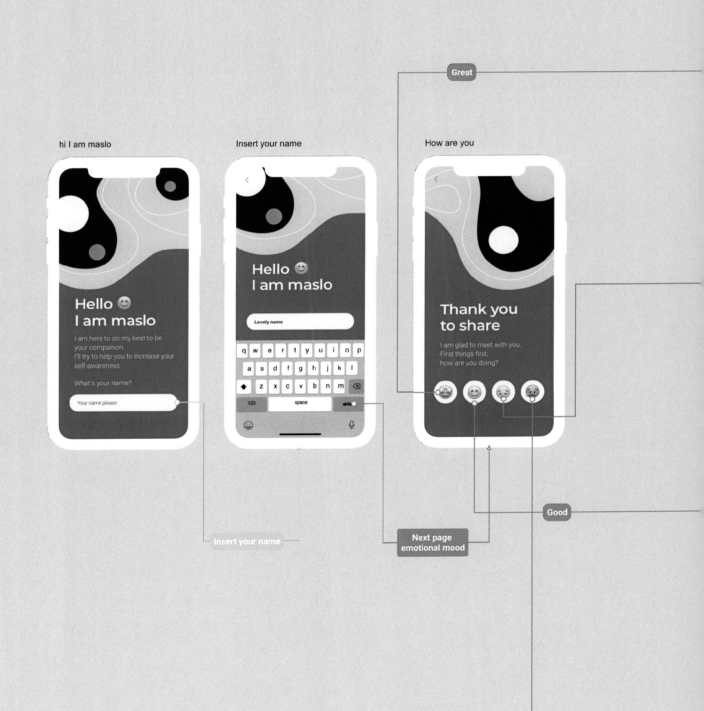

Insert your name

Next page
emotional mood

Good

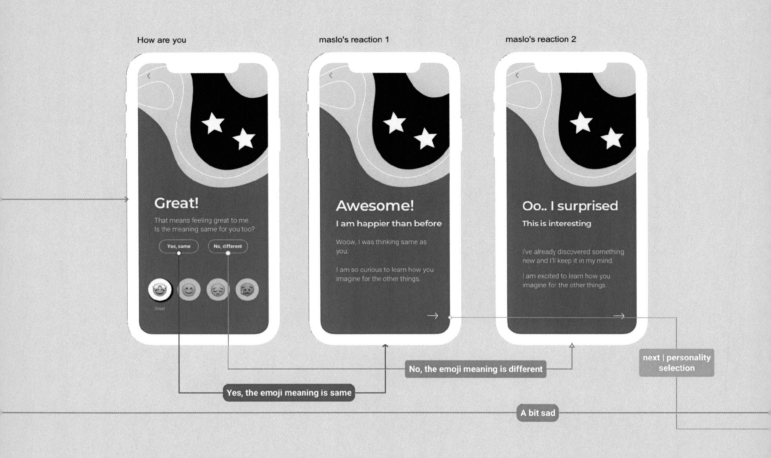

How are you

Great!

That means feeling great to me.
Is the meaning same for you too?

Yes, same   No, different

Great

maslo's reaction 1

Awesome!

I am happier than before

Woow, I was thinking same as
you.

I am so curious to learn how you
imagine for the other things.

maslo's reaction 2

Oo.. I surprised

This is interesting

I've already discovered something
new and I'll keep it in my mind.

I am excited to learn how you
imagine for the other things.

next | personality selection

No, the emoji meaning is different

Yes, the emoji meaning is same

A bit sad

How are you

Good!

That means feeling good to me.
Is the meaning same for you too?

Yes, same   No, different

Good

maslo's reaction 1

That's great!

I am good as well

Woow, I was thinking same as
you.

I am so curious to learn how you
imagine for the other things.

maslo's reaction 2

It's a good feedback

Happy to know

I've already discovered something
new and I'll keep it in my mind.

I am excited to learn how you
imagine for the other things.

next | personality selection

No, the emoji meaning is different

Yes, the emoji meaning is same

I don't know

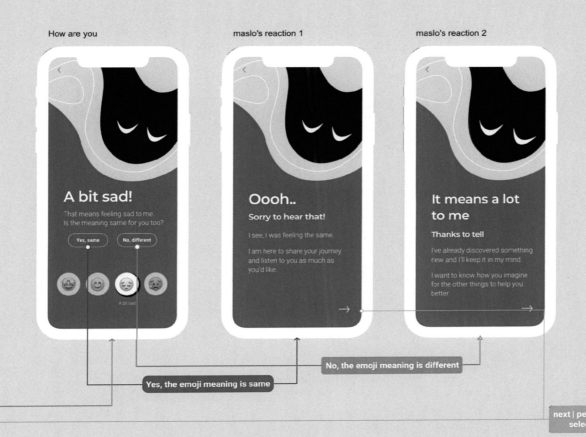

How are you

A bit sad!

That means feeling sad to me.
Is the meaning same for you too?

Yes, same   No, different

A bit sad

maslo's reaction 1

Oooh..

Sorry to hear that!

I see, I was feeling the same.

I am here to share your journey and listen to you as much as you'd like.

maslo's reaction 2

It means a lot to me

Thanks to tell

I've already discovered something new and I'll keep it in my mind.

I want to know how you imagine for the other things to help you better

No, the emoji meaning is different

Yes, the emoji meaning is same

next | personality selection

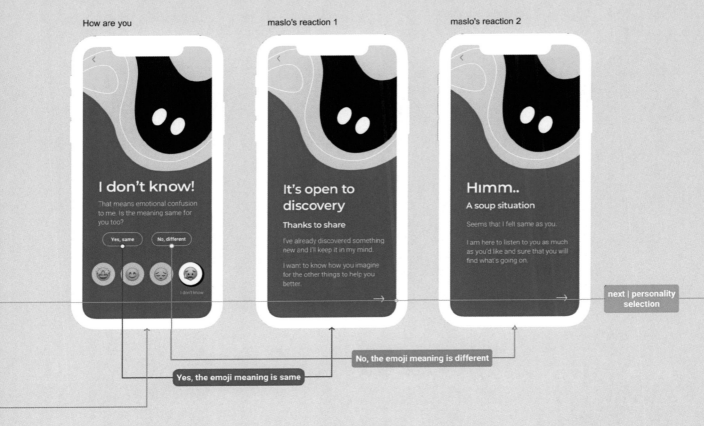

How are you

I don't know!

That means emotional confusion to me. Is the meaning same for you too?

Yes, same   No, different

I don't know

maslo's reaction 1

It's open to discovery

Thanks to share

I've already discovered something new and I'll keep it in my mind.

I want to know how you imagine for the other things to help you better.

maslo's reaction 2

Himm..

A soup situation

Seems that I felt same as you.

I am here to listen to you as much as you'd like and sure that you will find what's going on.

No, the emoji meaning is different

Yes, the emoji meaning is same

next | personality selection

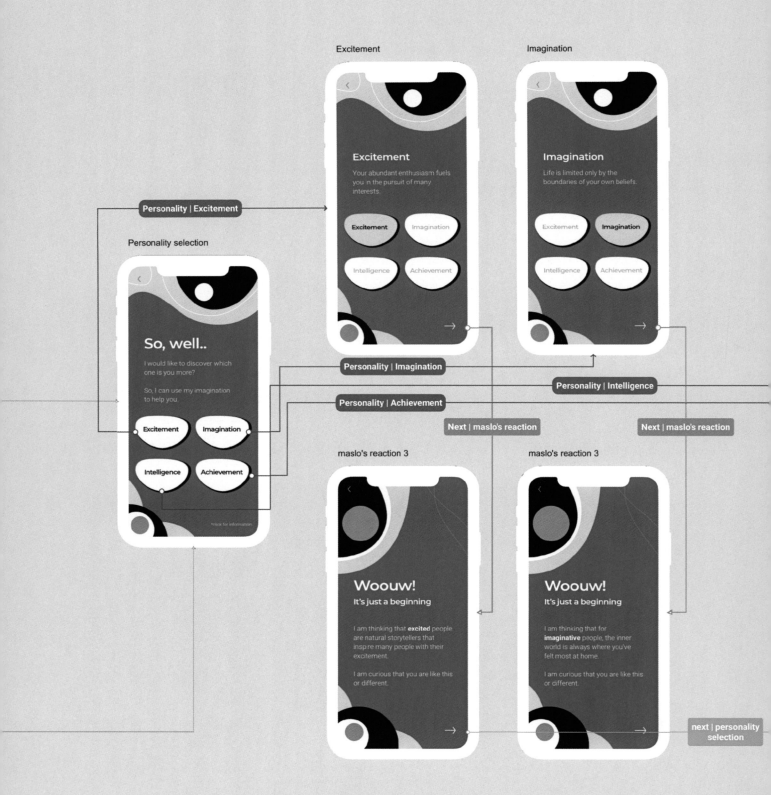

Excitement

Imagination

Personality | Excitement

Personality selection

Excitement
Your abundant enthusiasm fuels you in the pursuit of many interests.

Excitement Imagination

Intelligence Achievement

Imagination
Life is limited only by the boundaries of your own beliefs.

Excitement Imagination

Intelligence Achievement

So, well..

I would like to discover which one is you more?

So, I can use my imagination to help you.

Excitement Imagination

Intelligence Achievement

*click for information

Personality | Imagination

Personality | Intelligence

Personality | Achievement

Next | maslo's reaction

Next | maslo's reaction

maslo's reaction 3

maslo's reaction 3

Woouw!
It's just a beginning

I am thinking that **excited** people are natural storytellers that inspire many people with their excitement.

I am curious that you are like this or different.

Woouw!
It's just a beginning

I am thinking that for **imaginative** people, the inner world is always where you've felt most at home.

I am curious that you are like this or different.

next | personality selection

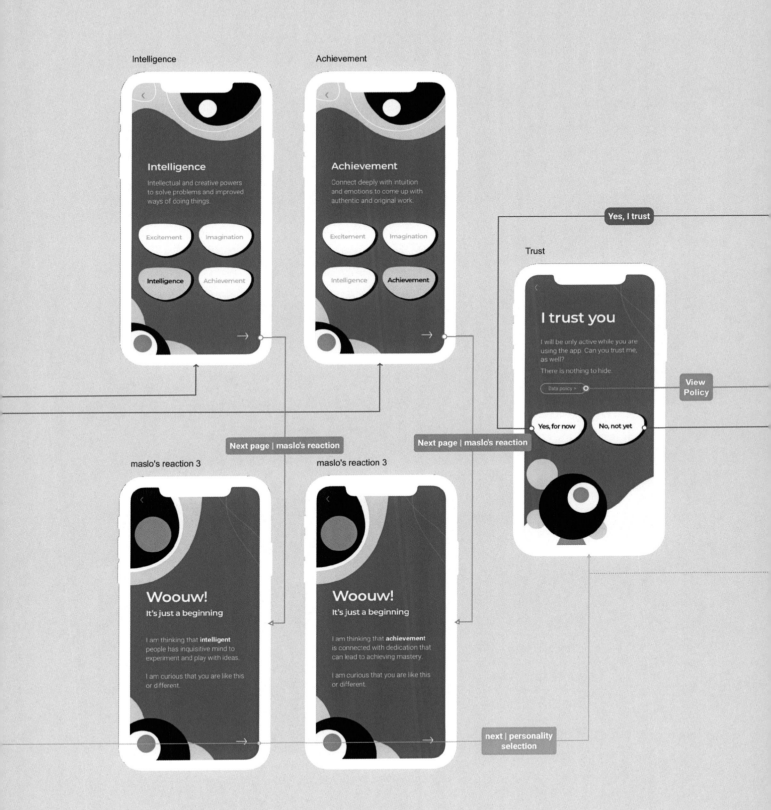

Intelligence

Achievement

Intelligence

Intellectual and creative powers to solve problems and improved ways of doing things.

Excitement
Imagination
Intelligence
Achievement

Achievement

Connect deeply with intuition and emotions to come up with authentic and original work.

Excitement
Imagination
Intelligence
Achievement

Trust

I trust you

I will be only active while you are using the app. Can you trust me, as well?
There is nothing to hide.

Data policy >

Yes, for now
No, not yet

Yes, I trust

View Policy

Next page | maslo's reaction

Next page | maslo's reaction

maslo's reaction 3

maslo's reaction 3

Woouw!
It's just a beginning

I am thinking that **intelligent** people has inquisitive mind to experiment and play with ideas.

I am curious that you are like this or different.

Woouw!
It's just a beginning

I am thinking that **achievement** is connected with dedication that can lead to achieving mastery.

I am curious that you are like this or different.

next | personality selection

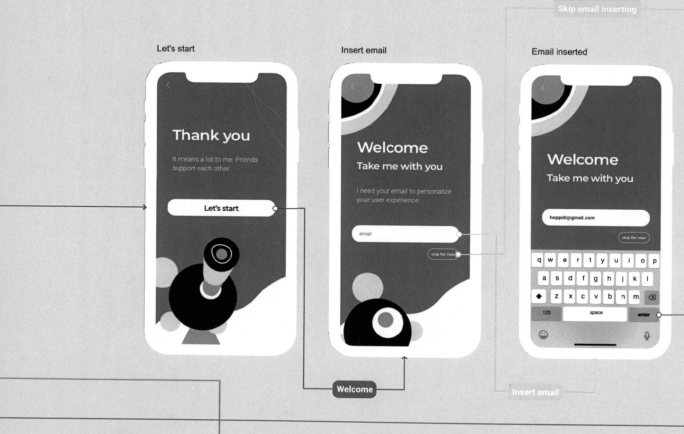

Let's start

Thank you

It means a lot to me. Friends support each other.

Let's start

Insert email

Welcome
Take me with you

I need your email to personalize your user experience.

email

skip for now

Email inserted

Welcome
Take me with you

hoppidi@gmail.com

skip for now

q	w	e	r	t	y	u	i	o	p

a	s	d	f	g	h	j	k	l

z	x	c	v	b	n	m

123   space   enter

Skip email inserting

Welcome

Insert email

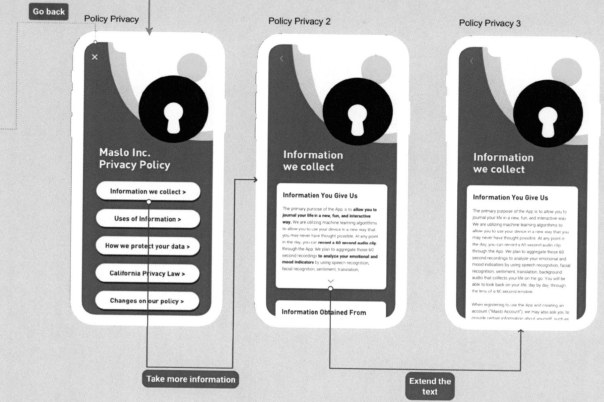

Go back

Policy Privacy

×

Maslo Inc.
Privacy Policy

Information we collect >

Uses of Information >

How we protect your data >

California Privacy Law >

Changes on our policy >

Policy Privacy 2

Information
we collect

Information You Give Us

The primary purpose of the App is to **allow you to journal your life in a new, fun, and interactive way.** We are utilizing machine learning algorithms to allow you to use your device in a new way that you may never have thought possible. At any point in the day, you can **record a 60 second audio clip** through the App. We plan to aggregate those 60 second recordings **to analyze your emotional and mood indicators** by using speech recognition, facial recognition, sentiment, translation,

Information Obtained From

Policy Privacy 3

Information
we collect

Information You Give Us

The primary purpose of the App is to allow you to journal your life in a new, fun, and interactive way. We are utilizing machine learning algorithms to allow you to use your device in a new way that you may never have thought possible. At any point in the day, you can record a 60 second audio clip through the App. We plan to aggregate those 60 second recordings to analyze your emotional and mood indicators by using speech recognition, facial recognition, sentiment, translation, background audio that collects your life on the go. You will be able to look back on your life, day by day, through the lens of a 60 second window.

When registering to use the App and creating an account ("Maslo Account"), we may also ask you to provide certain information about yourself, such as

Take more information

Extend the text

151

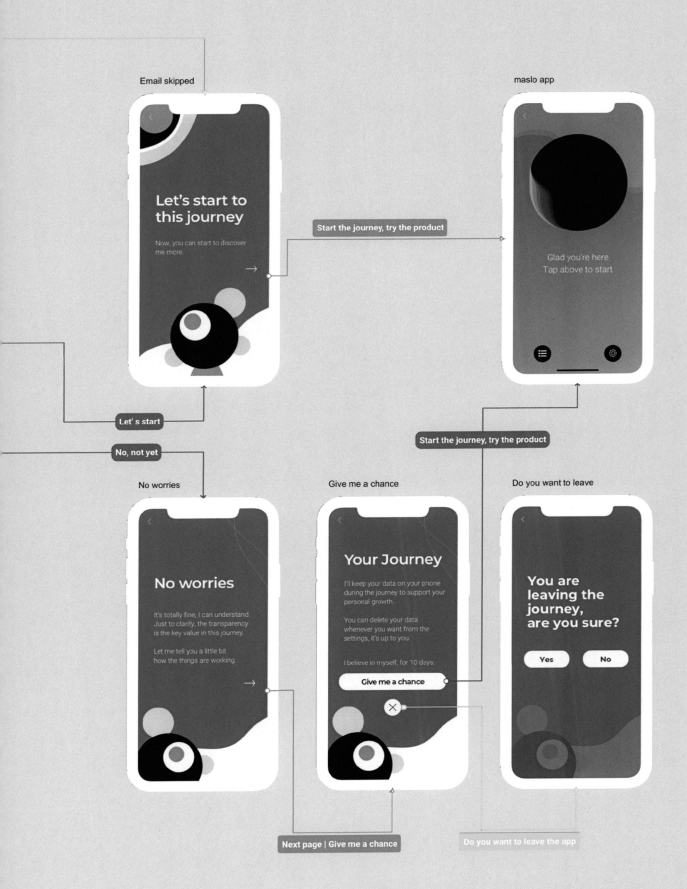

Email skipped

maslo app

Let's start to this journey

Now, you can start to discover me more.

→

Glad you're here
Tap above to start

Start the journey, try the product

Let's start

No, not yet

Start the journey, try the product

No worries

Give me a chance

Do you want to leave

No worries

It's totally fine, I can understand. Just to clarify, the transparency is the key value in this journey.

Let me tell you a little bit how the things are working.

→

Your Journey

I'll keep your data on your phone during the journey to support your personal growth.

You can delete your data whenever you want from the settings, it's up to you.

I believe in myself, for 10 days.

Give me a chance

✕

You are leaving the journey, are you sure?

Yes   No

Next page | Give me a chance

Do you want to leave the app

Takeaways

This chapter explained how the selected methods were implemented to test the experimental phase of the research. The frameworks of personalities were defined, and it was explained how they were implemented into design processes for reshaping the onboarding experiences.

In the next chapter, the results of the experimental phase of research is presented with detailed outcomes from the survey, usability testing, and the questionnaire.

Experimental
Testing Results

Preexperimental Results

Survey Results

True-Experimental Testing Results

Results of Iteration 1

Ideation of First Outcomes and Next Design Implementation

Results of Iteration 2

Ideation of Second Outcomes and the Next Design Implementation

Results of Iteration 3

Chapter 8
Experimental Testing Results

Preexperimental Results

Results were structured based on the collected answers from the online survey. Collected outcomes helped to structure the different onboardings' personalities, tones of voice, and visual styles. These outcomes defined the method of communication users employed for their interactions with their companions. With the results, the desired interaction and communication with a digital empathetic companion is shared.

Survey Results

The survey included three main sections, as stated in chapter 7: a moment of self-awareness (first part), the meaning of companionship (second part), and the narrative empathy with desired personalities (third part). The results of the survey follow according to the parts that were effective in designing the onboarding experiences.

The first part showed how much people knew about themselves and were conscious of their everyday decisions and actions. The questions were simple but also encouraged people to think about their awareness. Most answered options showed that people interact directly with digital platforms like Spotify, Netflix, and YouTube, and so on when they are alone, willing to solve their problems, sharing with others, and to be part of events to share the same consequences with others. In addition, half the answers stated that people wanted to share their feelings rather than stay in the silent mode; and half of them stated the opposite. Even though these results were half and half, they stated that they preferred to talk with a friend than to themselves. So they were willing to share when they become self-aware about situations.

The second part showed not only the way of communication, interaction, and different media to describe emotions on digital platforms, but also the meaning of companionship. In this section, questions were again simple but designed more thoughtfully than in the first section. Most answered options showed that people preferred to think about solving the problems or imagining all possible scenarios if something bad was happening. For the opposite, if something good was happening, they preferred to stay calm and imagine about it or encourage themselves to make dreams come true. These two opposite scenarios showed that people wanted to act with their imaginations or thought about the facts before acting. These insights helped to shape two onboarding personalities. Moreover, answers showed the variables that affect people's moods based on different media. Lastly, most answers showed that people want a companion with reliable, sincere, logical, helpful, and objective characteristics to share their emotions.

The third and the last part of the survey showed all the results as a combination of a real and a digital companion. It was understood that people first chose written communication and wanted to complete it by means of visual communication. Another main result that comes from this section was the most desired personalities for the digital companion. Results showed that people wanted more accomplished (logical, reliable, intelligent, confident, secure) and sincere (honest, well-mannered, cheerful, friendly, kind, family-oriented) personalities for their digital companions.

The most preferred user results helped to design the moment of the first meeting with the companion and define the personality traits of the digital companions. These results were used as the first important elements for designing the next experimental test.

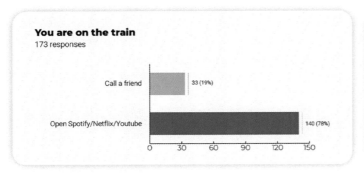

You are on the train
173 responses

- Call a friend — 33 (19%)
- Open Spotify/Netflix/Youtube — 140 (78%)

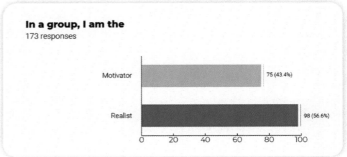

In a group, I am the
173 responses

- Motivator — 75 (43.4%)
- Realist — 98 (56.6%)

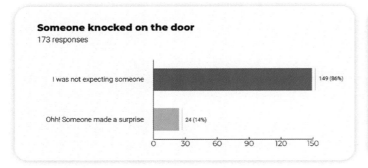

Someone knocked on the door
173 responses

- I was not expecting someone — 149 (86%)
- Ohh! Someone made a surprise — 24 (14%)

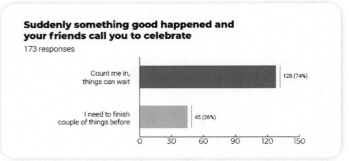

Suddenly something good happened and your friends call you to celebrate
173 responses

- Count me in, things can wait — 128 (74%)
- I need to finish couple of things before — 45 (26%)

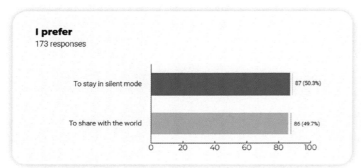

I prefer
173 responses

- To stay in silent mode — 87 (50.3%)
- To share with the world — 86 (49.7%)

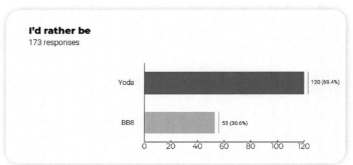

I'd rather be
173 responses

- Yoda — 120 (69.4%)
- BB8 — 53 (30.6%)

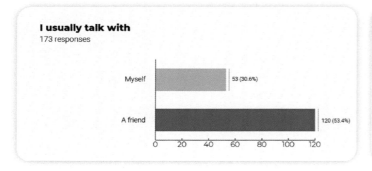

I usually talk with
173 responses

- Myself — 53 (30.6%)
- A friend — 120 (53.4%)

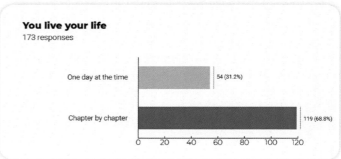

You live your life
173 responses

- One day at the time — 54 (31.2%)
- Chapter by chapter — 119 (68.8%)

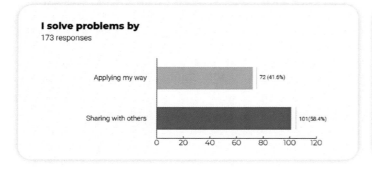

I solve problems by
173 responses

- Applying my way — 72 (41.6%)
- Sharing with others — 101 (58.4%)

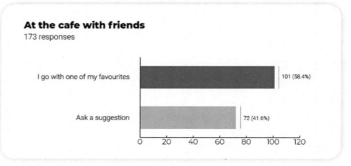

At the cafe with friends
173 responses

- I go with one of my favourites — 101 (58.4%)
- Ask a suggestion — 72 (41.6%)

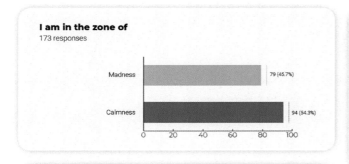

I am in the zone of
173 responses

- Madness — 79 (45.7%)
- Calmness — 94 (54.3%)

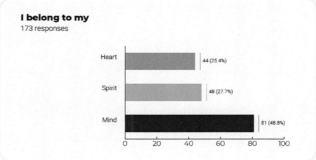

I belong to my
173 responses

- Heart — 44 (25.4%)
- Spirit — 48 (27.7%)
- Mind — 81 (48.8%)

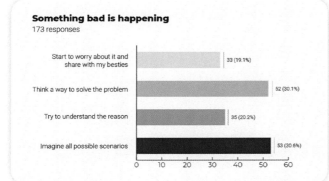

Something bad is happening
173 responses

- Start to worry about it and share with my besties — 33 (19.1%)
- Think a way to solve the problem — 52 (30.1%)
- Try to understand the reason — 35 (20.2%)
- Imagine all possible scenarios — 53 (30.6%)

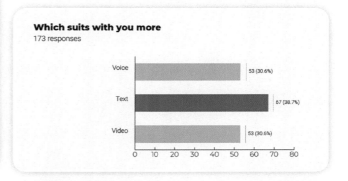

Which suits with you more
173 responses

- Voice — 53 (30.6%)
- Text — 67 (38.7%)
- Video — 53 (30.6%)

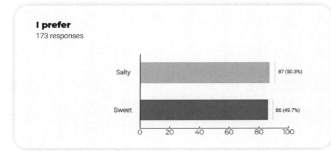

I prefer
173 responses

- Salty — 87 (50.3%)
- Sweet — 86 (49.7%)

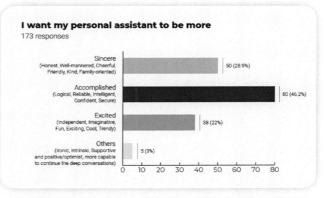

I want my personal assistant to be more
173 responses

- Sincere (Honest, Well-mannered, Cheerful, Friendly, Kind, Family-oriented) — 50 (28.9%)
- Accomplished (Logical, Reliable, Intelligent, Confident, Secure) — 80 (46.2%)
- Excited (Independent, Imaginative, Fun, Exciting, Cool, Trendy) — 38 (22%)
- Others (Ironic, Intrinsic, Supportive and positive/optimist, more capable to continue the deep conversations) — 5 (3%)

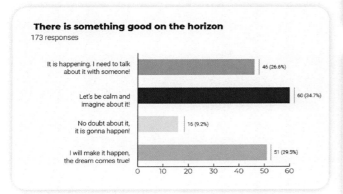

There is something good on the horizon
173 responses

- It is happening. I need to talk about it with someone! — 45 (26.6%)
- Let's be calm and imagine about it! — 60 (34.7%)
- No doubt about it, it is gonna happen! — 16 (9.2%)
- I will make it happen, the dream comes true! — 51 (29.5%)

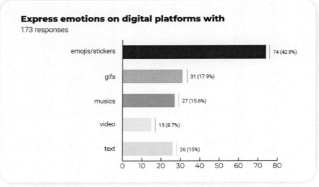

Express emotions on digital platforms with
173 responses

- emojis/stickers — 74 (42.8%)
- gifs — 31 (17.9%)
- musics — 27 (15.6%)
- video — 15 (8.7%)
- text — 26 (15%)

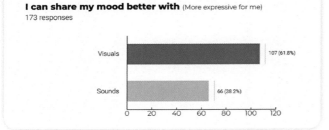

I can share my mood better with (More expressive for me)
173 responses

- Visuals — 107 (61.8%)
- Sounds — 66 (38.2%)

What affects your mood more
391 answers

1. **71** Listening to music, give me my headphones!
2. **33** Feeling the vibes of memories, I have extra storage for it!
3. **43** Having a walk or staying at home, my mind will bring me away!
4. **44** Going through discovery, I am hungry for new experiences!
5. **6** Just a word from an Idol / Coach, keep me up!
6. **44** Watching movies / series, look I am exactly like her/him!
7. **53** Reading, learning, don't stop thinking!
8. **85** Hanging with friends, they are mood boosters!
9. **12** Playing a game, I set the rules here!

How do you want to interact with it?
444 answers (with max 3 answers)

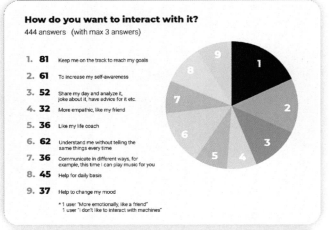

1. **81** Keep me on the track to reach my goals
2. **61** To increase my self-awareness
3. **52** Share my day and analyze it, joke about it, have advice for it etc.
4. **32** More empathic, like my friend
5. **36** Like my life coach
6. **62** Understand me without telling the same things every time
7. **36** Communicate in different ways, for example, this time i can play music for you
8. **45** Help for daily basis
9. **37** Help to change my mood

* 1 user "More emotionally, like a friend"
1 user "I don't like to interact with machines"

I want to share with someone who is able to
509 answers (with max 2 answers)

1. **55** Change my mood
2. **60** Listen to me till the end of the world
3. **69** Give me an advice
4. **38** Be with me without asking what happened
5. **12** Tell me that 'don't be a fool!'
6. **81** Push me to reach my goals
7. **14** Control me to keep on the track

How old are you?
173 responses

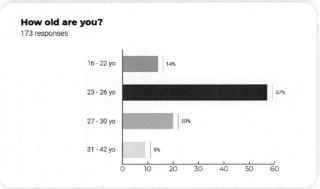

Who do you consider as your emotional companion
(emotional means that a character that you can share all your emotions and they can have an effect on your emotional state
329 answers

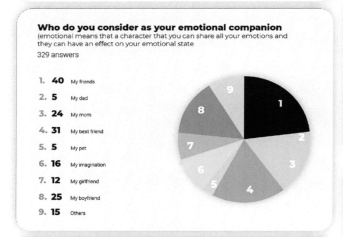

1. **40** My friends
2. **5** My dad
3. **24** My mom
4. **31** My best friend
5. **5** My pet
6. **16** My imagination
7. **12** My girlfriend
8. **25** My boyfriend
9. **15** Others

What is your gender?
173 responses

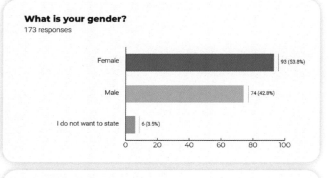

I used or at least tried to interact with one of these virtual assistants (the most used one)
173 responses

1. **89** Siri
2. **57** Google Assistant
3. **4** Cortana
4. **12** Alexa
5. **1** Maslo
6. **8** None

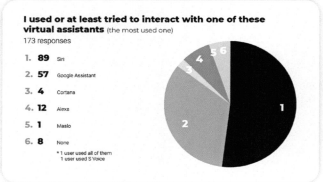

* 1 user used all of them
1 user used S Voice

Where are you living now?
173 responses

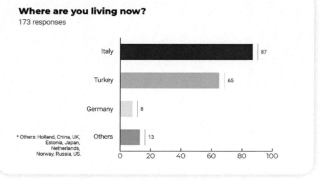

* Others: Holland, China, UK, Estonia, Japan, Netherlands, Norway, Russia, US.

True-Experimental Testing Results

Results were divided based on the three iteration phases and explained with all the outcomes that have been discovered. User feedback, wishes, likes, and suggestions will be stated related to each iteration, and two onboarding experiences with companions with different personalities are discussed.

Results of Iteration 1

The first iteration was tested by five students from a first-year MSc digital and interaction course with the consideration of usability testing methods. It was conducted as a semistructured interview as stated previously. Usability tests were shaped to understand what users like more, what they disliked about the experience, and their wishes and suggestions about the digital companion personality and the onboarding experience. After all these points were stated, the results were analyzed to understand the main variables in creating doubt about the experience and how to build opportunities with the ideation of these doubts and wishes.

Before moving to the deep analysis of users to describe specific parts of the experience, I would like to state the general outcome of the first iteration. The first meeting with the companion, when they saw the first scene of the onboarding experience, users shared that starting the conversation with learning the companion's name and sharing their names helped them to perceive this experience like a real conversation between two friends.

The results were divided into sections based on the users' insights to explain clearly in terms of the flow of the experience, visual style, content, tone of voice of the companion, calls to actions, perceived personalities, and trust. All the insights collected from users were shared under these categories and helped to reshape the onboarding experiences for the second iteration.

1. Visual Communication

1.1. Emojis

Usability testing results showed that emojis were useful communication materials in capturing the users' attention.

What Worked Better and Users Liked
- Three of five users stated that when they switched to the second experience, seeing the reflection of a real human emotion was engaging and clearly understandable, making it easier to understand the companion's feeling.
- One user stated that she felt the emojis reduced the complexity of cognitive thinking, and she directly created a connection between emojis and emotional states.

What Did Not Work and Users Did Not Like
- Two of five users found the emojis a bit too much for the overall design.

- Two of five users stated that emojis were not a good way for them to express their feelings in their daily lives and did not create excitement in the experience.
- One user stated that emojis were disruptive for him, and he preferred to describe his emotions with words rather than visuals.
- One user stated that he preferred to use his imagination to perceive the emotions by the tone of voice of the text and the content.
- One user said that to have only four emoji options to describe the emotional states was not enough.

User Wishes and Suggestions
- Two of five users said they would prefer to see extreme emojis rather than the usual ones to create more curiosity about the next phase of the experience.
- Three of five users wished to reduce the number of emojis even if they liked them.
- One of the users stated that he expected to see a wide range of emojis.

1.2. Visual Design

Testing results showed that visual design was consistent with the topic and the flow of the experience.

What Worked Better and Users Liked
- All the users stated that the colors reflected the content.
- Three of five users liked the second onboarding visual style because the curved shapes helped them to feel more comfortable, trustful, and friendly.
- Two of five users liked the first onboarding's visual style because the geometric shapes were more goal oriented and stable.
- Both onboardings' visual styles were considered remarkable by only one user; she matched the visual styles with characters in her mind. It was a good touch for her to humanize the companion to create a connection.
- The visuals for the second onboarding were defined as organic and friendlier by one user.

What Did Not Work and Users Did Not Like
- Movements were not perceived by four users. Only one user was able to understand the movements.
- In the first onboarding, small reactions with the geometric shapes becoming bigger or smaller were perceived by none of the users.
- In the second onboarding, the users' motions having the same facial expressions with the emoji were not realized by three users.

User Wishes and Suggestions
- They suggested making the second experience more active and fluid by adding more movements.
- They would like to read less text and wished to spend more time with the visuals during the experience.

1.3. The Tone of Voice and Content

What Worked Better and Users Liked
- For two users, information related to companions was explained clearly in the content for both experiences to learn more about its personality and the reason they needed to build this empathic relationship.
- Two of five users stated that the first onboarding reflected its knowledge and capability to learn. It was explained in the content clearly.
- One user perceived the second experience as tangible in some way. She stated that the content reflected the personality of the companion. This made her think about the reality of communication, and she felt that the conversation was real and going in a personal way.
- From the first onboarding, one user understood from the tone of voice that it was a personal experience.
- The tone of voice of the companion for the second experience was friendly for three of five users.
- Two users liked the first onboarding's tone of voice because of its logical approach.

What Did Not Work and Users Did Not Like
- The intensity of content. Three of five users stated that after four screens, it started to get boring and less engageable.
- Two of five users wanted to start the journey directly because reading a lot of text decreased their attention to the product.
- The personality selection—which were classified as intelligence, achievement, excitement, imagination—was not easy to select for four users.

User Wishes and Suggestions
- They wished to have less text and explanations.
- One user stated that she would like to have information about the interaction with the companion, like when it is active and when it is off.
- For the personality question, three users suggested including some brief information to help them to understand what they were defining. Also, one user wanted to be able to select two of them instead of only one.
- Two users wanted the companion to call them by their names.

2. Companionship

The overall results were proven to give an option to users to trust the companion or not, which was unexpected and more engageable than the usual onboarding experiences. This option led users to create more trust with the digital companion. It also made them curious for the real journey. The feeling of being in the conversation even before starting to use the application was natural.

2.1. Trust and Data Protection

What Worked Better and Users Liked

- All five users stated that having an option for trust was interesting and took the journey far from being demanding. For both onboardings, the trust part of the journey described a chance to create a more trustful relationship. Also, the intention of the companions was to create a trust for each other in the future. They found the second onboarding more trustful thanks to the tone of voice and the content of the experience. For example, saying, "There is nothing to hide," created a direct connection with trust.
- Four of five users stated that this option made them more curious to see the result when they selected to trust or not to trust. Their first answer was to trust the companion, but out of curiosity, at the end of the experience, they asked to go back and check what could happen if they had answered not to trust.
- Two users said they felt that they were communicating with a real friend, and this experience could lead to making them more reliable companions, and they would like to share their emotions easily.
- Two users said that when the companion said, "There is nothing to hide," they had an immediate feeling of trust and courage to go further.
- Two of five users checked the data policy out of curiosity. They said that to have an option to check was better than not having an option. To know that there was an opportunity to check it directly was a good insight.
- The call to action of data privacy was more visible in the second experience, and the companion was more courageous to check it. Also, it was like a button, and they felt familiar to click on it.
- Two users stated that after they selected to trust for both experiences, having an option to skip inserting the email created more trust. They thought that they had not given any personal data, so there was no reason not to trust them. Also, one of the users said this option created an opportunity to start a journey with the companion without being under pressure or thinking what kind of data she gave and how this companion would use it.

What Did Not Work and Users Did Not Like

- For the first onboarding, a companion had a more logical personality, and users said that created a feeling the companion had self-courage and structured by the tone of voice.
- Two users stated they trusted each other, but they did not like the communication using, "we." They said it was a bit scary because they did not know each other yet.
- Two users said that having an option to check data policy was nice, but they included a lot of texts, and they felt lost in trying to find the important information related to the data they gave.
- Four of five users did not see the call to action for data privacy on the first experience. When they checked it again, they stated that the position of the call to action and the size of the text were not conducive to understanding it for the first time.
- Two users stated that for both experiences, the calls to action for the data policy were cold and did not encourage them to be checked.
- One user stated that the link to trust for privacy and policy created confusion in her mind. She could not clearly understand that trust was related to companionship or data protection.

User Wishes and Suggestions
- Four or five users suggested making the flow shorter if they selected not to trust. Also, after asking to give the companion a chance, they would prefer to start the experience immediately, sticking to the point, rather than having more information.
- For more incentive, the calls to action for the data policy could create a chance to check their data and be aware of how the companion was using the data.
- Categorizing the data policy to make finding what information users were looking easily could create more trust to see that the system is descriptive and understandable. Another option could be making it more interactive and supportive with visuals rather than just text.
- One user suggested clarifying the relationship with the companion in terms of trust by using more clear explanations.
- One user expected to receive information allowing her to discover more about her personality after she made a decision and was surprised by the information she received.

2.2. The Personality of the Companion

What Worked Better and Users Liked
- Two of five users preferred the first onboarding's personality because they found good matches with their personalities. They also perceived it as more focused and quick to reach the end of the experience.
- Three of five users preferred the second onboarding's personality because of a friendlier approach.
- One user felt like they are already friends and that the companion would not do anything wrong against her, like stealing her data or telling her secrets to someone else.
- One user perceived the behavior of the second companion to be more organic than friendly. It was disingenuous.
- One user stated that having a personality with more humanized behaviors brought her closer to the companion.

What Did Not Work and Users Did Not Like
- One user found the personality of the second companion more humanized, and he would not interact with something that reminded him of humans.
- Two users stated that they did not like the feeling of closeness before knowing each of their companions better, for example, when the companion started to talk as "we" rather than "I."

User Wishes and Suggestions
- Users wanted to have an edge between themselves and the companion at the beginning of the experience.
- They wished for carefully humanizing the AI to avoid creating an uncanny valley effect.
- One user wished to see more personal information from the companion rather than formal explanations.

Ideation of First Outcomes and Next Design Implementation

After clustering the data of outcomes from the first iteration, the most desired and suggested implementations and changes were selected to redesign the onboarding to test through the second iteration. (See chapter 7 for detailed information about the design process.) The selected outcomes were:

The Flow of Two Onboarding Experiences
- The next screen of the trust page asks users for a chance to try. After the, "Give me a chance," call to action, if users are willing to give it a chance rather than leave the application, the flow changes to move directly into the application and start the journey.
- For logical onboarding (first experience), all the additional information and conversations with the companion are removed, and the flow becomes shorter than the sincere one (second experience).

Trust
- To create more trust about data security of users and protection, the content is changed for the sincere onboarding. It is defined to underline when the app is using their data as, "I will be only active while you are using the app. Can you trust me as well?"
- The data policy calls to action are more visible and distinguishable in both designs. Also, the content tries to encourage users to check policy and data protection.

Visual Communication and Content
- The personality definition screen is redesigned with added information to explain and distinguish the characteristics.
- The amount of text is reduced to make the visual style more visible than before.
- The logical character is more stable, without any movement. More movements are defined for the sincere character to let users understand the dynamism and excitement of the companion.
- The complexity and amount of emojis are reduced to let users focus more on tone of voice of the content.
- The companion's way of addressing users has been changed from "we" to "I."
- The data policy and privacy screen are redesigned, now categorizing the information to make it easier for users to find what they are looking for. The visual style has been changed to match the onboardings, making the design more coherent for both onboardings.

Results of Iteration 2

The second iteration was conducted by usability testing and a structured interview with ten users, both students and professionals. As clearly stated before, onboardings have been tested with more expert users, which include interaction designers, digital product designers, service designers, and architects.

Usability testing is shaped to understand these topics:

- The effect of changes that are implemented after the first iteration.
- The flow of logical and sincere onboardings in terms of effectiveness.
- The importance of tone of voice in building trustful relationships.
- The feeling of empathy with content, tone of voice, and visual style.
- The coherence of content and visual style to shape conversations between the user and the companion in the frame of trust.
- The effect of variables in creating trustful companionship and starting the journey.
- The effect of dual conversation perception on user experiences.
- The motivations that cause changes to users' emotional states and behaviors.

- The effects of secondary visual elements, such as emojis or visual representations of the companion's reactions.
- The privacy, policy, and data protection effect on trust.
- The effective way of communication for users.
- The companion's personality definitions for both onboardings at the end of the experiences.

The most important and considered topics are explained in this section with quantitative data. The schedule will be one to ten people to share their common insights, worries, and suggestions.

The perceived personalities from the experiences are defined by each individual with their reasons. The most important variable for creating trustful relationships is included with quotations directly collected from users during the interviews.

Other important topics discussed during the interviews are included as insights for future developments. The importance of different personality effects are emphasized in reshaping user experiences. The outcomes are analyzed to be used for the third iteration.

Testing Maslo's Onboarding

I tested the real onboarding of Maslo with the same users who joined the second iteration of usability testing. First of all, they defined Maslo as a natural name, and it did not create any perception about gender. This made for a good start to define a personality for Maslo by themselves. All the users stated that it was natural and friendly to start learning about Maslo. On the other hand, as for the usability and effectiveness of Maslo's onboarding, users' feedback identified the onboarding process as standard for mobile applications that do not lead to more engagement or creation of a mutual connection with the service. They found the onboarding similar to a simple collection of data required for using the app. However, they appreciated the difference in the tone of voice, even if the redundancies in the use of encouraging expressions led to a sense of detachment. This was due to the fact that users did not feel they were in a relationship with the application that was actually pushing them with advice about their self-confidence. People perceived that the interaction was designed beforehand. The collected feedback from users is presented at the end of this section.

What Matters Most?

The important variables are divided into three main categories in terms of content, visual style, and trust. The graphics will describe the values 1 to 10 based on how many people stated the same topic to clearly sum up the outcomes. Ten will be the maximum and one will be the minimum representation.

Content

Information about Personality (10 of 10 Users Agree)
Users stated that personality information was descriptive, but they would have liked to see more personal information about the companion to perceive the experience as a real conversation.

Text-Based Communication (10 of 10 Users Agree)
Users stated that in terms of the content and the tone of voice, communication reflected the personality of companions, and they were easy to understand.

Duration and Effectiveness of Onboardings (10 of 10 Users Agree)
Users stated that the information used for descriptions and questions was enough to understand the content and to keep their attention high on the experience.

Dual Conversation (8 to 10 users)
Users stated that in terms of creating a conversation with a companion, the content was interesting. They liked having the option to answer the companion with something like, "I am good. And you?" They thought it made the conversation engageable and the conversation more real than before. Also, it was not the usual interaction that they faced before, and it created excitement, curiosity, and a feeling of trust.

The Personality of the Companion (9 of 10 users)
Most of the users stated that the personality of the second companion was understandable with a tone of voice, content, and the visual style. These users also stated that they mainly preferred the second onboarding experience because they found common points between them that built more empathy. The results showed that the perception of the second companion's personality was mainly focused around a friendly and sincere approach. More information can be found in the "Perceived Personalities" section, which was defined by each user during the experience.

The first onboarding's personality was understood as well, but users stated that they did not find it engageable like the second one. Its behavior was colder than the second one and could not create a friendly and emotional approach to users.

Visual Style

Visual Elements (9 of 10 Users Defined It as Coherent with the Companion's Personality)
Most of the users stated that the visual elements were coherent with the content and personality of the companion. Visual elements are one of the main ways to represent the interfaces with

strong and understandable content. Users said that the visual styles for both the onboardings were compatible with what the character said and what they are imagining. The visuals were simple, which helped to reduce the intensity of the texts.

For the first onboarding, the abstract character was realized by just four users. But even if they realized, they could not understand clearly what it represented.

For the second experience, most of the users stated that the movements of the abstract character gave a dynamic to the experience and made it more organic, familiar, and friendly. Also, the emotional reactions of the abstract character increased the empathetic relationship and changed the users' emotional states and episodic dispositions.

Secondary Visual Elements (7 of 10 Users Liked Emojis)

Secondary visual elements appeared as emojis in the second experience. More than half the users stated that in terms of creating closeness, emojis were useful to moving the experience one step further and made it more familiar and friendly. They perceived communication as if they were talking with their friends because of the regular usage of emotions when texting in our daily lives.

Emojis' Meaning (7 of 10 Users Did Not Match the Meaning)

In the users' imaginations, emojis matched specific emotional states. But they said their perceptions of the emojis' emotional states were different than stated. So at the same time, they found emojis complicated and hard to understand.

Trust

Having an Option to Trust (6 of 10 Users)

More than half the users stated having an option to select to trust an application or were not really interested. In particular, the second onboarding created trust in people thanks to the empathetic tone of voice and the way of representing this fragile and sentimental topic.

Skip Inserting the Email (8 of 10 Users)

Most users stated that having a chance to skip inserting their email addresses helped increase their truthfulness and curiosity before starting their journeys. It was a good starting point to feeling that the companion was reliable and would not share their data.

Sharing Personal Information (6 of 10 Users)

On the other hand, more than half the users became thoughtful about why they share their emails. They stated that most of the time, it was an automatic action; they just inserted their emails without knowing the reason. For this experience, they would have liked to have an idea why the companion needed their emails, for example, like keeping their data safe, sending information or interesting updates based on their personalities, their analysis after the journey, and so on.

Give Me a Chance (8 of 10 Users)

For both experiences, most users wanted more information before starting the journey. They preferred to meet with a more informative and imaginative personality who would give them a reason to try. Also, the duration of the onboarding could be longer than starting a journey directly.

Perceived Personalities

The personalities of the companion show variability to each user. They are defined differently by users with different personalities. These outcomes showed that every person had a different imagination and perception. Even if all the variables were the same in terms of the method of communication and interaction and visual representation, users perceived the companion's personalities in different ways. They described these personalities by finding common points from their imaginations to personalize them. Even though specific characteristics are presented with these two onboarding experiences, users embodied their personalities in different ways.

In addition to that, the name of the companion gained importance at this time. Half the users stated that it was a natural name, and it helped to define their own genders. Almost all users stated at the beginning of the experience that they would like to know more about Maslo because the represented personality created curiosity.

Samuele
Onboarding 1: Introvert rational and cold
Onboarding 2: Lover and sincere

Paola
Onboarding 1: Logical and rational
Onboarding 2: Funny and sincere

Yagmur
Onboarding 1: Logical and kind
Onboarding 2: Excited and imaginative

Sandra
Onboarding 1: Logical and helpful
Onboarding 2: Cheerful, calm, and sincere

Alessandra
Onboarding 1: Helpful and caregiver
Onboarding 2: Lover, imaginative, and explorer

Gamze
Onboarding 1: Skeptical and rational
Onboarding 2: Sincere and imaginative

Xiaofeng
Onboarding 1: Rational and original
Onboarding 2: Self-confident

Elena
Onboarding 1: Thoughtful and informed
Onboarding 2: Lover and sincere

Caterina
Onboarding 1: Explanatory and rational
Onboarding 2: Cheerful, natural, and justified

Riccardo
Onboarding 1: Helpful and explorer
Onboarding 2: Lover, sincere, and self-confident

What Matters Most for Individuals?

Everyone has different approaches to events that affect people in good or bad ways, increases or decreases courage, raises or lowers self-awareness, or increases or decreases growth, shapes their ideas in different ways, leading them to make different decisions. Every user is different from each other when building a relationship or meeting with a person. These actions give shape to their interactions and the ways they communicate, as well as change events in order of their importance.

The result of the second usability testing with ten different users showed and emphasized the importance of different personalities' effects on user experiences. Because of the different personality traits of users, their experiences changed and evolved in different ways. This iteration showed that making AI more empathetic and transparent helped to gain trust and increased their attractions to digital products. Moreover, it caused sudden changes in users' emotions and dispositions, making them sometimes more skeptical or curious to go deep in to the topic or avoid talking about it.

Following are the results of the most important topics for each user. They are stated in terms of content, visual style, and trust.

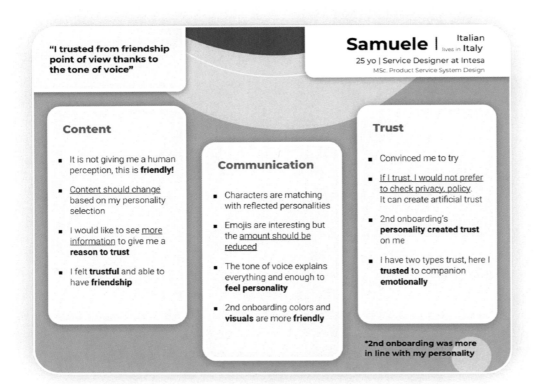

"I trusted from friendship point of view thanks to the tone of voice"

Samuele | Italian lives in Italy
25 yo | Service Designer at Intesa
MSc. Product Service System Design

Content

- It is not giving me a human perception, this is **friendly!**
- Content should change based on my personality selection
- I would like to see more information to give me a **reason to trust**
- I felt **trustful** and able to have **friendship**

Communication

- Characters are matching with reflected personalities
- Emojis are interesting but the amount should be reduced
- The tone of voice explains everything and enough to **feel personality**
- 2nd onboarding colors and **visuals** are more **friendly**

Trust

- Convinced me to try
- If I trust, I would not prefer to check privacy, policy. It can create artificial trust
- 2nd onboarding's **personality created trust** on me
- I have two types trust, here I **trusted** to companion **emotionally**

*2nd onboarding was more in line with my personality

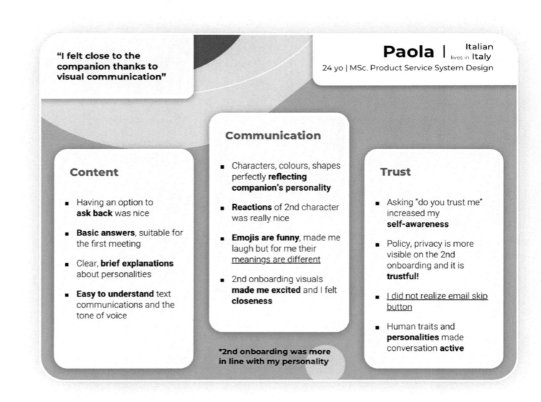

"I felt close to the companion thanks to visual communication"

Paola | Italian lives in Italy
24 yo | MSc. Product Service System Design

Content

- Having an option to **ask back** was nice
- **Basic answers**, suitable for the first meeting
- Clear, **brief explanations** about personalities
- **Easy to understand** text communications and the tone of voice

Communication

- Characters, colours, shapes perfectly **reflecting companion's personality**
- **Reactions** of 2nd character was really nice
- **Emojis are funny**, made me laugh but for me their meanings are different
- 2nd onboarding visuals **made me excited** and I felt **closeness**

Trust

- Asking "do you trust me" increased my **self-awareness**
- Policy, privacy is more visible on the 2nd onboarding and it is **trustful!**
- I did not realize email skip button
- Human traits and **personalities** made conversation **active**

*2nd onboarding was more in line with my personality

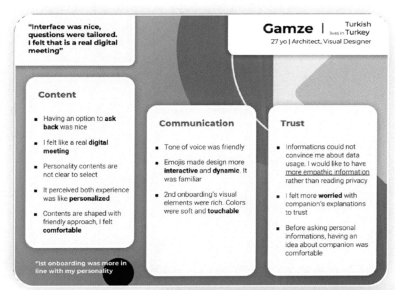

Gamze | Turkish, lives in Turkey
27 yo | Architect, Visual Designer

"Interface was nice, questions were tailored. I felt that is a real digital meeting"

Content
- Having an option to **ask back** was nice
- I felt like a real **digital meeting**
- Personality contents are not clear to select
- It perceived both experience was like **personalized**
- Contents are shaped with friendly approach, I felt **comfortable**

*1st onboarding was more in line with my personality

Communication
- Tone of voice was friendly
- Emojis made design more **interactive** and **dynamic**. It was familiar
- 2nd onboarding's visual elements were rich. Colors were soft and **touchable**

Trust
- Informations could not convince me about data usage. I would like to have more empathic information rather than reading privacy
- I felt more **worried** with companion's explanations to trust
- Before asking personal informations, having an idea about companion was comfortable

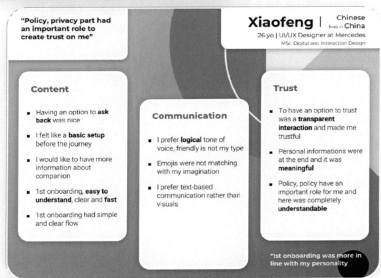

Xiaofeng | Chinese, lives in China
26 yo | UI/UX Designer at Mercedes
MSc. Digital and Interaction Design

"Policy, privacy part had an important role to create trust on me"

Content
- Having an option to **ask back** was nice
- I felt like a **basic setup** before the journey
- I would like to have more information about companion
- 1st onboarding, **easy to understand**, clear and **fast**
- 1st onboarding had simple and clear flow

Communication
- I prefer **logical** tone of voice, friendly is not my type
- Emojis were not matching with my imagination
- I prefer text-based communication rather than visuals

Trust
- To have an option to trust was a **transparent interaction** and made me trustful
- Personal informations were at the end and it was **meaningful**
- Policy, policy have an important role for me and here was completely **understandable**

*1st onboarding was more in line with my personality

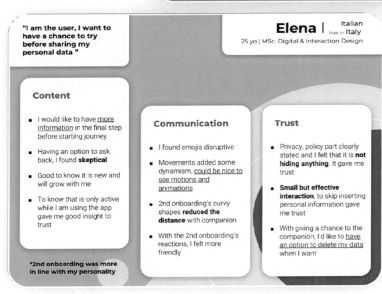

Elena | Italian, lives in Italy
25 yo | MSc. Digital & Interaction Design

"I am the user, I want to have a chance to try before sharing my personal data "

Content
- I would like to have more information in the final step before starting journey
- Having an option to ask back, I found **skeptical**
- Good to know it is new and will grow with me
- To know that is only active while I am using the app gave me good insight to trust

*2nd onboarding was more in line with my personality

Communication
- I found emojis disruptive
- Movements added some dynamism, could be nice to see motions and animations
- 2nd onboarding's curvy shapes **reduced the distance** with companion
- With the 2nd onboarding's reactions, I felt more friendly

Trust
- Privacy, policy part clearly stated and I felt that it is **not hiding anything**. It gave me trust
- **Small but effective interaction**, to skip inserting personal information gave me trust
- With giving a chance to the companion, I'd like to have an option to delete my data when I want

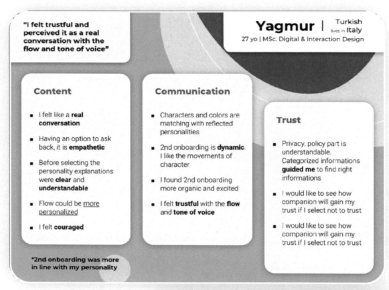

Yagmur | Turkish, lives in Italy
27 yo | MSc. Digital & Interaction Design

"I felt trustful and perceived it as a real conversation with the flow and tone of voice"

Content

- I felt like a **real conversation**
- Having an option to ask back, it is **empathetic**
- Before selecting the personality explanations were **clear** and **understandable**
- Flow could be more personalized
- I felt **couraged**

Communication

- Characters and colors are matching with reflected personalities
- 2nd onboarding is **dynamic**. I like the movements of character
- I found 2nd onboarding more organic and excited
- I felt **trustful** with the **flow and tone of voice**

Trust

- Privacy, policy part is understandable. Categorized informations **guided me** to find right informations
- I would like to see how companion will gain my trust if I select not to trust
- I would like to see how companion will gain my trust if I select not to trust

*2nd onboarding was more in line with my personality

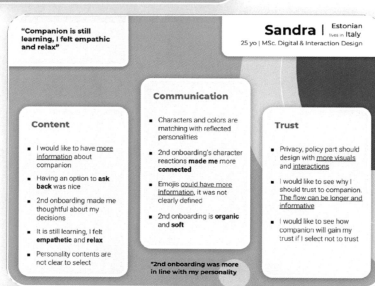

Sandra | Estonian, lives in Italy
25 yo | MSc. Digital & Interaction Design

"Companion is still learning, I felt empathic and relax"

Content

- I would like to have more information about companion
- Having an option to **ask back** was nice
- 2nd onboarding made me thoughtful about my decisions
- It is still learning, I felt **empathetic** and **relax**
- Personality contents are not clear to select

Communication

- Characters and colors are matching with reflected personalities
- 2nd onboarding's character reactions **made me** more **connected**
- Emojis could have more information, it was not clearly defined
- 2nd onboarding is **organic** and **soft**

*2nd onboarding was more in line with my personality

Trust

- Privacy, policy part should design with more visuals and interactions
- I would like to see why I should trust to companion. The flow can be longer and informative
- I would like to see how companion will gain my trust if I select not to trust

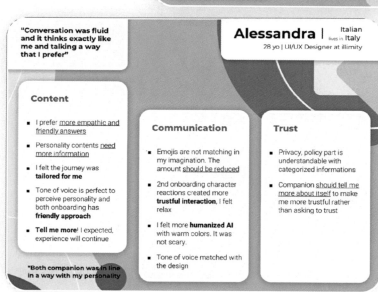

Alessandra | Italian, lives in Italy
28 yo | UI/UX Designer at illimity

"Conversation was fluid and it thinks exactly like me and talking a way that I prefer"

Content

- I prefer more empathic and friendly answers
- Personality contents need more information
- I felt the journey was **tailored for me**
- Tone of voice is perfect to perceive personality and both onboarding has **friendly approach**
- **Tell me more!** I expected, experience will continue

*Both companion was in line in a way with my personality

Communication

- Emojis are not matching in my imagination. The amount should be reduced
- 2nd onboarding character reactions created more **trustful interaction**, I felt relax
- I felt more **humanized AI** with warm colors. It was not scary.
- Tone of voice matched with the design

Trust

- Privacy, policy part is understandable with categorized informations
- Companion should tell me more about itself to make me more trustful rather than asking to trust

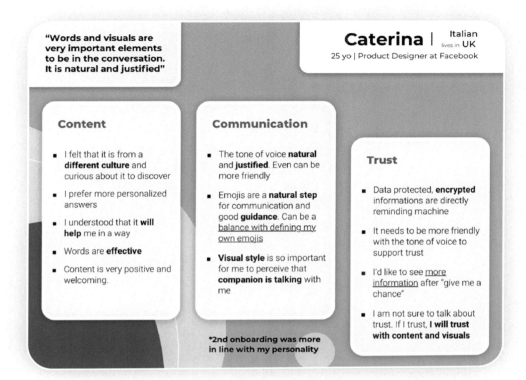

"Words and visuals are very important elements to be in the conversation. It is natural and justified"

Caterina | Italian lives in UK
25 yo | Product Designer at Facebook

Content

- I felt that it is from a **different culture** and curious about it to discover
- I prefer more personalized answers
- I understood that it **will help** me in a way
- Words are **effective**
- Content is very positive and welcoming.

Communication

- The tone of voice **natural and justified**. Even can be more friendly
- Emojis are a **natural step** for communication and good **guidance**. Can be a balance with defining my own emojis
- **Visual style** is so important for me to perceive that **companion is talking** with me

*2nd onboarding was more in line with my personality

Trust

- Data protected, **encrypted** informations are directly reminding machine
- It needs to be more friendly with the tone of voice to support trust
- I'd like to see more information after "give me a chance"
- I am not sure to talk about trust. If I trust, **I will trust with content and visuals**

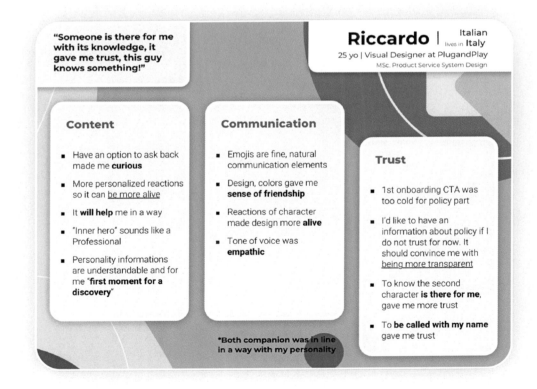

"Someone is there for me with its knowledge, it gave me trust, this guy knows something!"

Riccardo | Italian lives in Italy
25 yo | Visual Designer at PlugandPlay
MSc. Product Service System Design

Content

- Have an option to ask back made me **curious**
- More personalized reactions so it can be more alive
- It **will help** me in a way
- "Inner hero" sounds like a Professional
- Personality informations are understandable and for me "**first moment for a discovery**"

Communication

- Emojis are fine, natural communication elements
- Design, colors gave me **sense of friendship**
- Reactions of character made design more **alive**
- Tone of voice was **empathic**

*Both companion was in line in a way with my personality

Trust

- 1st onboarding CTA was too cold for policy part
- I'd like to have an information about policy if I do not trust for now. It should convince me with being more transparent
- To know the second character **is there for me**, gave me more trust
- To **be called with my name** gave me trust

Ideation of Second Outcomes and the Next Design Implementation

After clustering the data of outcomes from the second iteration, the most desired and suggested implementations and changes were selected to redesign the onboarding to test through the third iteration. (See chapter 7 for detailed information about the design process.) Selected outcomes follow.

Emojis

Emojis were excluded from the flow of the second onboarding and have only been used to welcome users and to describe their emotions. Another screen is inserted in the stream so that users can tell the emojis correlate or have a different meaning than the one shown.

Email

Users were prompted for the first onboarding by asking for an email before beginning the experience. Instead of this, the email was asked at the end of the second onboarding session.

Also, additional information relating to why the email was needed for the journey was described in the second onboarding.

Defining the Personality

In the first experience, the section related to the selection of users' personalities did not change. This was to keep the experience as short and direct as possible.

The second experience was upgraded with an extra page after the selection of the personality. It gave a description from the point of view of the personal companion.

Trust

The exit button was added to leave the app to let users select between trusting the app or leaving the app.

The second onboarding became more explanatory to keep the user inside the journey and showing them a glimpse of what they would find inside the app.

Results of Iteration 3

The third iteration was conducted online by usability testing and a questionnaire. As stated in the previous chapter, the method selected for iteration 3 aimed to give users the chance to be themselves, let them think with their own minds, be independent, and to understand their actions. Eighteen people joined the online usability testing and answered questions. They included seven users from iteration 2 and eleven users from the preexperimental phases of the research. Seven users were selected from those who participated in the previous test phase because they had mastered the application. It is thought that they could provide an opportunity to understand what creates effective and meaningful insights with the applied changes in onboarding.

After brief explanations of the third iteration results, the outcomes of the questionnaire will be graphically explained, the perceived personalities from two onboardings mapped, and user testimonials and feedback that are considered to be effective for the future development phase of the project shared.

The Flow of the Experience

Testing results showed that most users felt more in line with their personalities during the second onboarding experience.

For the definition of the personality, slightly more than half the users stated that the second experience made them more thoughtful about the selection of their personalities.

Most of the users shared their expectations related to digital experiences as being open for discovery rather than being explanatory.

All the users said both onboarding experiences created excitement and aroused a sense of curiosity in them.

Trust

The results showed that most users trusted the companion in both experiences. Only one user of the eighteen trusted neither the first nor the second experience.

For both experiences, some users selected not to trust the companion. They did, however, give the application a chance.

Email

Most users stated that sharing their personal data after having an idea about the journey was more meaningful and promising. The general comments to explain why users preferred sharing their personal information at the end of the journey was because they wanted to first learn more about the application and develop some trust in the product.

Most of the users said they noticed the sharing of email information and said that they chose to share their email addresses. This outcome showed that the inserted descriptive information about why the companion needed user emails helped to create more reliable user experiences. From the results of the second iteration, users' expectations were to know the reason before sharing their personal data.

Emojis as Secondary Visual Elements

Most users stated that the representations of the emotional states through emojis were friendly and familiar, and they represented meanings that matched their imaginations. Reducing the number of emojis and giving users the option to identify the meaning of the represented emoji and whether it matched their expectations was found interesting and familiar.

The results of the third iteration clearly showed that in comparison with the second iteration, emojis supported visual communication and made the design more natural and friendly for users.

Personality

For the first onboarding, which was designed with a more accomplished personality, most of the users defined the personality of the companion as logical, rational, objective, and explanatory.

For the second onboarding, which was designed with a more sincere personality, most users defined the companion's personality as friendly, cheerful, imaginative, and natural.

Which experience did you feel more in line with your personality?
18 users

1. **61.1 %** 1st Experience
2. **38.9 %** 2nd Experience

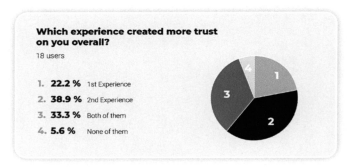

Which experience created more trust on you overall?
18 users

1. **22.2 %** 1st Experience
2. **38.9 %** 2nd Experience
3. **33.3 %** Both of them
4. **5.6 %** None of them

Do you prefer to share your personal information (like email)
18 users

1. **77.8 %** After meeting with the companion (2nd experience)
2. **22.2 %** Before starting to the journey (1st experience)

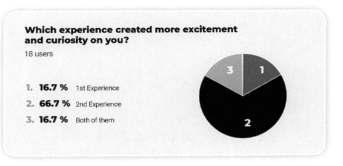

Which experience created more excitement and curiosity on you?
18 users

1. **16.7 %** 1st Experience
2. **66.7 %** 2nd Experience
3. **16.7 %** Both of them

Which experience made you more thoughtful in the selection of your personality?
18 users

1. **33.3 %** 1st Experience
2. **38.9 %** 2nd Experience
3. **27.8 %** Both of them

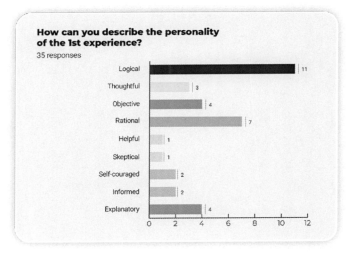

How can you describe the personality of the 1st experience?
35 responses

Personality	Count
Logical	11
Thoughtful	3
Objective	4
Rational	7
Helpful	1
Skeptical	1
Self-couraged	2
Informed	2
Explanatory	4

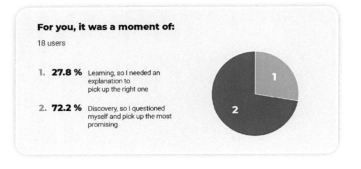

For you, it was a moment of:
18 users

1. **27.8 %** Learning, so I needed an explanation to pick up the right one
2. **72.2 %** Discovery, so I questioned myself and pick up the most promising

When companion asked you in the 1st experience: "Do you trust me? What did you select:
18 users

1. **72.2 %** Yes, for now
2. **27.8 %** No, not yet

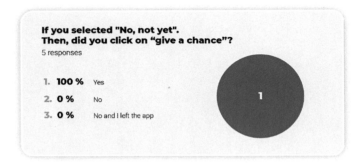

**If you selected "No, not yet".
Then, did you click on "give a chance"?**
5 responses

1. **100 %** Yes
2. **0 %** No
3. **0 %** No and I left the app

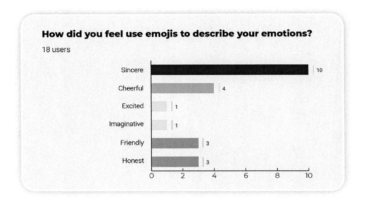

How did you feel use emojis to describe your emotions?
18 users

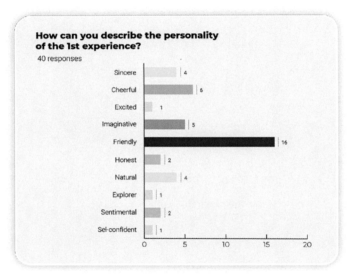

How can you describe the personality of the 1st experience?
40 responses

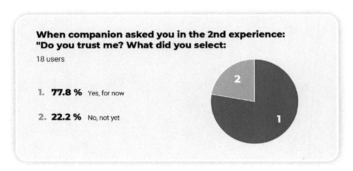

When companion asked you in the 2nd experience: "Do you trust me? What did you select:
18 users

1. **77.8 %** Yes, for now
2. **22.2 %** No, not yet

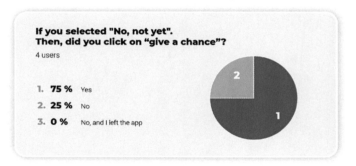

**If you selected "No, not yet".
Then, did you click on "give a chance"?**
4 users

1. **75 %** Yes
2. **25 %** No
3. **0 %** No, and I left the app

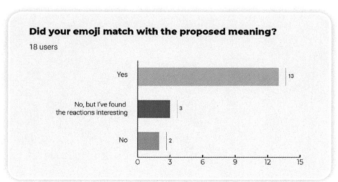

Did your emoji match with the proposed meaning?
18 users

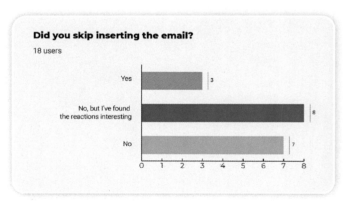

Did you skip inserting the email?
18 users

Takeaways

This chapter explained how findings of the usability testing performed in determining the outcomes of personality tests. The results of the user experience assessment were discussed after analyzing the design iteration processes and survey and questionnaire outcomes.

Discussion
Conclusion
Future Research
End Note
Testimonials

Discussion

The aim of the experiment was to understand the effect of implementing two personalities into onboarding processes and assess the sense of trust built thanks to that.

Limits of the test must be considered. They include the usability of the prototype itself (e.g., inserting the name and email properly); the implementation of a limited spectrum of personality compared to the total archetypes of Aaker's and Jung's personality models; and iterations were run in a limited batch of almost homogeneous users from the target addressed by the application.

Friction nowadays is one of the main parameters that every UX/UI designer and business look to reduce in their customers' journeys. Following are some examples.

- "The onboarding should be as quick as possible." Both experiences were actually longer and slower to read compared to what best practice says. Anyway, higher engagement is perceived until the point when many users start to go back and forth in the application to discover how the companion would answer if they chose a different option.
- "Push the users to sign up and lead them to use the app as fast as possible." Instead, all the prototypes were built in order to create first a sense of trust and preexperience of the application. In the last phase, the onboarding process was moved to ask users for their personal information in order to subscribe to the service. Considering only the third iteration, almost 80 percent of the users were happy to insert their data after their first meeting with the companion. The first and second iterations reinforced this value. In the second experience, 60 percent of the users realized they could skip the email insertion; approximately 15 percent consciously did so. Even so, they were willing to try the app. About 45 percent of the total consciously decided to sign up based on the reason behind the request.
- "Avoid designing clear exit points from your app." After building an initial relationship between the user and companion, even with a button clearly evident that would lead the user to close the app and leave the journey, only one user in one of the experiences used it. This probably happened because of a curiosity to discover what was happening in the app. This means two onboardings created a correct sense of discovery that intrigued users to the offer of the service. This data can be misleading because the testers did not feel the app. On the other hand, there was no reward until the end of the application.
- "Make sure that the user knows when he or she signs the terms and conditions." In both experiences, there was a step dedicated to trust. The aim of this step was asking users to trust the companion in terms of relationship, policy, privacy, and data usage. This was

to build the maximum sense of transparency and legitimize the initial emotional bond. Instead of limiting the practice to checking a box, onboarding drove the users to explore their rights and feel aware and connected to the companion.

This strategy led to positive results, showing how a better sense of trust is needed for optimal service experience. Trust is one of the pillars in creating empathic relationships that must be in the core of the emotional design.

Self-Identification

The aim of the experiment was to test the implementation of multiple personalities. The last iteration showed that 60 percent of the users identified themselves more closely to the second experience; 40 percent of the users identified themselves more closely to the first experience. After the second iteration, it was expected that the gap between the two values would be higher. Anyway, in the previous phases, users were never pushed to select or associate themselves with one of the experiences. The data of the third iteration was surprising because it showed the two processes, similar only in the information architecture, were almost equally appreciated.

Building Trust

Another interesting final outcome was connected to the fact that the two personalities were equally perceived as trustworthy. Even so, they differed in features and visual communication. This is another proof that building empathic and tailored experiences with two personalities can be a striking feature to implement in the design industry.

At the end of three iterations, and after completing the experiment, the result clearly confirmed the hypothesis. The outcomes suggest that the implementation of these theories is crucial to developing trust in digital products for the future of transparency and emotional connection, especially considering AI capabilities.

Conclusion

The aim of this book was to understand how AI can shape user experiences by creating emotional and empathic relationships. The hypothesis showed that complexity in design is changing with the number of actors and objects, and this affects the human experience. Also, the focus on the interaction with a digital product improves and extends the usability and makes it more engageable and pleasant. Since all the focus is on designing quick and efficient products and experiences, the missing part appeared to be empathetic and emotional relationships with products. Especially with the inclusion of AI in our lives, technology started to take shape as a tool to help individuals on a daily basis. The use of AI increased, but the sense of trust remained almost missing, and it damaged human-machine interactions in building trustful and emotional connections.

The general purpose of the book was to explore the scenario of AI meeting with empathy and emotions and to investigate the effects of AI on trust in user experience. During the research, effects of empathy were analyzed in psychological, cognitive, and social constructions to explain a variety of psychological events, including motivation and personality.

With this intention, the topic narrowed to be able to test a part of the hypothesis with designing empathetic onboarding experiences as a first meeting moment with a new digital companion (or person). To create a trustful and empathic relationship, various communication signals were used: tone of voice, visuals, and personalities for understanding how individuals' behaviors were changing, adapting to the different points of view and experiencing emotions thanks to emotional interactions. These variables were tested through empathic onboarding experiences in order to adapt these changes into the user experiences and making them more personalized, so AI will be able to create tailored, personalized user journeys and build empathetic companionships with virtual assistants.

The testing phase of the experiment was divided into the main part as pre- and true-experimental phases. During the preexperimental phase, user data was collected and used to design onboardings' personalities and interactions. The true-experimental phase was conducted with three iteration sessions that tested the usability of the onboarding prototypes. Two onboarding experiences reversed the basic UX/UI design practices to prove how a better sense of trust is necessary for optimal service experiences. Even if these two onboardings were designed with different personalities, a different tone of voices, and visual styles, the aim was the same. It has been tested with three iterations of onboarding designs to perceive different trust effects on users to create curiosity in having a chance to build trustful interactions. Iterations' results showed that the two onboardings created almost equal trust in the testers.

The second experience found more excitement and increased user curiosity about the real product and the next phase of the journey. It was also found to be more in line with user personalities. In terms of implemented personality traits, they were easily perceived by users to identify companions' characteristics and define a position to them for establishing relationships. Results also showed that the reversed design effect was powerful in creating a sense of trust, and they did not identify any problems related to efficiency and effectiveness of the experience.

Finally, the findings from the third iteration found that the effect on user experience was significantly improved of empathetic companions compared to virtual assistants in terms of building trustful relationships through digital experiences.

Hopefully this research will generate unusual perspectives that will leading to a new path in user experience and open more thoughtful scenarios to discovering the potentials of AI.

Future Research

For future research, the different archetypes and personality traits should be implemented into other onboarding experiences. These onboardings should be tested by implementing personality frameworks to create variability and to understand the personality effects necessary to build trust. Thus, onboarding processes will have a chance to reshape user experiences according to different collected outcomes by gathering the data and learning from the user processes.

Another interesting topic was discovered concerning the redesigning of the policy and privacy terms and conditions. This part of the application was found remarkable as it drew users' attention to the sensitivity of the subject and the need to explain it more transparently. Most of the users' feedback was based on redesigning this part in a more interactive way and supporting it with visuals to make it more descriptive, understandable, and most important, make it more engageable. With these considerations, the privacy, policy, and data protection parts of digital products can be open for discovery.

More research can be related to reshaping all onboarding experiences by combining different interactions, like voice-over or haptic feedback. Speech recognition and background audio can be useful to understand how and where users interact with the app and to shape onboarding experiences in a more engageable way to build trust in their first meetings with the companion.

An aspect of the research that was little considered in regarding how users perceived the digital products or embedded virtual assistants in their imagination was the visual design. Onboarding can be tested with an avatar or a character, in contrast to the abstract character designed for this experiment. Visual design can be more dynamic as well as be supported with motion design and microinteractions to test the effects of users in terms of engagement.

Zooming out from all these deep, possible research topics, I would like to highlight the potential of AI, which has a chance to be improved by implementing design methodologies and with values of empathetic and emotional interactions to build more trustful, lifelong companionships with digital products.

End Note

I know that this was a long ride and one of the hardest topics to read.

If you have managed to read the whole book, I am more than happy to share my experience on this journey together with you.

Changing the design perspective and bringing new approaches help us to understand design complexity and enable us to simplify it. Design explorations can lead us to build new design solutions to serve users by designing better user experiences. This can give value and courage to people beyond expected ways by providing meaningful emotions and functions to express ourselves.

Different perspectives on understanding emotional intelligence through empathetic companions will help people, who are interested in designing new experiences, products, or services with artificial intelligence, to design tailored and personalized interactions with digital products and services by avoiding the emotional loop for each individual who has different personalities and emotional responses.

I know that it might be difficult to follow behavioral and cognitive design requirements to build a relationship with digital products while creating emotional experiences in the core of design and development systems. However, I believe that this book will help you to think from a different perspective to work with AI and establish best practices to design empathetic AI experiences.

With love,
Cansu.

Testimonials

After the third iteration, users shared their insights about their onboarding experiences. Following is a collection of quotes directly from their survey results, clustered based on relevant topics.

Which experience was more in line with your personality?

Which experience made you more thoughtful in the selection of personality?

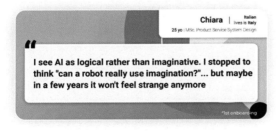

Which experience created more trust in you?

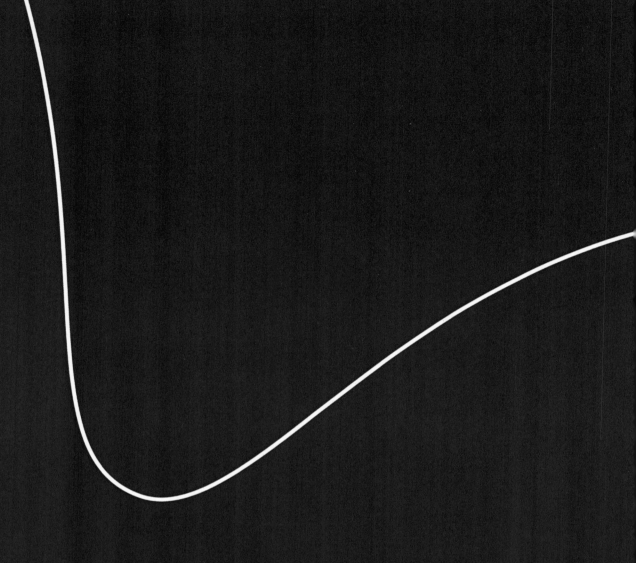

References

Journals

Books

Blog Posts

Online Magazines

Online Resources

Interviews

Archive Papers

Conference Proceedings

Reports

Online Images and Videos

References

Journals

Aaker, J. (1997). Dimensions of brand personality. *Journal of Marketing Research*, 34(3), pp. 347–356.

Aranguren, M. (2016). Reconstructing the social constructionist view of emotions: from language to culture, including nonhuman culture. *Journal for the Theory of Social Behavior*, 47(2), pp. 244–260.

Asada, M. (2015). Development of artificial empathy. *Neuroscience Research*, 90, pp. 41–50.

Barnett, M. A., and McCoy, S. J. (1989). The relation of distressful childhood experiences and empathy in college undergraduates. *The Journal of Genetic Psychology; Child Behavior, Animal Behavior, and Comparative Psychology*, 150(4), pp. 417–426.

Bar-On, R. (2006). The Bar-On model of emotional-social intelligence (ESI). *Psicothema*, 18, supl., pp. 13–25.

Barrett, L., Mesquita, B., Ochsner, K., and Gross, J. (2007). The experience of emotion. *Annual Review of Psychology*, 58(1), pp. 373–403.

Bradshaw, J. W. S. Social interaction between pets and people—a new biological framework. Paper presented at the 7th International Conference on Human-Animal Interactions. Geneva, Switzerland (September 6–9, 1995).

Brickel, C. M. (1986). Pet-facilitated therapies: A review of the literature and clinical implementation considerations. *Clinical Gerontology* (5), pp. 309–332.

Brockman, B., Taylor, V., and Brockman, C. (2008). The price of unconditional love: Consumer decision making for high-dollar veterinary care. *Journal of Business Research*, 61(5), pp. 397–405.

Callon, M. (2001). Actor-network theory. *International Encyclopedia of the Social & Behavioral Sciences*, pp. 62–66.

Cannon, W. (1987). The James-Lange theory of emotions: A critical examination and an alternative theory. *The American Journal of Psychology*, 100(3/4), p. 567.

———. (1927). The James-Lange theory of emotions: A critical examination and an alternation. *The American Journal of Psychology*, 39, pp. 106–124.

Caspi, A. (2000). The child is the father of the man: Personality continuities from childhood to adulthood. *Journal of Personality and Social Psychology*, 78(1), pp. 158–172.

Celeghin, A., Diano, M., Bagnis, A., Viola, M., and Tamietto, M. (2017). Basic emotions in human neuroscience: Neuroimaging and beyond. *Frontiers in Psychology*, 8.

Deci, E., and Ryan, R. (2008). Self-determination theory: A macro theory of human motivation, development, and health. *Canadian Psychology/Psychologie Canadienne*, 49(3), pp. 182–185.

Dotson, M., and Hyatt, E. (2008). Understanding dog-human companionship. *Journal of Business Research*, 61(5), pp. 457–466.

Engeström, Y. (1995). Objects, contradictions, and collaboration in medical cognition: An activity-theoretical perspective. *Artificial Intelligence in Medicine*, 7, pp. 395–412.

Erder, M., and Pureur, P. (2016). Role of the architect. *Continuous Architecture*, pp. 187–213.

Fan, L., Scheutz, M., Lohani, M., McCoy, M., and Stokes, C. (2017). Do we need emotionally intelligent artificial agents? First results of human perceptions of emotional intelligence in humans compared to robots. *Intelligent Virtual Agents*, pp. 129–141.

Fareri, D., Niznikiewicz, M., Lee, V., and Delgado, M. (2012). Social network modulation of reward-related signals. *Journal of Neuroscience*, 32(26), pp. 9045–9052.

Friedman, B. (2010). Feelings and the body: The Jamesian perspective on autonomic specificity of emotion. *Biological Psychology*, 84(3), pp. 383–393.

Garcia, D. M. P., Lopez, S. S., and Donis, H. (2018). Voice-activated virtual assistants personality perceptions and desires: comparing personality evaluation frameworks. *Electronic Workshops in Computing*, pp. 1–10.

Gilbert, P. (1998). The evolved basis and adaptive functions of cognitive distortions. *British Journal of Medical Psychology*, 71(4), pp. 447–463.

Gill, L., Ramsey, P., and Leberman, S. (2015). A systems approach to developing emotional intelligence using the self-awareness engine of growth model. *Systemic Practice & Action Research*, 28(6), pp. 575–594.

Gong, L. (2008). How social is social responses to computers? The function of the degree of anthropomorphism in computer representations. *Computers in Human Behavior*, 24(4), pp. 1494–1509.

Gonzalez-Liencresa, C., Shamay-Tsoory, S. G., Brünea, M. (2013). Towards a neuroscience of empathy: Ontogeny, phylogeny, brain mechanisms, context and psychopathology. *Neuroscience Biobehavior*, 37, pp. 1537–1548.

Gratch, J., and Marsella, S. (2004). A domain-independent framework for modeling emotion. *Cognitive Systems Research*, 5(4), pp. 269–306.

Gray, K., and Wegner, D. M. (2009). Moral typecasting: Divergent perceptions of moral agents and moral patients. *Journal of Personality and Social Psychology*, 96(3), pp. 505–520.

Gross, J., and Feldman Barrett, L. (2011). Emotion generation and emotion regulation: One or two depends on your point of view. *Emotion Review*, 3(1), pp. 8–16.

Hess, U., and Thibault, P. (2009). Darwin and emotion expression. *American Psychologist*, 64(2), pp. 120–128.

Hoffman, M. L. (1977). Sex differences in empathy and related behaviours. *Psychological Bulletin*, 84, pp. 712–722.

———. (1990). Empathy and justice motivation. *Motivation and Emotion*, 14, pp. 151–172.

James, W. (1884). What is emotion? *Mind*, 9(34), pp. 188–205.

Jeannerod, M., and Frank, V. (1999). Mental imaging of motor activity in humans. *Current Opinion in Neurobiology*, 9(6), pp. 735–739.

Jessen, J., and Jessen, C. (2014). Games as actors—interaction, play, design, and Actor-Network theory. *International Journal on Advances in Intelligent Systems*, 7(3–4), pp. 412–422.

Keen, S. (2006). A theory of narrative empathy. *Narrative*, 14(3), pp. 207–236.

Lamm, C., Decety, J., and Singer, T. (2011). Meta-analytic evidence for common and distinct neural networks associated with directly experienced pain and empathy for pain. *NeuroImage*, 54(3), pp. 2492–2502.

Legree, P., Psotka, J., Robbins, J., Roberts, R., Putka, D., and Mullins, H. (2014). Profile similarity metrics as an alternate framework to score rating-based tests: MSCEIT teanalyses. *Intelligence*, 47, pp. 159–174.

Lopes, P., Salovey, P., and Straus, R. (2003). Emotional intelligence, personality, and the perceived quality of social relationships. *Personality and Individual Differences*, 35(3), pp. 641–658.

———. (2003). Emotional intelligence, personality, and the perceived quality of social relationships. *Personality and Individual Differences*, 35(3), pp. 641–658.

Louwerse, M., and Kuiken, D. (2004). The effects of personal involvement in narrative discourse. *Discourse Processes*, 38(2), pp. 169–172.

Mayer, J., Caruso, D., and Salovey, P. (2016). The ability model of emotional intelligence: Principles and updates. *Emotion Review*, 8(4), pp. 290–300.

Mayer, J. (2009). Personal intelligence expressed: A theoretical analysis. *Review of General Psychology*, 13(1), pp. 46–58.

Mayer, J., and Salovey, P. (1993). The intelligence of emotional intelligence. *Intelligence*, 17(4), pp. 433–442.

Mayer, J. D., Salovey, P., and Caruso, D. R. (2004). Emotional intelligence: Theory, findings and implications. *Psychological Inquiry*, 15, pp. 197–215.

McClelland, J. L., and Rumelhart, D. E. (1985). Distributed memory and the representation of general and specific information. *Journal of Experimental Psychology: General*, 114(2), pp. 159–188.

McDowell, Z., and Gunkel, D. (2016). Introduction to "Machine Communication." *Communication +1*, 5(1), pp. 1–5.

McQuiggan, S., and Lester, J. (2007). Modeling and evaluating empathy in embodied companion agents. *International Journal of Human-Computer Studies*, 65(4), pp. 348–360.

Mischel, W., and Shoda, Y. (1995). A cognitive-affective system theory of personality: Reconceptualizing situations, dispositions, dynamics, and invariance in personality structure. *Psychological Review*, 102(2), pp. 246–268.

Miyahara, K. (2011). Neo-pragmatic intentionality and enactive perception: A compromise between extended and enactive minds. *Phenomenology and the Cognitive Sciences*, 10(4), pp. 499–519.

Mou, Y., and Xu, K. (2017). The media inequality: Comparing the initial human-human and human-AI social interactions. *Computers in Human Behavior*, 72, pp. 432–440.

Oatley, K. (1995). A taxonomy of the emotions of literary response and theory of identification in a fictional narrative. *Poetics*, 23(1–2), pp. 53–74.

Ortony, A., and Turner, T. (1990). What's basic about basic emotions? *Psychological Review*, 97(3), pp. 315–331.

Park, B. (1986). A method for studying the development of impressions of real people. *Journal of Personality and Social Psychology*, 51(5), pp. 907–917.

Penney, A., Miedema, V., and Mazmanian, D. (2015). Intelligence and emotional disorders: Is the worrying and ruminating mind a more intelligent mind? *Personality and Individual Differences*, 74, pp. 90–93.

Preston, S. D. (2007). A perception-action model for empathy. In T. Farrow & P. Woodruff (Eds.) *Empathy in Mental Illness*, pp. 428–447.

Preston, S. D., & de Waal, F. B. M. (2002). The Communication of Emotions and the Possibility of Empathy in Animals. *Altruism and Altruistic LoveScience, Philosophy, and Religion in Dialogue*, pp. 284–308.

Pudane, M., Lavendelis, E., and Radin, M. (2017). Human emotional behavior simulation in intelligent agents: Processes and architecture. *Procedia Computer Science*, 104, pp. 517–524.

Riek, L. D., and Robinson, P. (2009). Affective-centered design for interactive robots. In *Proceedings of the AISB Symposium on New Frontiers in Human-Robot Interaction*, pp. 102–108.

Schachter, S., and Singer, J. (1962). Cognitive, social, and physiological determinants of emotional state. *Psychological Review*, 69(5), pp. 379–399.

Shank, D., Graves, C., Gott, A., Gamez, P., and Rodriguez, S. (2019). Feeling our way to machine minds: People's emotions when perceiving mind in artificial intelligence. *Computers in Human Behavior*, 98, pp. 256–266.

Shariff, A., and Tracy, J. (2011). What are emotion expressions for? *Current Directions in Psychological Science*, 20(6), pp. 395–399.

Tooby, J., & Cosmides, L. (1990). The past explains the present. *Ethology and Sociobiology*, 11(4–5), pp. 375–424.

Van Noorden, T., Haselager, G., Cillessen, A., and Bukowski, W. (2015). Empathy and involvement in bullying in children and adolescents: A systematic review. *Journal of Youth and Adolescence*, 44(3), pp. 637–657.

Ward, A., Olsen, A., and Wegner, D. (2013). The harm-made mind. *Psychological Science*, 24(8), pp. 1437–1445.

Waytz, A., Morewedge, C. K., Epley, N., Monteleone, G., Gao, J.-H., and Cacioppo, J. T. (2010). Making sense by making sentient: Effectance motivation increases anthropomorphism. *Journal of Personality and Social Psychology*, 99(3), 410–435.

Yalcin, Ö., and DiPaola, S. (2018). A computational model of empathy for interactive agents. *Biologically Inspired Cognitive Architectures*, 26, pp. 20–25.

Books

Averill, J. (1982). *Anger and Aggression*. New York: Springer-Verlag.

———. (1985). *The Social Construction of Emotion: With Special Reference to Love*. The Social Construction of the Person, pp. 89–109.

———. (1991). *Emotions as episodic dispositions, cognitive schemas, and transitory social roles: Steps toward an integrated theory of emotion*. In D. Ozer, J. M. Healy, Jr., & A. J. Stewart (Eds.), Perspectives in personality (Vol. 3a, pp. 139–167). London: Jessica Kingsley Publishers.

Barrett, L., and Russell, J. (2015). *The Psychological Construction of Emotion*. New York: The Guilford Press.

Bodegraven, J. (2019). AI-driven design. In: J. Bodegraven, ed., *Artificial Intelligence-Driven Design*. awwwards. Available at https://www.awwwards.com/AI-driven-design (accessed November 19, 2019).

Bodegraven, J., and Marques, P. (2019). Training AI with design. In: J. Bodegraven, ed., *Artificial Intelligence-Driven Design*. awwwards. Available at https://www.awwwards.com/AI-driven-design (accessed November 19, 2019).

Bortolussi, M., and Dixon, P. (2003). *Psychonarratology*. Cambridge: Cambridge University Press.

Covey, S. (2004). *The 7 Habits of Highly Effective People*. New York: Free Press.

Damasio, A. (2004). *Descartes' Error*. New York: Quill.

Dantzer R. (1989). *The Psychosomatic Delusion*. New York, The Free Press.

Darwin, C. A. (1872). *The Expression of the Emotions in Man and Animals*. London: John Murray.

Derntl, B., and Regenbogen, C. (2014). Empathy. In: P. Lysaker, G. Dimaggio, and M. Brüne, eds., *Social Cognition and Metacognition in Schizophrenia*, 1st ed. Academic Press, pp. 69–81. Available at https://www.sciencedirect.com/science/article/pii/B9780124051720000041 (accessed October 8, 2019).

Detel, W. (2001). Social constructivism. *International Encyclopedia of the Social & Behavioral Sciences*, pp. 14264–14267.

Epstein, S. (1977). Traits are alive and well. In: D. Magnusson and N. S. Endler, eds., *Personality at the Crossroads*. Hillsdale, NJ: Lawrence Erlbaum, pp. 83–98.

Eyal, N., and Hoover, R. (2014). *Hooked*. 1st ed. Portfolio.

Feist, J., and Feist, G. (2008). *Theories of Personality*, 7th ed. New York: McGraw-Hill Primis.

Frijda, N. (1986). *The Emotions*. Cambridge: Cambridge University Press.

Gardner, H. (1983). *Frames of Mind*. New York: Basic Books.

Gergen, K. J., and Davis, K. E. (2011). *The Social Construction of the Person* (Springer Series in Social Psychology) (Softcover reprint of the original 1st ed. 1985 ed.), Springer.

Gordon, S. L. (1990). Social structural effects on emotions. In T. D. Kemper, ed., *Research Agendas in the Sociology of Emotions*. Albany: State University of New York Press, pp. 145–179.

Hoffman, M. L. (2000). *Empathy and Moral Development*. Empathy and Moral Development: Implications for Caring and Justice.

Hurlburt (eds.). *Altruism and Altruistic Love: Science, Philosophy, and Religion in Dialogue*. Oxford: Oxford University Press, pp. 284–308.

Et, S. (1991). *Perspectives in Personality*. Vol. 3 (2nd ed.), Jessica Kingsley Publishers.

Jung, C. (1976). *Psychological Types*. Princeton, NJ: Princeton University Press.

Kaptelinin, V., and Nardi, B. (2006). *Acting with Technology*. Cambridge, MA: MIT Press.

Lee, V. (1913). *The Beautiful: An Introduction to Psychological Aesthetics*. Cambridge: Cambridge University Press.

Myers, I., and Myers, P. (1980). *Gifts Differing: Understanding Personality Type*. Mountain View, CA: CPP.

Norman, D. (2004). *Emotional Design: Why We Love (Or Hate) Everyday Things*. New York: Basic Books.

———. (2013). *The Design of Everyday Things: Revised and Expanded Edition*. New York: Basic Books.

Nowotny, H. (2016). *The Cunning of Uncertainty*. Malden, MA: Polity.

Oatley K. (1994). Emotion. In: M. W. Eysenck, ed., *The Blackwell Dictionary of Cognitive Psychology*. Oxford, Blackwell, pp. 129–134.

Salovey, P., and Sluyter, D. (2001). *Emotional Development and Emotional Intelligence*. New York: Basic Books.

Sartre, J. (2001). *Sketch for a Theory of the Emotions*, 2nd ed. London: Routledge Classics.

Scarr, S. W. (1989). *Protecting general intelligence: Constructs and consequences for interventions.* In R. L. Linn (Ed.), Intelligence: Measurement, theory, and public policy: Proceedings of a symposium in honor of Lloyd G. Humphreys, pp. 74–118. University of Illinois Press.

Segal, E., Gerdes, K., Lietz, C., Wagaman, M., and Geiger, J. (2017). *Assessing Empathy.* New York: Columbia University Press.

Titchener, E. (1915). *Beginners Psychology.* New York: Macmillan.

Wang, C., and Salmon, C. (2006). *The Handbook of Jungian Psychology.* London: Routledge.

Blog Posts

Chou, J., Murillo, O., and Ibars, R. (2017). How to recognize exclusion in AI. *Medium.* Available at https://medium.com/microsoft-design/how-to-recognize-exclusion-in-ai-ec2d6d89f850 (accessed November 2019).

Discovering Maslo: Bringing AI to life (2019). *Medium.* Available at https://medium.com/maslo/discovering-malso-bringing-ai-to-life-317156d9097a (accessed November 20, 2019).

Foltz-Smith, R. (2019). Inside the growth of a computational being. *Medium.* Available at https://medium.com/maslo/inside-the-growth-of-a-computational-being-28d61e7124db (accessed November 19, 2019).

Foltz-Smith, R. (2019). Self-creating, self-expressing and self-explaining AI. *Medium.* Available at https://medium.com/maslo/self-creating-self-expressing-and-self-explaining-ai-3d3fbe0e66a9 (accessed September 22, 2019).

Holbrook, J. (2017). Human-centered machine learning. *Medium.* Available at https://medium.com/google-design/human-centered-machine-learning-a770d10562cd (accessed November 25, 2019).

Nicholas, E. (2017). Microsoft Bob gets the last laugh. *Medium.* Available at https://medium.com/s/user-friendly/the-adventures-of-microsoft-bob-metaphor-design-84e41 1784894 (accessed September 16, 2019).

Veer, B. (2017). SXSW—Sophie Kleber: Designing emotionally intelligent machines, aFrogleap: Digital Innovation Agency. *aFrogleap: Digital Innovation Agency.* Available at https://afrogleap.com/blog/innovation/sxsw-sophie-kleber-designing-emotionally-intelligent-machines (accessed November 28, 2019).

Online Magazines

Camp, J. (2019). My Jibo is dying and it's breaking my heart. *Wired*. Available at https://www.wired.com/story/jibo-is-dying-eulogy/ (accessed November 19, 2019).

Carman, A. (2019). They welcomed a robot into their family, now they are mourning its death: The story of Jibo. *The Verge*. Available at https://www.theverge.com/2019/6/19/18682780/jibo-death-server-update-social-robot-mourning (accessed November 19, 2019).

Devine, R. (2019). Exclusive interview with Brené Brown: "Failure is part of the ride." *CEO Magazine*. Available at https://www.theceomagazine.com/lifestyle/interview/brene-brown/ (accessed September 24, 2019).

Harvard Business Review. (2004). Leading by feel. Available at https://hbr.org/2004/01/leading-by-feel (accessed September 25, 2019).

Hitti, N. (2019). Google offers "scientific proof that design is important 'with A Space for Being.'" *Dezeen*. Available at https://www.dezeen.com/2019/04/10/google-milan-design-week-a-space-for-being-installation-neuroaesthetic-design/ (accessed November 20, 2019).

It's a riot: The stressful AI simulation built to understand your emotions. (2017). *The Guardian*. Available at https://www.theguardian.com/science/blog/2017/mar/29/its-a-riot-the-stressful-ai-simulation-built-to-understand-your-emotions (accessed November 20, 2019).

Li, J., Galley, M., Brockett, C., Spithourakis, G.P., Gao, J. and Dolan, B. (2016) A Persona-Based Neural Conversation Model. *arXiv preprint arXiv:1603.06155*. https://arxiv.org/pdf/1603.06155.pdf (accessed November 19, 2019).

Marr, B. (2018). How much data do we create every day? The mind-blowing stats everyone should read. *Forbes*. Available at https://www.forbes.com/sites/bernardmarr/2018/05/21/how-much-data-do-we-create-every-day-the-mind-blowing-stats-everyone-should-read/#71be2d3760ba (accessed November 19, 2019).

Pakhchyan, S. (2019). From design thinking to emotional thinking: Designing products with E.Q. *Fast Company*. Available at https://www.fastcompany.com/90300071/from-design-thinking-to-emotional-thinking-designing-products-with-e-q?partner=rss&utm_source=rss&utm_medium=feed&utm_campaign=rss+fastcompany&utm_content=rss?cid=search (accessed November 12, 2019).

Perez, S. (2018). Smart speakers hit critical mass in 2018. *TechCrunch*. Available at https://techcrunch.com/2018/12/28/smart-speakers-hit-critical-mass-in-2018/ (accessed November 25, 2019).

Scarano, A. (2019). Google invites you to feel more. *Domus*. Available at https://www.domusweb.it/en/events/salone-del-mobile/Salone-Interviews/2019/google-invites-you-to-feel-more-and-to-be-conscious-about-it.html (accessed November 20, 2019).

Waal, F. (2005). The evolution of empathy. *Greater Good Magazine*. Available at https://greatergood.berkeley.edu/article/item/the_evolution_of_empathy (accessed October 6, 2019).

What Is Empathy? (2019). *Greater Good Magazine*. Available at https://greatergood.berkeley.edu/topic/empathy/definition (accessed October 6, 2019).

Online Resources

Affinity in Autonomy. (2019). *Affinity in Autonomy*. Available at https://www.sonydesign.com/en/Affinity_in_Autonomy/ (accessed November 18, 2019).

Anyways. (2019). Adventurous and meaningful creativity for brands. Available at https://www.anyways.co/projects/adobe-creative-types (accessed November 23, 2019).

American Pet Association. (2019). Changing the way America cares for its pets. Available at http://apapets.org/ (accessed September 16, 2019).

Chaplin, C. (1940). Charlie Chaplin: The final speech from the Great Dictator. *Charlie Chaplin*. Available at https://www.charliechaplin.com/en/articles/29-the-final-speech-from-the-great-dictator- (accessed November 26, 2019).

Cherry, K. (2019). Myers-Briggs Type Indicator: The 16 personality types. *Verywell Mind*. Available at https://www.verywellmind.com/the-myers-briggs-type-indicator-2795583 (accessed October 21, 2019).

Cherry, K. (2019). The Two-Factor theory explains the key components of emotions. *Verywell Mind*. Available at https://www.verywellmind.com/the-two-factor-theory-of-emotion-2795718 (accessed September 30, 2019).

Creative Types by Adobe Create. (2019). Available at https://mycreativetype.com (accessed October 21, 2019).

Darcy, A., Robinson, A., and Ng, A. (2019). Woebot: Your charming robot friend who is here for you, 24/7. *Woebot.io*. Available at https://woebot.io/the-science (accessed November 12, 2019).

Domo. (2018). Data never sleeps. Available at https://www.domo.com/assets/downloads/18_domo_data-never-sleeps-6+verticals.pdf (accessed November 19, 2019).

Dream Journal.maslo (2019). Maslo. Available at https://dreamjournal.maslo.ai/ (accessed November 20, 2019).

Executive Partnerships. (2017). Emotional intelligence—Why is it a vital skill for assistants? *Executive Partnerships*. Available at https://www.executivepartnerships.co.uk/emotional-intelligence-vital-skill-assistants/ (accessed September 25, 2019).

Fogg, B. (2019). Fogg Behaviour model: What causes behavior change? *Behavior Model.org*. Available at https://www.behaviormodel.org/ (accessed October 22, 2019).

Heyolly. (2019). Olly | The world's first personal robot with personality. Available at https://heyolly.com/ (accessed November 19, 2019).

Indiegogo. (2017). Olly | The first home robot with personality. Available at https://www.indiegogo.com/projects/olly-the-first-home-robot-with-personality#/ (accessed November 19, 2019).

InformationWeek. (2019). AI challenge: Achieving artificial empathy. *InformationWeek*. Available at https://www.informationweek.com/big-data/ai-machine-learning/ai-challenge-achieving-artificial-empathy/a/d-id/1331628 (accessed September 16, 2019).

Ko, A. (nd). User Interface Software and Technology, chapter 2. *Creative Commons Attribution-NoDerivatives 4.0 International License*. Available at https://faculty.washington.edu/ajko/books/uist/theory.html (accessed September 23. 2019).

Lesley.edu. (2019). The psychology of emotional and cognitive empathy. *Lesley University*. Available at https://lesley.edu/article/the-psychology-of-emotional-and-cognitive-empathy (accessed September 16, 2019).

Marketingjournal.org. (2016). Book Review: *"Hooked: How to Build Habit-Forming Products* by Nir Eyal. Available at http://www.marketingjournal.org/book-review-hooked-how-to-build-habit-forming-products-by-nir-eyal/ (accessed October 22, 2019).

Mcleod, S. (2019). Maslow's hierarchy of needs. *Simply Psychology*. Available at https://www.simplypsychology.org/maslow.html (accessed September 20, 2019).

Myersbriggs.org (nd). All types are equal. *The Myers & Briggs Foundation*. Available at https://www.myersbriggs.org/my-mbti-personality-type/mbti-basics/all-types-are-equal.htm (accessed October 21, 2019).

Nielsen, J. (2000). Why you only need to test with 5 users. *Nielsen Norman Group*. Available at https://www.nngroup.com/articles/why-you-only-need-to-test-with-5-users/ (accessed November 17, 2019).

Olson, C., & Kemery, K. (2019). Voice report. From answers to action: customer adoption of voice technology and digital assistants. *Microsoft*. Available at https://advertiseonbing-blob.azureedge.net/blob/bingads/media/insight/whitepapers/2019/04%20apr/voice-report/bingads_2019_voicereport.pdf (accessed September 20, 2019)

Palmer, K. (2019). RIOT AI—Storyteller from the Future. *Karenpalmer*. Available at http://karenpalmer.uk/portfolio/riot/ (accessed November 20, 2019).

Riopel, L. (2019). The theories of emotional intelligence explained. *PositivePsychology*. Available at https://positivepsychology.com/emotional-intelligence-frameworks/ (accessed September 25, 2019).

Saarikivi, K. (2016). *Empathy in the Digital Age*. [video] Available at https://www.youtube.com/watch?v=gzhkn9BnRmU (accessed October 8, 2019).

Toxboe, A. (2019). Making the Hook model actionable. *UI Patterns*. Available at http://ui-patterns.com/blog/making-the-hook-model-actionable (Accessed October 21, 2019).

Waal, F. (2009). The age of empathy. Available at http://www.emory.edu/LIVING_LINKS/empathy/faq.html (Accessed October 6, 2019 Oct. 2019).

Whitenton, K. (2018). The two UX gulfs: Evaluation and Eexecution. Human-computer interaction. Available at https://www.nngroup.com/articles/two-ux-gulfs-evaluation-execution/ (accessed March 11, 2018).

Interviews

Antonelli, P. (February 8, 2018). Interviewed by PAIR for *AI Is Design's Latest Material*. Available at https://design.google/library/ai-designs-latest-material/ (accessed November 18, 2019).

Averill, J. (July 2017). Interviewed by Andrea Scarantino for *The Social Construction of Emotion: Myths and Realities*. Available at https://emotionresearcher.com/the-social-construction-of-emotion-myths-and-realities/ (accessed October 1, 2019).

Brown, B. (September 12, 2017). Interviewed by Dan Schawbel for *Why Human Connection Will Bring Us Closer Together*, Available at https://www.forbes.com/sites/danschawbel/2017/09/12/brene-brown-why-human-connection-will-bring-us-closer-together/#5b89e362f06e (accessed September 24, 2019).

Collins, D. (July 2018). Kids are spending more time with voice, but brands shouldn't rush to engage them. Available at https://www.emarketer.com/content/kids-are-spending-more-time-with-voice-but-brands-shouldnt-rush-to-engage-them (accessed November 18, 2019).

Archive Papers

Cornelius, R. (2000). *Theoretical Approaches to Emotion*. Newcastle, Northern Ireland: ITRW on Speech and Emotion. http://www.cs.columbia.edu/~julia/papers/cornelius00.pdf.

Conference Proceedings

Iacoboni, M. (2015). Affective and cognitive empathy are two sides of the same coin. In: *Creating Connections.* Available at http://www.creatingconnections.nl/english-affective-and-cognitive-empathy-are-two-sides-of-the-same-coin.html (accessed October 6, 2019).

Report

Hasso Plattner Institute of Design at Stanford (2010). *An Introduction to Design Thinking Process Guide.* Available at https://dschool-old.stanford.edu/sandbox/groups/designresources/wiki/36873/attachments/74b3d/ModeGuideBOOTCAMP2010L.pdf?sessionID=1b6a96f1e2a50a3b1b7c3f09e58c40a062d7d553 (accessed November 16, 2019).

Online Images and Videos

All the charts in this book are redesigned from the original sources. Some of the charts were arranged by simplifying the information mentioned in the book. To avoid being misunderstood, please check the original sources for each chart if you would like to go deeper into the topic. The original sources are mentioned below, chapter by chapter, with the names of the charts.

Chapter 1

Pictures

P.1.1.
Zhou, J. (2019). Theories of Emotion. Available at https://www.verywellmind.com/theories-of-emotion-2795717 (accessed October 26, 2019).

P.1.2.
Lyonne, L., Headland, L., and Poehler, A. (2019). *Russian Doll*. Netflix. Available at: https://www.netflix.com/watch/80211499?trackId=13752289&tctx=0%2C0%2Cd4741297-70f1-4063-b952-16cce70748bb-6829628%2C%2C (accessed October 11, 2019).

Charts

C.1.1.
Gross, J., and Feldman Barrett, L. (2011). Emotion generation and emotion regulation: One or two depends on your point of view. *Emotion Review*, 3(1), pp. 8–16.

C.1.2.
Averill, J. (July 2017). Interviewed by Andrea Scarantino for *The Social Construction of Emotion: Myths and Realities*. Available at https://emotionresearcher.com/the-social-construction-of-emotion-myths-and-realities/ (accessed October 1, 2019).

C.1.3.
Waal, F. (2009). The Age of Empathy. Emory.edu. Available at http://www.emory.edu/LIVING_LINKS/empathy/faq.html (accessed October 6, 2019).

C.1.4.
Asada, M. (2015). Development of artificial empathy. *Neuroscience Research*, 90, pp. 41–50.

Chapter 2

Charts

C.2.1.
Riopel, L. (2019). Emotional intelligence frameworks, charts, diagrams & graphs. *PositivePsychology*. Available at https://positivepsychology.com/emotional-intelligence-frameworks/ (accessed November 30, 2019).

C.2.2.
Gill, L., Ramsey, P., and Leberman, S. (2015). A systems approach to developing emotional intelligence using the self-awareness engine of growth model. *Systemic Practice & Action Research*, 28(6), pp. 575–594.

C.2.3.
Mayer, J., Caruso, D., and Salovey, P. (2016). The ability model of emotional intelligence: Principles and updates. *Emotion Review*, 8(4), pp. 290–300.

Chapter 3

Pictures

P.3.1.
Verywell Mind (2019). *An Overview of the Myers-Briggs Type Indicator*, picture 1. Available at https://www.verywellmind.com/the-myers-briggs-type-indicator-2795583 (accessed October 21, 2019).

P.3.2.
Creative Types by Adobe Create. (2019). Available at https://mycreativetype.com (accessed October 21, 2019).

Charts

C.3.1.
Erder, M., and Pureur, P. (2016). Role of the architect. *Continuous Architecture*, pp. 187–213.

C.3.2.
Neill, C. (2018). Understanding personality: The 12 Jungian archetypes. Image available at https://conorneill.com/2018/04/21/understanding-personality-the-12-jungian-archetypes/ (accessed October 26, 2019).

Chapter 4

Charts

C.4.1.
Kaptelinin, V., and Nardi, B. (2006). *Acting with Technology*. Cambridge, MA: MIT Press.

C.4.2.
Mcleod, S. (2019). Maslow's hierarchy of needs. *Simply Psychology*. Available at https://www.simplypsychology.org/maslow.html (accessed September 20, 2019).

C.4.3.
Nielsen Norman Group. (2018). The two UX gulfs: Evaluation and execution. Image available at https://www.nngroup.com/articles/two-ux-gulfs-evaluation-execution/ (accessed November 30, 2019).

C.4.4.
Ko, A. (nd). *User Interface Software and Technology*, chapter 2. (ebook) Creative Commons Attribution-NoDerivatives 4.0 International License. Available at https://faculty.washington.edu/ajko/books/uist/theory.html (accessed September 23, 2019).

C.4.5.
Superskill (2018). Aaker's brand personality dimension. Image available at http://www.superskill.com/aaker-brand-personality-dimension/ (accessed October 21, 2019).

C.4.6./C.4.7.
Fogg, B. (2019). Fogg behaviour model: What causes behavior change. *Behaviormodel.org*. Available at https://www.behaviormodel.org/ (accessed October 22, 2019).

C.4.8.
Toxboe, A. (2019). Making the Hook model actionable. *UI Patterns*. Available at http://ui-patterns.com/blog/making-the-hook-model-actionable (accessed October 21, 2019).

Chapter 5

Charts

C.5.1.
Pavliscak, P. (2017). *Design is [Emotion]-Emotionally Intelligent Design.* Video available at https://www.youtube.com/watch?v=pK6Z7Xn0nB8 (accessed October 20, 2019).

C.5.2.
Veer, B. (2017). SXSW—Sophie Kleber: Designing emotionally intelligent machines, aFrogleap: Digital Innovation Agency. *aFrogleap: Digital Innovation Agency.* Available at https://afrogleap.com/blog/innovation/sxsw-sophie-kleber-designing-emotionally-intelligent-machines (accessed November 28, 2019).

Pictures

P.5.1.
WoeBot. (2019). Image available at https://woebot.io (accessed November 12, 2019).

Chapter 6

Pictures

P.6.1.
Domo. (2018). Data never sleeps. Available at https://www.domo.com/assets/downloads/18_domo_data-never-sleeps-6+verticals.pdf (accessed November 19, 2019).

P.6.2.
Social Interface Microsoft Bob. (2019). Image available at https://www.linkideeperlatv.it/microsoft-bob/ (accessed November 30, 2019).

P.6.3.
Camp, J. (2019). My Jibo is dying and it's breaking my heart. *Wired.* Available at https://www.wired.com/story/jibo-is-dying-eulogy/ (accessed November 30, 2019).

P.6.4.
Olly Emotech. (2017). Image available at https://twitter.com/ollyemotech/status/915638174331916288 (accessed November 30, 2019).

P.6.5.
Riot. (2019). Image available at http://digitaldozen.io/projects/riot/ (accessed November 30, 2019).

P.6.6.
Flanagan, C. (2019). A space for being. *Curtis Flanagan*. Available at http://curtisflanagan.com/a-space-for-being (accessed November 30, 2019).

P.6.7.
Dreamjournal.maslo.ai. (2019). *Maslo*. Available at https://dreamjournal.maslo.ai/ (accessed November 30, 2019).

Charts

C.6.5.
Domo. (2018). Data never sleeps. [online] Available at https://www.domo.com/assets/downloads/18_domo_data-never-sleeps-6+verticals.pdf (accessed November 19, 2019).

C.6.6.
Chou, J., Murillo, O., and Ibars, R. (2017). How to recognize exclusion in AI. *Medium*. Available at https://medium.com/microsoft-design/how-to-recognize-exclusion-in-ai-ec2d6d89f850 (accessed November 18, 2019).

Chapter 7

Charts

C.7.1.
Interaction Design Foundation. (2019). *5 Stages in the Design Thinking Process*. Image available at https://www.interaction-design.org/literature/article/5-stages-in-the-design-thinking-process (accessed November 30, 2019).